Defiant Indigeneity

Defiant Indigeneity

The Politics of Hawaiian Performance

Stephanie Nohelani Teves

The University of North Carolina Press CHAPEL HILL

This book was published with the assistance of the Anniversary Fund of the University of North Carolina Press.

The University of North Carolina Press has been a member of the Green Press Initiative since 2003.

Library of Congress Cataloging-in-Publication Data
Names: Teves, Stephanie Nohelani, author.
Title: Defiant indigeneity : the politics of Hawaiian performance / Stephanie Nohelani Teves.
Other titles: Critical indigeneities.
Description: Chapel Hill : University of North Carolina Press, [2018] | Series: Critical indigeneities | Includes bibliographical references and index.
Identifiers: LCCN 2017033929 | ISBN 9781469640549 (cloth : alk. paper) | ISBN 9781469640556 (pbk : alk. paper) | ISBN 9781469640563 (ebook)
Subjects: LCSH: Hawaiians—Ethnic identity. | Hawaiians—Social life and customs. | Hawaiians—Social conditions. | Hawaiians—Government relations.
Classification: LCC DU624.65 .T48 2018 | DDC 305.899/42—dc23
LC record available at https://lccn.loc.gov/2017033929

Cover illustration: *Nā Mokuna Palaweka* (riso, watercolor, and ink) by Amberlee Kūʻiʻolani Cotchay. Used courtesy of the artist.

Portions of this book were previously published in a different form. An earlier version of chapter 1 was published as "Aloha State Apparatuses," *American Quarterly* 67, no. 3 (Fall 2015): 705–26; chapter 2 originally appeared as "'Bloodline Is All I Need!' Defiant Indigeneity and Hawaiian Hip-Hop," *American Indian Culture and Research Journal* 35, no. 4 (2011): 73–101, and is used here courtesy of the American Indian Studies Center, UCLA, © Regents of the University of California Press; and chapter 3 was published as "Cocoa Chandelier's Confessional: Kanaka Maoli Performance and Aloha in Drag," in *Critical Ethnic Studies: An Anthology*, edited by Nada Elia, David M. Hernández, Jodi Kim, Shana L. Redmond, Dylan Rodriguez, and Sarita Echavez See (Durham, NC: Duke University Press, 2016), 280–300.

For my parents

Contents

Figures

Preface
Throwing Mangoes at Tourists

I grew up across the street from the most visited tourist site in the Western Pacific, the USS *Arizona* Memorial, a U.S. National Monument located at Pearl Harbor, where two million tourists visit annually. Kānaka Maoli (Native Hawaiians) called this area Puʻuloa (the many waters of the long hill), known for its abundance of fishponds, loʻi kalo (taro patches), and oyster beds.[1] Soon after the Hawaiian Kingdom was overthrown in 1893, the U.S. Navy took formal control in 1899, turning Pearl Harbor into the Pacific seat of U.S. empire, making it a military target. As the story goes, Pearl Harbor was bombed by the Japanese in 1941 in what was then considered the most deadly attack on "U.S. soil," leading to the institution of martial law and solidifying the idea that Hawaiʻi needed the United States for protection. For Kānaka Maoli especially, Pearl Harbor serves as an enduring reminder of our multiple levels of loss—of our kingdom, of the sovereignty of the land and ocean, and of our status as a people. As kids in the 1980s, we would watch from behind chain-link fences as busloads of tourists unloaded to pay homage to *their* fallen. We would stare at them—mostly haole and Japanese tourists in their generic aloha attire—and gather rotten mangoes from nearby trees, throwing them over the fence. Our collective aim was poor, but a couple of times we hit the tour buses. We mostly spattered the sidewalk with rotten mangoes.

We were kids who lived in public housing, in three-story walk-ups, in the shadow of U.S. empire. We were the descendants of Hawaiians who grew up in the territory and statehood period, whose parents and grandparents witnessed Oʻahu's accelerated urbanization, during a time when people were told to stop speaking Hawaiian, to embrace the United States, when tourism it was said, was good for Hawaiʻi and that we needed to share our aloha. Our parents did not have Hawaiian names, but we did. Hawaiians, back then, didn't call themselves "Kānaka Maoli," and many still don't. They grew up listening to American rock and roll and Motown.[2] They joined the U.S. military; they listened to the music of The Sunday Mānoa; they reveled in the opening of the Ala Moana Shopping Center; they went to the "Hawai'i Woodstock" in Diamond Head Crater; they were against the ongoing military usage of Kaho'olawe but were suspicious of the general fight for Hawaiian sovereignty. They told us that if it weren't for America, Japan would have taken us over. They made fun of us for believing in Hawaiian sovereignty at the same time they wore shirts with Hawaiian warriors on them.

These conflicting messages were in full bloom in the late 1980s and early 1990s as the seeds of the Hawaiian Renaissance materialized in the Hawaiian sovereignty movement, causing enormous political and cultural rifts across Hawaiian, local, and haole communities. In 1993 a number of public events commemorated the overthrow of the Hawaiian Kingdom, including a five-act dramatization of the overthrow, the draping of 'Iolani Palace in black, the lowering of the American flag at the state capitol, and a march through the streets of Honolulu, where over 20,000 people rallied for Hawaiian sovereignty, forcing all of Hawai'i to see that "we [Hawaiians] are still here." These were public displays and performances of Hawaiian unrest and defiance. I was inspired! As a young teen, I watched these events on the evening news with my parents, who shook their heads at the so-called rowdy Hawaiians. My father joked with me: "What, Lani, you tink you sovereign?"

This period of time in Hawai'i presented a number of paradoxes for young Kānaka Maoli like myself. Our teen angst attempted to reconcile expressions of Hawaiian pride and sovereignty alongside the pervasive feeling that such expressions were futile in the face of U.S. colonialism. I mostly learned about sovereignty by watching the local news and listening to songs on Hawaiian radio stations. No one in my family seemed to be influenced by it; in fact, they seemed against it. Hawaiian sovereignty became everyday conversation because the local media villainized Hawaiian activists such as the famous Trask sisters, Haunani-Kay and Mililani, or Bumpy Kanahele, before he essentially played himself in the Cameron Crowe flop *Aloha* (2015). As a teenager, I borrowed Haunani-Kay Trask's *From a Native Daughter* (1994) from the public library. I read it cover to cover and created handwritten copies of many of the pages, which I then recited on the city bus, irritating all of my friends. I did not understand what sovereignty or nationalism was, but I knew it meant Hawaiians had to fight for our rights. I sang Hō'aikane songs about Hawaiian independence while hanging off the back of my dad's El Camino. I went to punk shows with mostly haoles and some locals and other Kānaka Maoli who hated how mainstream everybody was.

Hawaiian musicians in the early 1990s especially filled their music with fervent calls for sovereignty, oftentimes to the tune of a Jawaiian (Jamaican Reggae-infused genre) beat. Imagine hearing songs on the radio every day calling for Hawai'i to come together, for Hawaiians to assert our rights, for us to sing a "Song of Sovereignty" and to "Keep Hawaiian Lands in Hawaiian Hands."[3] These songs became the soundtrack of our youth alongside hip-hop. The call for sovereignty attempted to address the Hawaiians on the edges, those on the bottom, and even the emergent Hawaiian middle class, telling us all that we do have a voice, a kuleana (responsibility), and rights—and that now was the time to assert them. While some Hawaiians took to the streets, others were more subtly influenced. Music and performance allowed our political consciousness to conceal itself and percolate, transforming not only Hawaiian musicians and performers but Kānaka Maoli everywhere.

The emergence of Hawaiian pride occurred alongside an increasing stranglehold on what Hawaiian indigeneity is supposed to look like and mean in a Hawaiian nationalist environment that emphasized the expression of "revitalized" or "real" Hawaiian culture over the tourist-driven vision of Hawai'i. This fueled growing divisions within Hawaiian communities over "authenticity" and began to foreclose what kinds of expressions and cultural productions are legitimately "Hawaiian." Kānaka Maoli who do not perform "tradition" or revitalization in obvious ways to express their Hawaiian indigeneity continue to be unacknowledged or even ostracized for their cultural relevance by the dominant public, performers especially. The tension around this lack of acknowledgment can be felt by Kānaka Maoli daily. During my time as a performer in the Hawai'i underground music scene in the late 1990s and early 2000s, I met many Kānaka Maoli who expressed that being involved in certain kinds of music, looking a certain way, being "alternative," made their Hawaiian indigeneity suspect. People would question why they liked certain things, why they acted "white," why, when they liked hip-hop, they wanted to "be black," and why they didn't dance hula. I recall a similar experience working as a research associate at Kamehameha Schools—an elite private school system whose admissions policy prioritizes Native Hawaiian children—where I also met many young Kānaka who told me they did not feel "Hawaiian enough." I have even had this experience as a professor, meeting Kānaka Maoli students who differentiate themselves as "less Hawaiian" because of their limited cultural knowledge or outward performance of indigeneity. These brief examples signal the constraints around what it means to be Hawaiian today, which extends beyond a personal account of who your ancestors were, and now must require an identity and performance informed by popular culture and emergent forms of nationalism that influence how Kānaka Maoli see and recognize one another. In many ways, feelings of anxiety and fears of not being a "real" or "authentic" Native are a symptom of a Native experience itself. This book analyzes Indigenous performances on stage and in everyday life, not merely to rewrite inaccurate depictions and replace them with "authentic" or "real" Hawaiians, but to take stock instead of the multiple ways in which we cultivate our indigeneity and defy the expectations colonialism has handed down to us.

Specifically, I elaborate on the double-binding pressures of the performance of indigeneity and how these performances are contested in the political and cultural context of Hawaiian indigeneity. I shift the gaze away from the mass-produced imagery of tourism embodied in hula performance and idyllic landscapes, as well as performances that promote an "authentic" Hawaiian identity articulated through cultural nationalism, to attend to the performers, performances, and performativity on the fringe, in the countercultural spaces of Hawaiianness. These performances and the spaces that generate them are ignored and undervalued within dominant Hawaiian critical traditions. Much attention has been focused on the recovery and revitalization of the Hawaiian language and the revival of spiritual and cultural practices, as well as useful analyses of kingdom law or other forms of community-based governance. This focus on "Hawaiian" culture, however, can also occlude. There are so many perspectives, aspects, and enclaves of Hawaiian worlds that generate strategies of survival from the margins. This work provides an account of contemporary Kanaka Maoli performance by working between and across the quotidian spaces where Kānaka Maoli perform the routines of everyday life; the often overlooked performance zones of the Hawaiian undercommons (punk clubs, drag shows, and hip-hop venues); and the officially sanctioned domains of Hawai'i's culture industries (regional theater and Hollywood films). These artists use performance to contest, (re)produce, and proliferate new possibilities for what it means to be Kanaka Maoli in the (ongoing) time of Hawai'i's colonization and U.S. military occupation. Our Indigenous belonging and survival as a lāhui, as a nation, are wrapped up in these contentious spaces of cultural performance. Our survival must involve creating space for conversations and critiques of the forms of Hawaiianness that are used to confine and over-determine us.

To guide my inquiries, I draw on the ʻōlelo noʻeau (wise saying) "I ulu nō ka lālā I ke kumu," translated as "The branches grow because of the trunk," which describes how we are connected to our roots, to our culture and ancestors. This central trunk of Hawaiian indigeneity is rooted in the land and routes our genealogies up through the trunk and into the branches and leaves of a tree.[4] These routes can also take us to hip-hop, to living on Turtle Island, to the seeming whiteness of LGBTQ life, to isolation in our own land. The routes and roots take many directions, but we always know that their base is our genealogical connection as Kānaka Maoli. It is in our kinship and genealogies that we are Kānaka Maoli, and despite our divergent opinions, Kānaka Maoli know and share this. These are practices of belonging and Indigenous recognition that occur through the performance of aloha, maintaining and motivating our commitment to be Kānaka Maoli. As Noelani Goodyear-Kaʻōpua describes, the branches nourish and are nourished by the tree and bring together a gathering of distinct and preexisting elements that can combine to create a new entity.[5] This ʻōlelo noʻeau is often invoked as a call to return to one's roots, but we must expand this interpretation to attend to the smaller branches that often go unnoticed in the struggle to rebuild a vibrant lāhui.[6]

The struggle for lāhui does not happen just in secret boardrooms, during court proceedings, or even at protests; it exists in performance space—staged and lived—and it is a reminder to all Hawaiians that we are Indigenous people, politically and culturally. As an Indigenous political and cultural group—not merely as entertainers or remnants of a kingdom that time forgot—we clench our fists around our sovereignty, knowing that colonialism has not killed us. As Haunani-Kay Trask reminded us in the speech she gave on the centennial commemoration of the overthrow, "The intention was to kill every one of us. And we are still here, one hundred years to the day that racist American country took our sovereignty."[7] This beautiful moment has been replayed, retold, relived, and reaffirmed within the Hawaiian community for over two decades. I return to Trask's words when Hawaiʻi feels far away from me, when I feel my understanding of aloha is fading and my sense of what it means to be Kanaka Maoli is waning, when my access to aloha feels far off. Her words speak to aloha's unmatched power; they speak to what aloha is fundamentally about, living and dying as Hawaiians, as Kānaka Maoli. Not as Americans. When I return to

Trask's words, I know aloha again, despite the fact that she never utters the word at all. This sense of what it means to be Kanaka Maoli—through aloha—at times emerges in defiance and at other times is barely recognizable. Sometimes it does not even need to be named, but those who are present, those who share the psychic and physical spaces of Hawaiian indigeneity, *know*.

Acknowledgments

The aloha and kōkua of so many people supported this research. The labor of these performers, writers, and thinkers is often overlooked and dismissed within Hawaiian worlds, as is the extended community of folks who share these performance spaces. I want to acknowledge especially Cocoa Chandelier, Krystilez, Lopaka Kapenui, Kristiana Kahakauwila, and Amber Ku'iolani Cotchay for her amazing cover art, and all the unnamed artists in Hawai'i who continue to buck convention and test the boundaries of Hawaiian expression. Their innovation and community presence make so much possible. I hope that my interpretations do their contributions justice.

This research was graciously supported by the Center for the Study of Race, Indigeneity, and Transnational Migration at Yale University; the Ford Foundation dissertation and postdoctoral fellowships; the Center for the Study of Women and Society at the University of Oregon; the Women of Color Project, and the University of Oregon College of Arts and Sciences. Those I name here do not begin to account for the numerous people who have assisted me. To my mentor and friend, Vicente Diaz, I am grateful for your unending advocacy and reminders to theorize at the edge and to never hesitate to come up with inappropriate essay titles. In addition, Sarita See, Andrea Smith, Amy Stillman, and Evelyn Alsultany provided much-needed guidance throughout graduate school and continue to offer support. I am so thankful for Mark Simpson-Vos and all the wonderful people at UNC Press who shepherded this project early on, and mahalo to Kēhaulani Kauanui and Jeani O'Brien for their inclusion of this work in the Critical Indigeneities series. Special gratitude to my mentors and friends Hokulani Aikau, Johanna Almiron, Constancio Arnaldo, Rick Baldoz, Matthew Chin, Kelly Fayard, Mishuana Goeman, Theo Gonzalves, Lloyd Grieger, Shari Huhndorf, Karen Kosasa, Mindy Mizobe, Michael Nakasone, Michelle Raheja, Lianne Rozzelle, Kiri Sailiata, Audra Simpson, Danica Smith, David Stannard, Harrod Suarez, Dawn Sueoka, Haunani-Kay Trask, Ty Kāwika Tengan, Leeann Wang, and Mari Yoshihara.

I have been lucky to call many great people at the University of Oregon colleagues and friends. Thanks to Donella Alston, Kemi Balogun, Yvonne Braun, Kirby Brown, Eryn Cangi, Ed Chang, Charise Cheney, Lynn

Fujiwara, Michael Hames Garcia, Angie Hopkins, Dan Ho-Sang Martinez, Michelle Jacob, Loren Kajikawa, Brian Klopotek, Sharon Luk, Ernesto Martinez, Theresa May, Angie Morrill, Josie Mulkins, Kari Norgaard, Jennifer O'Neal, Jeff Ostler, Laura Pulido, Julee Raiskin, Shoniqua Roach, Leilani Sabzalian, Alai Reyes Santos, and Margaret Rhee. Special thanks to the Many Nations Longhouse, the Native Strategies group, and the Women of Color Project.

I send my deepest mahalos to my Hinemoana of Turtle Island sisters Maile Arvin, Natalee Kehaulani Bauer, Kehaulani Natsuko, Fuifuilupe Niumeitolu, Joyce Pualani Warren, and Liza Keanueanueokalani Williams, and to my writing hui bruddahs Dean Saranilio and Kealani Cook. I am honored to know and learn so much from all of you. I owe an immeasurable debt to Kathleen and Mele and to my entire ʻohana, whose support never wavered—mahalo nui.

Defiant Indigeneity

Introduction
How to Do Things with Aloha

A-L-O-H-A, a little aloha in our day, spread a little aloha around the world.
—MANAʻO COMPANY, "Spread a Little Aloha"

What ideological forces are there, if any, that would enable the individual representative of an ethnic minority to move beyond, or believe she could ever move beyond, the macro sociological structures that have already mapped out her existence—such as, for instance, forces that allow her to think of herself as a "subject" with a voice, as a human person? What makes it possible for her to imagine that her resistance-performance is her ultimate salvation, her key to universal humanity, in the first place?
—REY CHOW, *The Protestant Ethnic and the Spirit of Capitalism*

In Hawaiʻi, the commercialized spirit of aloha is both pervasive and a little perverse, its invocations deployed to sell everything from hula skirts to plumbing services. My personal favorite is Aloha Exterminators, a termite and pest control company on the island of Oʻahu. Aloha is also used to sell promises of spiritual enlightenment and fantasies of diversity to eager tourists. Loosely translated since the mid-nineteenth century as "welcome" or "love," aloha is everywhere, and seems to mean just about everything.

This seeming universality is possible because the word "aloha" and the concept it represents have been removed from their Hawaiian cultural context, harnessed to the purposes of others, and used to the detriment of the Kanaka Maoli people. This has been part of the historical, cultural, and political process that Jonathan Kamakawiwoʻole Osorio describes as the "dismembering" of the lāhui.[1] Still, aloha is something we Kānaka Maoli continue to believe deeply in, fiercely protecting and defending aloha above other Hawaiian concepts as the essence and personification of who we are. That said, what Kānaka Maoli do with aloha varies greatly. Protesting U.S. militarization might be the purest expression of aloha to one Kanaka Maoli, whereas it would be seen as disrespectful by others. A hotel hula show could be interpreted as a meaningful and culturally grounded expression of aloha by the performers sharing their culture and by the audience of tourists watching, yet some Kānaka Maoli would also critique this commodified performance. For many, aloha signifies a deep, abiding kinship within Hawaiian culture based on practices of reciprocal care and the work it takes to be in community, but we also know that aloha has been turned into a concept for tourism, emptied of its cultural context when displayed in advertisements or postcards.

But one thing is clear: aloha is a performance, negotiated at the intersection of ancestral knowledge and outsider expectations, manifest in the daily contradictions and complexities of Kanaka Maoli indigeneity. Usually conferred through the sharing of a lei, a kiss on the cheek, or perhaps a smile, aloha is supposed to transfer an overall feeling of welcome and warmth. This imagined performance affirms in the global imagination the existence of something that is real, that represents Hawai'i, that comes from Hawaiians, but that is now a gift given to the world.

This is the dominant tension noted in the juxtaposition of the epigraphs above. The first is a lyric penned by a Hawaiian music group, the Mana'o Company, about the joys of aloha and what it means to spread it; it was the sound track for an Aloha Airlines commercial in 2007. The second comes from the scholar Rey Chow, who has written powerful critiques of ethnic performances as representative of resistance. These two examples represent a modern Indigenous contradiction: culture is what makes Indigenous people special, so it should be a source of pride and shared; however, it is cultural difference that made Indigenous peoples subject to colonization and continues to keep "the Native" locked in Western discourse, even when Indigenous people are resisting. This is an understandable reaction to histories and processes of racial discrimination and disempowerment, and inasmuch as it is an effort to prove ourselves worthy and as a culturally distinct Indigenous people with inherent rights to sovereignty, the imperative to produce more "authentic" forms of culture only means that it is "culture" and not "race" that now (doubly) disempowers indigeneity.[2] This critique has substantial implications for Kānaka Maoli (and other Indigenous peoples), whose primary form of identification is through the performance of "culture" (for example, hula, seafaring, music, relation to land), and, as this book explores, is exceptionally tied to cultural values such as aloha.

While the historical appropriation and commodification of aloha have been justifiably criticized, this book looks instead at the conditions that require Kānaka Maoli to perform aloha and how aloha can be reclaimed as a practice of insurgent world-making that exceeds the limits set by the colonial order of things. This practice is what I term "defiant indigeneity," and it is the focus of this work.

Since the mid-1970s Hawaiian politics and culture have been undergoing a renaissance and renewal of a number of cultural forms, such as hula, martial arts, language revitalization, lo'i kalo (taro patch) restoration, seafaring, and spiritual practices. These performances create a space for Kanaka Maoli people to contest the ongoing effects of American colonialism.[3] Referred to under the banner of the Hawaiian Renaissance in its early days, this contestation drew inspiration from the American civil rights movements and agitations of African Americans, Asian Americans, Latinx, and other Indigenous people, who demanded an acknowledgment of their distinct political and cultural histories and identities. Over the past thirty years, a growing library of works in the Kanaka Maoli academic and activist worlds have labored to push back against inauthentic or offensive representations of Hawai'i and Kānaka Maoli, offering a revision of those images and a literal rewriting of Hawaiian history.[4] The excavation of purposefully overlooked primary source documents (for example, Hawaiian-language newspapers and memoirs) and changes in academic and legal discourses have brought institutional and mainstream legitimation to the Hawaiian sovereignty movement, showing that many Kānaka Maoli have never consented to the occupation of our homeland and that Kānaka Maoli are so much more than how we are stereotyped and represented.

Acknowledging and telling this story of resistance, resilience, and revitalization have propelled numerous Hawaiian nationalist[5] projects in both academic and community-activist circles. While this work and the ideas behind it have produced much-needed changes to how Hawaiian culture and politics are understood and expressed, such narratives (while productive) can sometimes still work in the service of hegemonic forces that aim to incorporate—and thus contain, manage, and even exploit—Hawaiian indigeneity under the guise of celebrating "authentic" Hawaiian culture without translating such celebrations into Kanaka Maoli political power.

Ongoing efforts to federally recognize the Kanaka Maoli people similar to a Native American tribe have been consistent since the early 1990s as a result of the "Apology Resolution" adopted in 1993 by the U.S. Congress and signed by President Bill Clinton. This act apologized for the United States' role in the illegal overthrow of the Hawaiian Kingdom, thus opening the door to a federal process to recognize Native Hawaiians as an Indigenous group with claims to self-determination. The Native Hawaiian

Government Reorganization Act of 2009, popularly known as the Akaka Bill, named after U.S. Senator Daniel Akaka, became a rallying point for many within the Kanaka Maoli community who view federal recognition or a "nation within a nation" structure as necessary to protect Hawaiian entitlement programs. I have had conversations with many Kānaka Maoli who view federal recognition as a way to pursue nationhood without a total upheaval of Hawai'i's current cultural and political environment; others view it as yet another way that the United States will control Kānaka Maoli and Hawai'i. As pro-independence activists and scholars have warned, growing federal and state support for Hawaiian recognition is indicative of the settler-colonial forces that seek to further incorporate Hawaiian indigeneity, settle Hawaiian ceded land claims, and solidify military control of Hawai'i and the rest of the Pacific with a pivot toward Asia.

Federal recognition, in theory, would grant Kānaka Maoli specific rights as a domestic dependent nation under U.S. federal jurisdiction (without giving back any land or permitting for gaming as a means of economic development), "allowing" us to form our own government as well as granting a number of other protections, but it would simultaneously obfuscate Kanaka Maoli rights to self-determination and national sovereignty on a global stage. Over the past decade, many Kānaka Maoli have become critical of federal recognition, preferring to think of Hawai'i—as it is framed by legal scholars and activists—as illegally occupied by the U.S. military. Extinguishing Hawaiian independence claims through the federal recognition process coincides with efforts to articulate certain forms of Hawaiian culture that do not challenge settler colonialism and can be easily accommodated. With respect to the various activists and scholars who spent their lives articulating these divergent visions and paths toward our Hawaiian liberation, the performances in this book resist easy categorization. Instead, I offer a rendering of performances that resist the architecture of colonialism and the binaries at its core, documenting the expressions of being that confound these processes to turn state-based forms of recognition and commodified versions of aloha itself on their head.

Corporations, engineering firms, film studios, state agencies, and nonprofits are all actively recruiting Hawaiian cultural specialists to advise and administrate "authentic" Hawaiian culture to combat all the hypercommodified imagery of Hawai'i. The product of activist and scholarly critiques, this so-called embrace of authenticity might be understood as "inclusion." Inclusion under capitalism and settler colonialism, however, represents an additive model of multiculturalism that depends on and generates community by inserting the history of the oppressed into an American and increasingly global narrative in the name of commerce, not sovereignty or decolonization.[6] Thus, while it might appear that the cultures of "the other" are now being accepted and celebrated, this often happens through a frame of liberal multiculturalism that depoliticizes and diminishes difference by emphasizing a surface-level celebration of cultural diversity that does not fully engage a transformative struggle against racism and white supremacy. This kind of celebration is dangerous because the recognition of cultural or ethnic difference can actually culturally bind the subaltern subject (that is, the Indigenous subject).[7] This means that Indigenous peoples have to properly perform culture in order to be seen as Indigenous to begin with, thus binding indigeneity solely to cultural difference and denying Indigenous political self-determination. Through performance, Kanaka Maoli subjectivity is packaged, bought, and sold within the tourist economy in a fashion that simultaneously justifies the colonial occupation of Hawaiʻi and reduces the range of possibilities for Kanaka Maoli subjectivity.

The employment of cultural advisers might be viewed as an improvement, but this is yet another example of the shape-shifting nature of settler colonialism and capital accumulation. In the current neoliberal multicultural color-blind era, settler colonialism cannot blatantly appropriate, but it can hire cultural experts to provide authentication and an illusion of inclusion. Through co-optation by "experts," Indigenous culture is dispossessed again for the capital accumulation of settlers. We must be critical of the representational apparatuses in which this "authentic" culture is promoted and aware of what is foreclosed in the process. As Brendan Hokowhitu notes, some expressions of Indigenous precolonial pride—and, I would add, cultural revitalizations—require the death of Indigenous subjectivities that threaten strategic traditionalism.[8] Indigenous peoples, and performers especially, live with this threat of double jeopardy because conversations about us are almost always framed in dichotomies of authentic versus inauthentic and traditional versus modern.[9] This divides Indigenous communities, privileges anthropological discourse of Indigenous people as static, and supports settler narratives that use "authenticity" to argue that our Indigenous political, cultural, and legal claims are irrelevant. Worse yet, in the Hawaiian context, aloha is appropriated by the tourist industry and is in turn employed as a barometer of Hawaiianness that is used to quiet dissent and encourage the maintenance of the settler-colonial state. Our performances of culture can thus function as a tool or weapon of the dominant culture, which forces Indigenous people to perform within the limited and often negating frames it sets in order to be seen or recognized as subjects (read Native/Indigenous) at all. These are the catch-22s of indigeneity. Settlers employ definitions of Indigenous cultures that limit Indigenous claims to our resources, lands, and sovereignty. Indigenous people must prove themselves as "real" or "authentic" to secure political recognition and, unfortunately, cultural belonging. Indigenous peoples have in turn utilized these same definitions to access the social, economic, and political resources that are necessary for survival.[10] Native people "playing Indian" might seek to alter stereotypes, but such performances often work to reaffirm stereotypes and expectations of what indigeneity "ought" to look like for stubborn non-Native audiences (be they in the classroom or the courtroom or at the beachside bar) who are profoundly attached to the fantasy of the premodern Native.[11]

SITUATED AT THE turn of the twenty-first century, *Defiant Indigeneity* examines performances that reveal the ways in which indigeneity is interpellated by tourism, the settler state, and ourselves, performed and rearticulated in a supposedly postracial America. This book documents the defiant indigeneity of Kanaka Maoli performers and writers and the communities they represent. I focus on examples that are dissonant or out of sync—the hip-hop cipher, the gay nightclub, the streets of Waikīkī, the kitchen, the hotel, the haunted stage, online commenting spaces—in order to expose the violence enacted through the "spirit of aloha" while also highlighting the creative and innovative ways Kānaka Maoli are disarticulating and rearticulating Hawai'i. I look at two Kanaka Maoli performers: Krystilez, a rapper from a Hawaiian homestead, and Cocoa Chandelier, a performance artist, drag queen, and theater scholar. I conducted ethnography of multiple performance spaces from 2006 to 2012 in urban Honolulu in a performance community I was familiar with when I began this research, but which I do not consider myself a member of. From 1997 to 2005, I was a fan, organizer, and performer in Hawai'i's underground music scene, notably within the punk scene. This participation overlapped with the LGBTQ performance and hip-hop scenes, but while I was certainly present in these scenes, I was more of a spectator than a performer or an organizer. Still, because of the small size of these communities and their differentiation from the mainstream Hawaiian music scene in Hawai'i, there is a sense of radical marginality within these spaces. My knowledge of these environments, because I grew up in them, informed the research I conducted. These alter/native spaces are sites of contestation, as they expose the limits of aloha for making decolonial claims to life and land. They are also sites of love and belonging. These sites call us to account for the ways in which the "spirit of aloha" silences, erases, and renders invisible those members who do not measure up to our yardstick of Hawaiian indigeneity. These are not places where Hawaiianness is known in advance. These are of course mixed spaces. Sometimes there are lots of Kānaka Maoli, lots of Asian settlers, lots of haoles who may be tourist voyeurs, and all of these groups may or may not have grown up in Hawai'i and identify themselves as "local." These performance spaces allow people to negotiate their relationship to the spaces of "authentic" and revitalized Hawaiian culture. My reading of these spaces centers a suspicion of the state-sanctioned celebrations of representation as evidence of social change or progress.

In addition to ethnography and analysis of performance space, I engage in close readings of how texts perform, including the 2015 play *Ka'iulani*, staged in downtown Honolulu, juxtaposed with the 2011 film *Princess Kaiulani*, as well as a ghost tour of Waikīkī that traverses the multilayered nā wahi pana (storied place) of a famed tourist environment that sits on the lands of Princess Ka'iulani. Finally, I examine the short story "The Old Paniolo Way" from the book *This Is Paradise* (2013) by the Kanaka Maoli writer Kristiana Kahakauwila. I focus on these Kanaka Maoli artists and performances to document their defiance in the face of often restrictive expectations of Hawaiian performance and the multiple forces that compel Indigenous people to prove their humanity and to seek governmental forms of recognition as the measurement of indigeneity and to legitimate our existence. As Mishuana Goeman explains, these performances allow us "to examine the complex power relations that rely on assumptions about Native/ Indigenous peoples to uphold exploitive structures of settler-states."[12] The double bind for Kānaka Maoli is in how our indigeneity has become attached to aloha on a personal level and through popular culture and statecraft. Aloha, as the next section explains, can be a tool of subordination as well as a stabilizing force that connects us to our indigeneity.

Performing Aloha

J. L. Austin wrote in *How to Do Things with Words* (1975) that speech acts are performative and that they perform an action through speech—they do things.[13] The performance of aloha—on stage and in everyday life—does something to and for Kānaka Maoli. Both a blessing and an obligation, aloha also constrains, often prescribing how Kānaka Maoli are supposed to act.

In the global imagination and in the Hawaiian community, aloha is believed to convey love and understanding, an open invitation. Such definitions of aloha support the colonial and gendered logic that is reinforced unwittingly and purposefully by many different performances that represent Hawai'i, Kānaka Maoli, and the Pacific as always readily available for white colonial narratives to possess. Aloha and the region and people it stands in for, in order to maintain U.S. settler colonialism and American political hegemony, must give themselves to you naturally. In response, Hawaiian activists and scholars have labored to situate the place of aloha within a wider Hawaiian worldview. Activists highlight the practice of aloha 'āina (love of the land) as an act of Hawaiian patriotism to centralize how aloha 'āina represents the active practice of caring for the land that provides for you. But aloha (without the 'āina) operates as a signifier and a practice that moves and restricts in so many ways. Maile Arvin and I have written elsewhere that sometimes aloha is performed as a refusal that prioritizes our resistance to incorporation into the settler state. Instead, the expression of aloha can be felt through the expression of a loud "a'ole" or "no!"[14] Noelani Arista and Judy Kertesz have proposed that Kānaka Maoli say "no more love; aloha denied" to non–Kānaka Maoli or especially to tourists who feel entitled to our lands, ocean, and culture.[15]

Aloha's uses as a moniker (the Aloha State) and as a disciplining force in state law (the Aloha Spirit Law) exemplify the complexities of this cultural affect for Hawaiian indigeneity. I flag it here to frame a deeper discussion of how the advancement of certain cultural attributes—in the name of asserting aloha as our "gift to the world"—easily falls into a trap that further ensconces extractive practices of settler colonialism and capitalist exploitation. Aloha remains highly contested in these sites and many others because despite aloha's commodification, aloha still maintains a relationship to some kind of originary Hawaiian essence, to an imagined real, which is what generates its power in the hearts and minds of tourists, settlers, and Kānaka Maoli working to demarcate what is and what isn't "Hawaiian." Beyond aloha's representation in multiple discourses, we perform it because we believe that it is what makes us Hawaiian (and it does). By focusing on this negotiation and performance of aloha, I intend to map how Hawaiian indigeneity itself is performed into existence through aloha.

Rather than debate what counts as "traditional" or "contemporary" Hawaiian culture, I prefer to analyze how a performance of aloha emerges out of, and can help us rethink, prevailing social matrices. All of the performances in this book arose during a particular moment in the late twentieth century when Hawaiian nationalism and the consolidation of global mass media converged in public discourse. Understanding that identities are constituted through performance makes possible a critique of how Hawaiian indigeneity is defined vis-à-vis performances of aloha. This offers opportunities to think critically about the ways that Kānaka Maoli articulate Hawaiian indigeneity with aloha and with certain kinds of performances that cohere at critical historical moments and in everyday life, getting us out of discourses that posit Kānaka Maoli as simplistically performing aloha as duped by colonialism.

An example of the constraints of indigeneity today can be observed in the Hawaiian principle and practice of "Kapu Aloha." Kapu Aloha was a guiding principle of the protectors of Mauna Kea who in the spring of 2015 stood firm in the face of the state and university partners endeavoring to build a thirty-meter telescope on the sacred mountain. Now, I have to give the full disclaimer that this is a practice that I and others were not familiar with until it reemerged (or should I say resurged?) during the 2015 struggle to protect Mauna Kea. I learned about Kapu Aloha through social media. In an interview, the Kanaka Maoli activist Lanakila Mangauil was asked whether the concept of Kapu Aloha was a "traditional" practice.[16] When questioned on the authenticity of the concept, Mangauil responded with respect and precision, explaining what Kapu Aloha is and why it is significant. Pressed further by an interviewer about where this concept came from and whether it is a verifiable "traditional" Hawaiian concept, since no one had allegedly heard about it until now, Mangauil appeared to find humor in the charge and responded that if it was made up, "Well aren't you glad we came up with it then?"

This interaction is representative of the tensions and accusations that are imposed on Indigenous peoples daily, whether as a reaction to social protest, partaking in revitalization efforts, or simply living a life that does not register as "Indigenous." Indigenous peoples and other communities of color are accused of betraying their heritage when they step into arenas that were not intended for them or when they act in ways that somehow disrupt the outdated, so-called real or traditional modes of how they are supposed to act. Mangauil explains that Kapu Aloha is a practice he and many others learned in Hawaiian-language immersion school. The Hawaiian philosopher Manulani Meyer expounds that Kapu Aloha has been around for a long time. When people question its authenticity, the protectors of Mauna Kea are steadfast, linking it to Hawaiian knowledge and community concerns. They cite Kapu Aloha's genealogy while also highlighting the ability to fashion new concepts if necessary. This is why a theory of Indigenous performance and performativity is so crucial. The power of Indigenous performativity is its ability to create, modify, alter, and revive practices or to make completely new ones out of a reverence for your culture while also critiquing the need to perform a pure indigeneity. Standing firm in their purpose, the protectors of Mauna Kea perform Kapu Aloha and their resistance, serving as reminders of the ways our kupunas (ancestors) survived too. They did this through a myriad of performances, many of which prompted debate, just as they do today. These debates, transformations, and contestations might make us uncomfortable, and they certainly make us disagree, but they do not compromise our indigeneity. They make us vibrant and ever-changing, reaching into an Indigenous, a Kanaka Maoli, future for all of us. Hawaiians know that our kupuna were exceptional navigators and explorers; they were interested in new things and had an incorrigible thirst for knowledge. Yet we have internalized this notion that we must think and behave a particular way, a way that is culturally Hawaiian, without outside influences. As David Chang explains, Hawaiians were especially eager to explore the outside world, affirming their sovereignty through a global vision; they "elaborated a critical geography that was both deeply Indigenous and broadly global."[17] The performers in this book are doing this cultural exploratory work. In a cultural environment that prioritizes revitalization and authenticity, they articulate indigeneity with new performance genres, representing the outward-looking global thinking that our kupuna partook in. The struggle at Mauna Kea shored up many of the criticisms Kānaka Maoli face when they challenge settler colonialism—preeminently that they are supposed to exist in a pure state of Indigenous culture and tradition. There is no such thing as Indigenous subjects untouched by the ideologies of the world or culture they inhabit. So why then do Indigenous peoples continue to get held to this standard—by the state and, worse, by each other? Rather than seeking a Native essence or truth, Kapu Aloha is an example of the ways that aloha can be rearticulated away from the state and back into the Indigenous episteme in which it is rooted/routed. In a defiant affirmation of indigeneity, Mangauil's response reminds us all of ancestral laws and kuleana to our kupuna and community. At the risk of falling into a trap that asserts a kind of precolonial Hawaiian purity, his response beautifully maps out the ways that we all transform and perform things that are necessary for our survival, and it does not matter whether such actions are "traditional" or "real"; what makes them both these things is our commitment to being Indigenous. Without asserting a formation of aloha that is limiting or overly expansive, his defense of Kapu Aloha is a reminder that aloha can be defiant and still be used to convey a profound connection, to express our aloha for Hawaiian culture and our commitment to survival as a people.

Defiant Indigeneity

Kapu Aloha is defiant indigeneity par excellence. Defiant indigeneity is an amorphous performance that challenges settler colonialism and refuses the elimination of the Native.[18] It is a performance of indigeneity that constantly deconstructs, resists, and at times recodifies itself against and through state logics. It is all of these things and some of these things simultaneously. It is a performance that intends to help your people survive. That is what makes it fundamentally defiant and its performance so crucial. Sometimes this defiance can be simply about asserting Indigenous presence, and at other times it can collude with the forces of heteropatriarchy or capitalism. Sometimes it invokes blood quantum to defend a land claim. Other times it prioritizes kinship and being in community and includes those whom the government does not count as your family. Defiant indigeneity is a chant at sunrise, it is a Disney princess that inspires Native youth, it is doing the haka[19] before a football game, it is the "protesters" protecting a sacred mountain, it is marching in an LGBTQ pride parade in full regalia. It is all this and many more performances I have yet to witness or imagine.

Defiant indigeneity emerges from the space between performance's emancipatory will and its capacity to reproduce conditions of domination. As a theory, it attempts to account for the world-making and reifying capacities of performance that affirms the ongoing existence and defiance of Indigenous people. Offering its own sets of practices and ways of seeing/doing in the world, defiant indigeneity resists and reorganizes the conditions and limits prescribed by the colonial order, materializing heterogeneous possibilities of Kanaka Maoli being. Defiant indigeneity is a method and theory of the ways that Kānaka Maoli mobilize performance (in both the quotidian and the aesthetic realm) to survive the annihilating conditions of colonization and occupation, and also to affirm and reproduce collective forms of Indigenous being, belonging, and becoming.

This book brings together critiques of indigeneity and performativity from Native studies and performance studies, advocating that the fields have much to learn from one another. To decolonize understandings of indigeneity, we must centralize the tenets of what constitutes indigeneity and trouble those understandings deeply. Akin to the kind of epistemological critique of gender performed by Judith Butler in *Gender Trouble* (1990) and *Bodies That Matter* (1993), Native studies and performance studies must trouble "the Native." In Butler's critique of sex and gender, she argued that the inability to see that gender construction was co-constituted with the illusion of biological sex has doubly disempowered feminist philosophy (as well as the "women's movement" in general) and re-entrenched the dominance of gender binaries in which "woman" is subordinate under heteropatriarchy. Applying how gender works on bodily surfaces to become a site of both "the natural" (biological sex) and the dissonant (gender performance) is critical for thinking through how "the Native" and what is now termed "indigeneity" are worked on the bodies of Indigenous peoples.[20]

My customization of Butler's theories to the category of "the Native" is indebted to the theoretical contributions of Native Pacific cultural studies. I employ Teresia Teaiwa's game-changing articulation of "the Native." She writes: "The Native may have been produced in colonial discourse as an 'other' for the European, the colonizer, the civilized; it may have been used in nationalist movements to counterpose the civilization of the colonial European; it may be left behind by immigrants and diasporic subjects, but it will not go away. The Native will not go away—not only because its 'original' referent still exists, but because I believe it has always had multiple significations—the Native is many things before and 'after' colonialism, before and 'after' migration and diaspora."[21] The Native emerges through colonialism and has meaning now as a subject position that has been infused with Indigenous innovation in the face of efforts to exterminate Indigenous peoples. Indigeneity, especially in the Indigenous Pacific, may have always been about movement, fluidity, and innovation in spite of colonial efforts to affix it in time and space.[22] And yet, even when we acknowledge that "the Native" was created through colonial discourse and that we are so much more complex than the colonizers marked us, we retain "the Native" as an essential stability that existed in a "true" prior state.

I add to Teaiwa's and Native Pacific cultural studies an additional layer of analysis, that is, the notion that indigeneity is a *performative process*. It requires work, doing. Indigenous people would not have been able to survive if they had not continued to do or perform what it is that made them "Native," and this process will never end. Indigeneity requires action, a performance, and such actions are informed by the knowledge of our culture and our genealogies; but performance also avails itself of new interpretations and techniques that ensure our survival. This is why it is *in process, constant movement, and change.* This is also resistance to measurement and containment. As a performative process on an individual level, indigeneity is representative of a genealogy that is routed through colonialism that manifests in any number of contemporary performances or behaviors. I invoke performance here as action, not as a pure social construction, as many poststructuralists and performance theorists have argued. This is vital because when indigeneity is understood solely as a subject position as determined by legal administrative measures or even by the observation of cultural activities that are legible as "Native" in a specific place and time, we neglect to understand that it is a categorization that formed through colonialism and that Natives have challenged these definitions consistently. When we see indigeneity as a performance, we see that it will always survive even if it involves things that seem to challenge our Indigenous authenticity. It exposes "authenticity" as a colonial measurement that we now unfortunately carry out on each other. Giving an account of indigeneity should be a story about Indigenous resurgence and living rather than a story about Indigenous inauthenticity, disappearance, or death. So, rather than a book about all the terrible things that happened to us, I wanted to write instead about all the beautiful ways that we live and love each other and what we have to do in order to continue to do so into the future.

"Performance" refers to both staged performances and the enactment of everyday life. The latter focuses on how social forces structure the perceived behaviors of certain groups—that is, sexuality, gender, age, race, class, and indigeneity.[23] Performance itself does not merely reflect social realities; it also creates them. Within Native studies there has been more recent attention to the processes of performing indigeneity and how "Indigenous" as a global category emerged in the Cold War era, because of human rights concerns leveraged by Indigenous peoples around the world interested in preserving distinct cultures and knowledges and a growing attention to the importance of the natural environment.[24] Seeking recognition by a state or federal entity especially puts Indigenous subjects in a position of performing their culture, always asking to be seen and known, rather than controlling the terms of relationship. These performances have high stakes, often requiring a romanticized performance of indigeneity that Indigenous peoples in turn problematically use to police one another and begin to regard certain behaviors as "traditional" or "natural."[25]

It is the constant performance of expected behaviors and their repetition that create "performativity," which works through repetition, becomes subconscious, and appears natural. Performativity creates norms and transgressions, which contribute to what becomes calcified as the "real" through repetitious acts. In the Hawaiian context, any transgression from the happy aloha-filled Native is figured as "against Aloha" or "un-Hawaiian." For example, the idea that Kānaka Maoli are natural "performers," that our aloha is supposed to emanate from us, is part of a political and discursive practice intended to create a population that can "naturally" serve tourists. This is policed among ourselves too, thus further dividing the Kanaka Maoli community as disorganized or not really "Hawaiian," or just as lost remnants of our former "Native" selves in the service of deeming us always as unfit for self-government. Our Indigenous performance then operates in two tonalities simultaneously; it is the mechanism by which Kānaka Maoli are hailed as docile and happy Natives while also being a means by which we authenticate ourselves as an original Indigenous group when making claims to sovereignty on the world stage. Thus, one of the most pernicious myths of indigeneity is that everything we do is supposed to be "natural" because we have some kind of unwavering ability to listen to the heartbeat of the earth and talk to the wind (even if we do).

As Indigenous people, Kānaka Maoli of course have a special relationship with nature or the land. Certainly it is this relationship that anchors Kanaka Maoli sovereignty claims, and it is this relationship that differentiates Kānaka Maoli from Asian settlers and haoles[26] in the islands. But, as Hokowhitu explains, the Native's relationship to the land is misinterpreted as "primitive inertia," which implies that Natives cannot evolve or be civilized.[27] When Natives are looked to as resources for particular kinds of knowledges (such as the ability to *have* aloha), they become equated with nature—a first step in rendering indigeneity as a static object that possesses an essential truth.[28] Advocating for a reframing of the essentialist/nonessentialist debate, Hokowhitu reanalyzes performance through Indigenous sovereignty. He explains that Indigenous peoples represent their worlds through both hybrid and essential notions of culture, both of which are "critical to strategic decolonization and fluid epistemologies."[29] Instead of fearing dilution and a loss of the "authentic," he focuses instead on the sovereignty of Indigenous peoples and communities to represent themselves alongside a commitment to be self-reflexive.[30] Thus, while affirming authenticity and realness can sometimes be a necessary tactic to push back against stereotypical imagery of Kānaka Maoli, it re-embeds a belief that our "real" selves existed prior to colonization, and it is dangerously similar to imperialist ideas of the noble savage. This is also a reinvestment in the notion that "real" Natives exist in their natural state somewhere, uncorrupted by the ills of the West. We must dislodge the flattening of "the Native" as the prediscursive foundation upon which modern subjectivity asserts itself.

The performative status of the "natural" Native needs to be exposed because the power of this myth extends to all facets of Indigenous life. Rather than overemphasizing that how we perform is "natural," a theory of performance allows us to see that what is considered "natural" was created in opposition to the more advanced modern subject, the foil to the Indigenous subject. By denaturalizing what indigeneity is supposed to look like, we allow indigeneity to be performed in very strategic ways. Without presuming a realm of representation as distinct from the realm of the real, we sharpen our tools of analysis to identify the underlying currents of any performance as it emerges out of a particular social formation.[31] In other words, we can acknowledge that performance creates and sustains identities, rather than searching for a subject that existed before the performance. Performance creates knowledge through action; creating subjectivities, it is a simultaneous process of world-making.

Indigenous authenticity is a complicated, necessary, and messy response to representations that posit Natives as somehow less Native when they perform in ways that defy dominant representations of themselves. When Natives step out of the frames made for them, they are subject to attack, to having their authenticity and backgrounds evaluated.[32] This is also why no one wants to believe that Hawaiian indigeneity is something that is "performed." It makes us feel like artificial cultural representatives who are "vanishing" and must perform a "real" or "authentic" version of Hawaiian culture in counterdistinction to the massively commodified performances. The desire to be "recognized" as "real"—in both formal statecraft and everyday life—is as much a reaction to heavily mediated (mis)representations of Kānaka Maoli as it is to deep existentialist determinations of indigeneity. This desire for recognition and respect speaks to a need among Kānaka Maoli, one that seeks to move beyond stereotypes and one that acknowledges our varied articulations. The ever-present tourist gaze marks Kānaka Maoli as happy Natives, and the "justice" system positions Kānaka Maoli as criminals, while the media oscillate between the two in their own representations of Hawaiian indigeneity. Such perceptions of indigeneity, when internalized, keep communities demobilized, contained, and motionless in the same ways that anthropological notions of culture and "the Native" do.

We must turn our attention to the social processes that create identities, which means a move away from conceptions of Natives as "things" that can be studied, as Scott Lyons explains.[33] As a reaction to colonialism, we do, at times, privilege notions of purity and authenticity because they offer us a sense of stability; but when that stability is exposed as a colonial-necessitated desire, we should turn our focus to the multitude of strategies employed to survive. In the service of cultural nationalism and tourist artifice, we have adopted a rigidity around Hawaiian indigeneity and, inadvertently in the process, we have marginalized many of our own. To the extent that such cultural forms are posited as having historical depth that reaches into "precolonial" contact, there is also an identification or a bonding that is constructed between the precolonial Kanaka Maoli subject and the contemporary Hawaiian nationalist. This cultural connection may be seen by the latter to legitimize and authorize the struggle to "reclaim" Hawaiian nationhood through the forms of its cultural differences from the settler state. Indeed, it is through culture that many of us pursue our liberation; but culture also runs the risk of constituting the form by which Kānaka Maoli will once again be shackled. Not surprisingly, there is no shortage of Kānaka Maoli lined up to show you how they perform on the market. Indigenous performers and performances sustain state budgets, tribal economies, and individuals' ability to feed their families. Because of this political economy of cultural difference, many Kānaka Maoli would shudder to think that we "perform" our indigeneity (that is, our "Hawaiianess"). To be sure, this is a normal reaction to the mass-mediated artifice of Hawaiian culture via tourism. It makes sense that we would be invested in saying that our ways of being Hawaiian, of practicing our culture, are not performance, that they are *real*. A better way to think about it is to ask, Why are we worried that people will say we aren't real? Why are we so worried people will say we aren't authentic? Why are we letting the touristic and colonial visions of what our culture is define who we are? These questions are useful for thinking about indigeneity in general and Hawaiian indigeneity in particular.

An analysis of racial performativity is also necessary to assess how "the Native" is routed through colonialism and Indigenous identity and performance. Racial performativity, as described by E. Patrick Johnson, informs the process by which bodies are invested with social meaning. Indigenous performativity is similarly informed by social meanings and popular representations. Depending on the context, this might invoke the image of the crying Indian or the hula girl. Both of these tropes do damage that I need not rehearse here, but we must be cognizant of the arbitrariness of authenticity and the dangers of foreclosing possibilities. It is more useful to look at the ways that Indigenous peoples deploy authenticity as a shifting set of ideas that work for certain ends, not as a measuring stick.[34] Understanding the processes of performativity offers nuanced methodologies and interpretative modes in which to theorize how dominant modes of indigeneity allow for a narrow set of notes to be sung before they become incoherent and unacceptable. It is also critical to focus on the dissonant sounds that exceed the dominant frame so that we can see how indigeneity is made and remade through multiple registers.

Ma Ka Hana Ka ʻIke

There is another ʻōlelo noʻeau that I want to add to my thinking on Hawaiian indigeneity and performativity: Ma ka hana ka ʻike. The translation of this phrase is "In working one learns." I expand this definition to also mean that knowledge comes from doing, from action. Performance as an event, as a set of forms and practices, actually works to make knowledge possible. Defiant indigeneity creates new forms of knowledge. This knowledge and its subsequent defiance must be performed; it is an action that is learned and practiced. Not only does an analysis of Indigenous performativity allow us to articulate the various performances that keep us alive, but Indigenous performances (even if they are not identified as such) contribute to the process of learning and obtaining knowledge about what it means to be Indigenous in a specific time and place. The knowledge comes from practice. Put another way, this learning to be Indigenous through performance takes form through the material experiences of being in community, of being Kānaka Maoli. This way of knowing defies modes of analysis focused on visible representation and measurable results.[35] Thus, forms of knowledge are influenced by and created through performances; these things cannot always be measured, but they do create worlds and possibilities. What Hawaiians call "kaona"—a rich and interconnected system of signification and hidden meanings—is another dynamic Hawaiian way of knowing that is present in these performances.[36] According to Noelani Arista, the prevalence of such deep and hidden and shifting systems of thought and the multiple meanings must be taken into account when analyzing any Hawaiian text.[37] Kaona reflects a Hawaiian way of knowing that begins with fluidity, complexity, and contradiction, which is in contrast to Western ways that seek categorization, compartmentalism, fixity, and truth. When we focus on ontology instead of identity, we open up space for much more nuance and acceptance of incommensurability. The performers, writers, artists, and musicians I discuss here all contribute to this growing movement of Indigenous ingenuity but seldom are recognized as "Hawaiian." "Hawaiian performance" is constantly evolving, interrogating boundaries, and challenging dominant representations. As kuʻumealoha hoʻomanawanui explains, Hawaiian poets—present and past—are more interested in the metaphors, images, and kaona of poetry than in the forms it employs.[38]

There is kaona in defiant indigeneity and in the Hawaiian performance of aloha in particular spaces. Kaona is in many ways a Hawaiian reading practice that integrates ancestral and cultural knowledges to read against the grain of what appears to be presented. As a decolonial aesthetic practice, kaona "draws on the collective knowledges and experiences of Hawaiians" in a range of contexts and experiences.[39] Brandy Nālani McDougall describes "kaona connectivity" as a continuum that permits Kānaka Maoli to connect to one another and to our kupuna through an interpretation of kaona.[40] For instance, in chapter 4 I look at the cultural memory of Princess Kaʻiulani, the heir to the Hawaiian Kingdom during annexation in 1898. I investigate what the 2009 film *Princess Kaiulani* performs for Kanaka Maoli audiences. I argue that while the film has been critiqued within the Hawaiian community for its historical inaccuracy, it actually enables a radical and necessary form of kaona that challenges the legitimacy of the settler state and allows Kanaka Maoli audiences to reconnect to the kingdom and their kupuna.

These performances push the boundaries of what is permissible, laying the foundation of resistance, anticipating and sometimes preparing for more political action.[41] I reject the narrow understanding of political involvement because traditional avenues of engagement such as voting, grassroots organizing, and other forms of public social protest can overlook the everyday actions of people, including those of artists who chose to articulate their politics in a different manner. These cultural productions are not outside of the governmental aspirations or the political environment that are informing them, even if they do not appear to be ascribing anything "political." As Audra Simpson describes, sovereignty and nationhood can be expressed differently from the essentialized modes of expectation—the performance of bounded culture—and this different mode of expression pushes against narrow forms of judicial interpretation.[42] Hawaiian cultural productions thus create spaces of connection and contestation for those within the community who may not be interested in the governance process or who do not have access to the language and conversations that are taking place in formal political spaces. Defiant indigeneity can be seen throughout these chapters, exercised through the creation of sounds, drag shows, websites, and fashion. These spaces—from the beach to the nightclub—develop alternatives to mainstream Hawaiian performances. Attending to the ephemeral spaces where Indigenous peoples gather is crucial because what happens in these spaces cannot be contained or recuperated through the archive. These spaces contain various forms of embodied acts that always reconstitute themselves, and they transmit communal memories, history, and values to future generations.[43] As I explore in chapter 5, knowledge and belonging are negotiated in multiple performance spaces, including the home. I focus on a short story about Hawaiian LGBTQ life, "The Old Paniolo Way" by Kristiana Kahakauwila, to examine how belonging is performed in the Hawaiian diaspora through aloha and how this manifests in quotidian spaces, whether in Hawai'i or on the continent.

Kanaka Maoli cultural performances are the products of over 200 years of Hawaiian culture actively resisting, incorporating, and expanding literary, musical, and dance repertoires.[44] It is the sharing of cultural knowledge through Hawaiian performance that preserved aspects of Hawaiian culture when Christian missionaries initially sought to obliterate it—via the "banning" of the hula (1857–70) and the outlawing of a number of Hawaiian spiritual practices.[45] The suppression of all things "Hawaiian" (including language) in the late nineteenth and early twentieth centuries had huge ramifications for Hawaiian communities. Hula, in particular, went underground until the 1880s, when King David Kalākaua revived it. In the face of increasing European influence, Kalākaua sought to revitalize hula to show the resilience and greatness of Hawaiian culture.[46] As Kānaka Maoli had become Christian and hula became secularized, hula became the centerpiece of an emergent tourism industry. Kānaka Maoli were active agents in these growing performance opportunities. Hawaiian music troupes and dancers traveled across the continental United States after annexation in 1898 and were especially prominent at the Hawai'i Pavilion during the 1915 Panama Pacific Exposition in San Francisco, resulting in a nationwide fad of Hawaiian music. Hawaiian musicians and performers were inventive and appropriated other expressive forms. This continued in the 1920s during the Tin Pan Alley era when composers wrote pseudo-Hawaiian songs, and later in the 1940s when soldiers returned from World War II with nostalgia for the islands (and women) they met in the Pacific.[47] What we now understand as "contemporary" Hawaiian music and performance were first used in the late 1960s with the rise of the rock counterculture as Kanaka Maoli musicians began to integrate aspects of American rock and roll into Hawaiian music compositions.[48] This diverse history of Hawaiian performance was motivated by performers' ability to be innovative and to adapt to performance expectations of non-Native audiences as well as Indigenous ones.

The rise of global media technologies in the 1960s allowed the public performance of certain kinds of Hawaiian culture to become the mainstream fantasy. This is why the Hawaiian Renaissance was so important, because it politicized the performance and revival of Hawaiian music and other spiritual and cultural practices, pushing against the touristic visions of Hawaiian culture. The legacies of the Hawaiian Renaissance continue today in multiple forms, and while its impact on the Hawaiian community cannot be overstated, it also created within the Hawaiian community a focus on performances of revitalized Hawaiian culture that makes it appear that there are specific ways in which one must perform one's Hawaiian indigeneity. My intention is not to delegitimate cultural revitalization, but we need to be careful not to allow it to divide communities in the name of authenticity. We must also recognize that the knowledge transferred in both these realms of performance aided in saving our culture.

Today, practitioners and performers continue a strategic interplay among the performers' intent, what is permissible as "Hawaiian," and what sells tickets. The Kanaka Maoli performers I examine in this book are forced to participate in this political economy of difference, using their indigeneity to their advantage in some cases. For example, described in chapter 2, Krystilez stakes his identity through blood quantum because he grew up on a Hawaiian homestead on the island of Oʻahu, but he still finds his music unappreciated because it is not "Hawaiian." In chapter 3, Cocoa Chandelier, celebrated widely as a drag performer, regularly performs in a way that does not identify her as "Hawaiian," seeming to disguise her Hawaiian indigeneity altogether. At the same time, she is known in the theater community as a practitioner of butoh (Chinese opera) and in 2015 was part of Lāʻieikawai, a live production staged completely in the Hawaiian language. I show how in the process of resisting the straitjacket of "Hawaiian culture" or the "Aloha spirit" these Hawaiian performers seem to disavow Hawaiianness while also performing aloha by working to build these countercultural spaces. These performers are not only defying what is perceived to be their "nature"; they are producers of theory and worlds.

I am often tortured and haunted by aloha and what it might demand. I am weary of the heralding of aloha in numerous formations, but everything in my na'au (guts; heart) reminds me that we need aloha—not the wasteful forms of aloha spread through tourism, but the kind of aloha that is sustainable and has actually allowed us to survive. We need to center, perform, and cultivate this kind of aloha. As described in *A Hawaiian Survival Handbook* (2014): "Sustainable Aloha is the spiritual aspect to our survival. It is the part of our existence that cannot be physically seen but is revealed in our actions and interactions with ourselves, our community and our environment . . . It is the bond a community has during chaos. It is the resilience a nation has in wartime. It is what keeps us going when we are hungry, angry, lonely or tired. It is the intuitive and inherent knowledge that if we love something, we will never give up on it, and we will share this love for generation upon generation."[49] In this book, I present examples of how we perform our aloha as an experiential knowledge that need not appear "Hawaiian" but is nonetheless Hawaiian because of our shared connections and consciousness of what it means to be Kānaka Maoli. This shared consciousness is not without conflict. We must remember too that conflict is also evidence of our survival and that robust political debate is crucial to the lāhui.[50]

This book will not excavate Hawaiian knowledge or teach you about the "true" power of aloha. Aloha is an Indigenous way of knowing and relation that we utilize to sustain one another. The performances in this book are not the forms of Indigenous knowledge production that many seek to "preserve" or even fund, but they are representative of modes of Indigenous knowing, performances of aloha that have helped us see each other and, by extension, recognize, build, and enrich our communities because of our genealogy as Kanaka Maoli people. This book is ultimately about our defiant indigeneity, embodied and performed in the context of Hawai'i. I look closely at four sites where indigeneity contests juridical and community forms of policing that foreclose Hawaiian indigeneity. By disrupting indigeneity through performance, the artists described allow spaces to emerge that challenge how the state manages us, how the media and popular culture stereotype us, and how we even divide ourselves. I hope this book encourages us to look to how we create spaces in which we see one another, honoring the ways that we communicate and maintain who we are through performance.

CHAPTER ONE

F-You Aloha, I Love You

> There are these things that are
> important to me and they speak of
> how all is not right with the world
> yet still all is right.
>
> At the hardcore show the singer
> was screaming fuck-you-aloha-I-
> love-you-fuck-you-aloha-I-love-
> you.
>
> —JULIANA SPAHR, "Things"

This excerpt from a poem by Juliana Spahr, a haole woman from Ohio and a University of Hawai'i English professor from 1997 to 2003, encapsulates the paradox of the aloha spirit. Moving from stating the significance of "things" and then to an acknowledgment of how those things expose something not being "right with the world," and that yet, somehow, things are "right," these lines flag a somber contradiction. Following the lines "fuck-you-aloha-I- / love-you," the poem takes the spirit of aloha head-on and expresses the complexities of the investment in and relationship to aloha. I was hesitant to begin a chapter about Hawaiian culture's supposedly most prized essence or *spirit*—aloha—with a haole woman's words and the unnamed hard-core music band she cites. It is noteworthy that the sentiment "fuck you aloha, I love you" emerges in a subcultural space where juxtaposing "fuck you" with aloha might be possible. No information about the hard-core band who is screaming these words is available, raising a number of questions about who harbors these feelings about aloha and when and how aloha is invoked in multiple spaces. This chapter explores the ways that Kānaka Maoli experience the sentiment "fuck you aloha I love you" as it encapsulates the contradictions of aloha and its subsequent performance in especially deep, personal ways at the limits of discourse. As a seminal Hawaiian concept of love and inclusion, aloha, ironically, serves to obscure troubling lived realities that Kānaka Maoli experience, such as increasing poverty, houselessness, low educational attainment, and overall poor health.[1]

Aloha has a history that Kānaka Maoli embody. Aloha has undergone a historical transformation that has problematically contributed to the dispossession of Hawaiian lands, culture, and identity. Aloha is a burden and a gift, rife with tension because of the ways in which Kānaka Maoli are called by religion, the settler state, and the tourism industry to *live aloha*. Kanaka Maoli belief in aloha has enabled a Hawaiian cultural and political resurgence, and it is a force that we use to hold each other up and together. Aloha is also the way that Kānaka Maoli police and regulate the behavior of our broadly defined community. The function of aloha as a disciplining force that manages and encourages particular kinds of Hawaiian cultural expressions is seldom critically analyzed. It is only celebrated or mourned.

Why do Kānaka Maoli continue to be emotionally, financially, and performatively invested in aloha even when we are aware of the damage it has wrought across the Indigenous Pacific and the impact it has on our own Hawaiian indigeneity? My approach circumvents ethnographic practices invested in accessing or excavating a "pure" Hawaiian cultural essence, usually named "aloha," by interrogating instead the ways that the performance of aloha has become a barometer of Hawaiian indigeneity. The debate or question that is most critical is not what aloha truly is or means or when it is "real"; rather, we need to ask how and why the performance of aloha has become a marker of Hawaiian value within and outside of Hawaiian communities. It is crucial to map the historical and political terrain upon which this value was assigned and the manner in which Kānaka Maoli have internalized this as our worth. I trace the convergence and the demands of modernity, labor, and performance, which transformed "aloha" into a so-called expression of our true inner selves. I proceed with an outline of Louis Althusser's thoughts on interpellation, applying them to the processes of colonization, Christianity, capitalism, the settler state, tourism, and public education in Hawai'i. Specifically, I describe two ways in which the state has attempted to enshrine aloha, by naming Hawai'i the Aloha State in 1959 and by passing the Aloha Spirit Law in 1986. I recommend that we rethink aloha as the Hawaiian "gift to the world," ending the chapter with a reconsideration of why we continue to perform aloha. My analysis of aloha in this chapter provides a foundation for understanding the performances of aloha I examine in the subsequent chapters.

The Hawaiian dictionary defines "aloha" as love, affection, compassion, mercy; to love, to venerate, to show kindness; and as a salutation, to greet, and to hail.[2] *No Nā Mamo* (2011) by Malcolm Nāea Chun documents that the meaning of aloha as a Hawaiian word transformed over time. Calvinist missionaries, first arriving in Hawai'i in 1820, were directly involved in the translation of the Hawaiian language into English. One of their primary goals was to translate the Bible into the Hawaiian language. As Chun explains, aloha was a concept that got translated into a casual greeting while also retaining its meaning of "love," but prior to this transformation, "welina" and "anoʻai" were the more common modes of address among Kānaka Maoli. As George Kanahele has discussed, missionary translation turned aloha into a word that focused on agape love, in other words, love of God and unconditional love. Aloha is now a product of this evolution and commingling between the "ancient traditional" meaning of aloha, a Polynesian concept, and its Christian translation.[3]

Christian missionaries had been traversing the Pacific since the late seventeenth century. Similar translations of "aloha" can be found across the Pacific, meaning love, pity, and compassion. "Aloha" was similar to "aroha" in Maori, "alofa" in Samoan, "aroha" in Tahitian, and "alōfa" in Tongan, thus displaying the etymological links and kinship across Polynesia. However, as Kanahele and Mary Kawena Pukuʻi explain, aloha was just one aspect of precolonial Hawaiian life, and it came from a philosophical matrix of Hawaiian ideas and values.[4] Pukuʻi, largely regarded as *the* authority on Hawaiian language, culture, and life, was the author of numerous texts, worked as an ethnologist at the Bishop Museum from 1938 to 1961, and was an informant for white anthropologists who staked their careers on the translations and access to Hawaiian culture she provided.[5] She writes in *Nānā I Ke Kumu* that "ʻohana" may have been a more important way that Kānaka Maoli related to one another than "aloha." Put best by Pukuʻi, Haertig, and Lee, "eating, drinking, singing and talking together, the ties of man to fellow man are strengthened in the mutual regard and love summed up as aloha."[6] Aloha thus meant kindness and sharing, especially in the family or ʻohana setting where people are welcomed and all is shared, with the understanding that people gather to provide mutual helpfulness for collective benefit. This understanding of aloha alongside ʻohana reiterates the importance of community and the responsibility that comes with membership. Additionally, as Kanahele infers, loyalty to family might have been more important than aloha in precolonial Hawaiian life.[7] Stripped of this epistemological context, aloha is misused and misrepresented. The definition put forward by Pukuʻi and Kanahele differs clearly from the missionary translation that turned aloha into a word focused on a love of God. The missionary translation empties aloha of its reciprocal ethos, and, as this chapter elaborates, the transformation of aloha was carefully orchestrated and later entrenched in the settler state and the tourism industry as part of the settler-colonial project to abuse our concepts for their own gain.

Aloha State Apparatuses

Aloha demands something of everyone in Hawai'i; it does not discriminate—that's kind of the point. Aloha calls everyone in Hawai'i to behave in a manner that is kind, loving, open, and nonconfrontational. We are constantly reminded of the aloha spirit—in public, to express it at work, and in private, to "live aloha." The pressure to be friendly all the time can sometimes feel like a command that in turn can produce a backlash, such as in the sentiment "fuck you, aloha." As the Indigenous people of Hawai'i, and as the so-called repositories of the famed "aloha spirit," Kānaka Maoli are held to a higher standard when it comes to aloha. This section explains how aloha became the Hawaiian calling that serves an ideological function for the state of Hawai'i. Althusser's now famous "Ideology and Ideological State Apparatuses," when applied to Hawai'i, exposes the ways in which aloha has seeped into all aspects of daily life. Althusser explains that ideology functions through institutions such as the church, the education system, and the family unit. These institutions create subjectivities through a process of "interpellation," an act that hails subjects into ways of being that are notably reinforced through ideological state apparatuses (ISAs). He explains that hailing occurs at the moment that one is "called" or hailed. ISAs hide systems of domination to normalize (oppressive) modes of power in everyday life in both public and private spheres.[8] In Althusser's configuration, subjects are "hailed" into their identities by the state via modes of address, in his now iconic calling "hey you" when a police officer or the state calls you. Remember, one of the definitions of aloha is "to hail." In Hawai'i when aloha is spoken, it conjures Hawaiian indigeneity and what people believe aloha to mean (informed by lived experience and popular culture), and it in turn holds users to an expectation of behavior that is welcoming and loving. The voice hails subjects in a state or secular voice and is harnessed by ISAs that in turn interpellate subjects into believing in aloha.[9]

Interpellation is built upon an older concept of being "called" by God. As Judith Butler explains in *The Psychic Life of Power*, ideology is established through a religious metaphor of being called (that is, hailed or interpellated). Being called happens in a voice that is impossible to refuse—the voice of God.[10] This voice of God called Kānaka Maoli and required their submission to aloha to ensure their salvation. Max Weber's *The Protestant Ethic and the Spirit of Capitalism* outlined how religion has helped to develop and grow the spirit of capitalism through the process of establishing one's "calling." Weber describes the calling as a divine ordinance and the only way of living acceptable to God, wherein man was to ensure salvation "solely through the fulfillment of the obligation imposed upon the individual by his position in the world."[11] As a product of the Reformation, the calling was also defined as a skill or task that a person would perform to his or her fullest capacity, such as working hard in order to earn a place in heaven. In Rey Chow's reading of Weber, she finds that the drive toward material gains via capitalist enterprises is an outcome of internal disciplining forces that accompany a secularizing West.[12] In other words, with the rise of the secular West, one's calling by God was replaced with interpellating practices of the state. Through the workings of colonialism, the imposition of capitalism, statehood, narratives of multiculturalism, and now tourism, Kānaka Maoli have been taught that performing aloha is a natural extension of who we are as a people.

Being interpellated and called to perform aloha is the context in which Kānaka Maoli believe that performing aloha will save us, will set us free. This occurs through a performance of aloha. Althusser contended that the subjects' acts are practices that are governed and defined by material ISAs that create subjects.[13] Put another way, interpellation happens through bodily movements and through the performance of skills that have a material basis. Citing the seventeenth-century French mathematician, physicist, and Catholic philosopher Blaise Pascal, Althusser asserted that physical gestures, attitudes, and beliefs are material practices that form through habit. He draws on Pascal's description of religious belief captured in the injunction "Kneel down, move your lips in prayer, and you will believe" to show how interpellation is a corporeal practice.[14] Pascal's example of kneeling to pray in order to produce belief emphasizes how something becomes unquestioned and natural through repetition, which is what Judith Butler later claims is the basis for "performativity."[15] In short, ISAs proliferate through individual subjects' internalization of a given ideology that we then use to discipline one another. The constant performance of aloha as a natural form of "Hawaiianness" has caused us to internalize the idea that performing aloha makes us who we are, when, in fact, it has been through a performative process of doing that this has become the measure of our ability to be Hawaiian. But not all is lost; while performativity constitutes and sustains the subject, it also "becomes the occasion for further making," leaving space open for transgression, which I explore in the other chapters.[16]

One of the reasons that aloha is performed today as *natural* is because of the transformation of land tenure in Hawai'i in the mid-nineteenth century. Private land ownership and the plantation system replaced Kanaka Maoli relationships with the 'āina, inhibiting the way Hawaiians related to the land and what they had to do to subsist under this new system.[17] Once capitalism had become normalized in Hawai'i and was practiced as the predominant form of "production," living sustainably off the land and sea was no longer possible because many Kānaka Maoli lost their lands during the "Great Mahele" to plantation owners. Recall too that not long before this, Christian missionaries translated aloha to mean unconditional love and selflessness. The call of aloha through Christianity and then capitalism combined to encourage Kānaka Maoli to perform culture—for example, to perform "aloha" as it is manifested in cultural performances. As early as the mid-nineteenth century, Kānaka Maoli were being encouraged to perform hula for money for high-ranking visitors.

Hula was the cornerstone of Hawaiian religious culture and was of course at first shunned by Calvinist missionaries, who pressured Hawaiian royalty to discourage (and later criminalize) hula's public performance. Noenoe Silva has clarified that the legal restrictions put on hula in the mid-nineteenth century allowed the Hawaiian Kingdom (and later the state of Hawai'i) to control Kanaka Maoli sexuality and spiritual practices and to regulate hula for public and commercial purposes. In 1859 the public performance of hula became restricted to hula hālau (troupe) who were granted licenses and to spaces where hula shows were generating a paid audience (as in Honolulu and Lāhaina) with harsh consequences for those in violation. Hula subsequently went underground until the 1880s, when King David Kalākaua revived it.[18] In addition, as Kānaka Maoli adopted Christianity and hula became secularized (for example, the need for hula licenses, and the criteria of recreational rather than spiritual performances), the stage was set for transforming hula into a potent symbol of Hawaiian aloha for tourism.[19]

After the illegal overthrow of the Hawaiian Kingdom in 1893, the territory and statehood period proliferated the idea, rooted in the racism of the time, that Kānaka Maoli are "skilled" only at certain things—performing culture and physical labor. These perceptions stood in stark contrast to what we know was a highly literate Hawaiian population. Estimates show that nearly 80 percent of the Hawaiian population could read and write by the mid-nineteenth century, an exceedingly high proportion for any population.[20] Instruction in Western ways of communicating as well as in the Hawaiian language was fostered by Hawaiian royalty, but by the late nineteenth century, shortly after the illegal overthrow of the Hawaiian Kingdom by American businessmen, Hawaiian-language schools steadily declined. In 1896 the Republic of Hawai'i named English the official language of Hawai'i and closed all Hawaiian-language schools. The decline of the Hawaiian language continued as English was emphasized as a language of economic opportunity, which solidified the so-called superiority of Western knowledge and the delegitimation of Hawaiian ways of knowing and being. The devaluation of Hawaiian knowledge occurred at the same time aloha remained a prominent element of Hawaiian indigeneity, as other concepts and practices went underground or were stopped altogether.

With the imposition of American education, as Ty Kāwika Tengan and Noelani Goodyear-Ka'ōpua have explained, Hawaiian men were groomed for physical labor or military service, and Hawaiian women were taught domestic duties.[21] Akin to the civilizing projects enacted on Native Americans in boarding schools (such as Carlisle Indian School) and on African Americans at the Hampton Institute, Hawaiian education was in many ways controlled by missionaries who prioritized Christianity and Western thought, which carried often-racist Eurocentric values and practices that pipelined Hawaiians into certain sectors of the economy. After the overthrow, public education promoted the Hawaiian Kingdom as something that belonged in the past. Julie Kaomea's study of public schools in modern Hawai'i also examines the role of ISAs—in particular, public education—in reifying Hawaiian stereotypes and affirming state power. Kaomea found that educators promoted negative depictions of Kānaka Maoli in textbooks and curriculums, wherein Kanaka Maoli chiefs are depicted as merciless rulers and Hawaiian life as unjust and scary (as a product of this school system, I can attest to this).[22] The texts work to obscure the realities of American colonialism by discrediting Kanaka Maoli rulers of the past and present, which in turn continues to justify the overthrow of the Hawaiian Kingdom and undermines modern Hawaiian sovereignty struggles.[23] Kaomea also adds that these standardized textbooks look like tourist "appreciation kits" that manufacture Hawaiian culture as naturally giving and entertaining.[24] Such textbooks subsequently serve the economic interests of the state by helping to create attitudes favoring an abundant supply of cheap labor and docile Kānaka Maoli as willing and able "ambassadors of aloha."[25] In a state where tourism is the preeminent industry, school curriculums must reflect the desires of the state and corporate interests to duplicate power relations—producing behavioral expectations that both Kānaka Maoli and settlers internalize to support aloha as an ideology—to promote and reinforce the image of Hawai'i as a paradise in every sense.

Throughout the territory period up through the present, Kānaka Maoli found opportunity and agency through the performance of culture. Kānaka

Maoli actively pursued performance opportunities to share Hawaiian culture and to travel and see the world. These performances might be summed up in any number of ways, but to the tourist—to the non-Hawaiian audience—it is "aloha." Kānaka Maoli are then called and required to perform this aloha, especially in the tourism industry. Such performances produced a paycheck and a value that Kānaka Maoli could hold onto when so much of our culture was being discarded because of colonization. Participation in such activities, however, lent credence to the notions that the only value of Kānaka Maoli was their ability to perform aloha and that such performances were "natural," indicative of who we used to be and should be. The latter is evidence of colonialism and capitalism working together to transform and co-opt Hawaiian culture, which was achieved through the disciplining and exhibition of Kanaka Maoli bodies in a process that has become naturalized.

By the early twentieth century, aloha became one of the few cultural practices that Kānaka Maoli had left, and they were encouraged to perform it for money (by dancing hula and expressing aloha). This is precisely how aloha got attached to the definition of Hawaiianness and Hawaiian culture, because under capitalism Kānaka Maoli are required to perform it as their worth. That is not to say that Kānaka Maoli were duped completely as they "performed" aloha. Giving aloha came to be a skill that Kānaka Maoli were perceived to be good at (and they were). It also provided one of the few available sources of financial benefits. As Adria Imada has discussed, many Kānaka Maoli secured a measure of agency through the hula tours in the 1930s and 1940s, but giving and performing "aloha" on these tours also so-lidified the relationship between Hawaiʻi and the United States, creating a fantasy of reciprocal attachment, making U.S. military and tourist expansion appear "benign."[26] Still, when tourism became Hawaiʻi's primary in-dustry after statehood, controlling how "aloha" was invoked became quite difficult as it became a widely disseminated sign of Hawaiianness. The con-stant performance of aloha as a natural extension of Kanaka Maoli identity was internalized by Kānaka Maoli. While many Kānaka Maoli work in all types of professions, aloha has come to represent an unwavering internal character trait of Kanaka Maoli identity, regardless of whether we earn money for it directly. Aloha became, through a process of repetition and performance, an expression of Hawaiian cultural difference. Over time, per-forming aloha became a way to sustain a relationship to Hawaiian culture. The state of Hawaiʻi has been integral in this process by appropriating and co-opting aloha to quiet dissent and to police Kanaka Maoli behavior and identity.

The Aloha State

On March 13, 1959, Reverend Abraham Akaka delivered an inspiring sermon that motivated the naming of Hawai'i as "the Aloha State." The governor, members of the territorial senate, Hawaiian civic clubs, and the Royal
Hawaiian Band all convened for an interdenominational sermon at Kawaia-
hao Church during which Akaka addressed fears about what the future
would hold for Hawai'i as a U.S. state.[27] Akaka also named what has now
come to personify Hawai'i's hypercommodified artifice, "the spirit of aloha."
He said:

> We need to see that Hawaii has potential moral and spiritual contri-
> butions to make [to] our nation and to our world. The fears Hawaii
> may have are to be met by men and women who are living witnesses
> of what we really are in Hawaii, of the spirit of aloha, men and
> women who can help unlock the doors to the future by the guidance
> and grace of God. This kind of self-affirmation is the need of the
> hour. And we can affirm our being, as the Aloha State, by full
> participation in our nation and in our world. For any collective
> anxiety, the answer is collective courage. And the ground of that
> courage is God.[28]

Inspired by the sermon, a law was soon passed that designated Hawai'i the
Aloha State. By this time, aloha had already been solidified as Hawai'i's cultural essence via tourism. As Akaka's sermon stated and as subsequent
events exhibit, the state of Hawai'i was always invested in the Christian undertones of aloha and its influence on state politics. Further, the intertwin-
ing of aloha with the state created the ruse that the state represented the
interests of aloha and coded aloha as the epitome of what is "Hawaiian"
to an increasingly globalized media and as a universal cultural gift that
Hawaiians are obliged to share.

The dispossession of aloha from Kānaka Maoli took place as aloha became the foundation for Hawai'i's racial coexistence and tolerance. Throughout the territory period (1898–1959), Asian settlers began to stake their
place in Hawai'i's racial hierarchy as part of a "local" community to differentiate themselves from haole people. At this time, Asian settlers clung to
aloha to negotiate their sense of belonging in Hawai'i.[29] As aloha was celebrated as an expression of "Hawaiian values of love, generosity, and open-
mindedness," it was then promoted as the central value of Hawaiian culture
and island life.[30] Hawai'i, as a place, and its residents, because of aloha,

marked the distance between Hawai'i's residents and the continental United States.[31] Aloha in this sense indexes the difference of Hawai'i for all its inhabitants. Buttressed by Hawaiian culture, aloha is honored at the expense of Kanaka Maoli claims to sovereignty and self-determination because aloha makes Hawai'i available to everyone in a way that dispossesses Kānaka Maoli of cultural authority.

By perpetuating the myth of the Aloha State, the local government prioritizes a false sense of belonging among Hawai'i's multicultural population while actively ignoring and erasing Kanaka Maoli sovereignty struggles. The latter is evidenced in Hawai'i's reputation of cultural diversity and, by extension, our so-called kindness toward one another. This reputation, which I would argue is in most cases *real*, is most heinously personified in statecraft, as in the naming of the Aloha State and in the Aloha Spirit Law, which is then used in the Foucauldian sense to discipline the self and others.[32] The ideal of aloha as emblematic of inclusion and racial harmony has been referred to as the "Hawai'i multicultural model," and it has served as a model for American race relations and the world since the mid-twentieth century.[33] Hawai'i's multicultural population was imagined to reflect the biological diversity of the natural environment and was celebrated by sociologists and historians who characterized Hawai'i as a "racial melting pot" and posited that Hawai'i's multiracial population lived in harmony in a way unmatched anywhere in the world.[34]

In combination with Asian political and economic ascendancy and the supposed lack of racial violence, Hawai'i's exceptional multiculturalism is cited as evidence of the aloha spirit at work.[35] The multicultural model, as Jonathan Okamura explains, is highly limited because it ignores ongoing institutional discrimination, racism, prejudice, and ethnic hostilities that are common features of everyday life in Hawai'i.[36] Through academic discourse, journalism, and literary works, tales about the "power of aloha" and Hawai'i's multiculturalism proliferated throughout the post–World War II era.[37] In this context, Kānaka Maoli became valued because of what their culture could offer the United States, especially during the Cold War, as a representation of America's multicultural character. The foregrounding of Hawai'i's multiculturalism was critical to the statehood project, and after statehood in 1959, aloha as an expression of goodwill, love, and inclusion for all became coterminous with the promotion of Hawai'i as a tourist destination.[38]

Tourism continues to be Hawai'i's largest industry (along with the U.S. military). With tourism as Hawai'i's primary economic base and aloha as its so-called gift to the world, the performing bodies of Kānaka Maoli (Hawaiians)—or whoever can pass as "Hawaiian"—became necessary. In her most-cited work, "Lovely Hula Hands" (1993), Haunani-Kay Trask argues that the state of Hawai'i pimps Hawaiian culture through tourism.[39] Of course, the state has always been in the business of promoting tourism. In 1903, just a few years after Hawai'i was declared a U.S. territory, the new government set up the Hawaii Promotion Committee—which became the Hawai'i Tourism Authority in 1915—to begin marketing Hawai'i as a tourist destination. In Trask's scathing critique of tourism and American colonialism, she writes, "Our country has been and is being plasticized, cheapened, and exploited. They're selling it in plastic leis, coconut ashtrays, and cans of 'genuine, original Aloha.' They've raped us, sold us."[40] Narrating the prostitution of the Hawaiian culture, Trask's insights lay bare the ways in which aloha has become so distorted, as representative of what Rona Halualani describes as "a hegemonic political relationship of power," which produced the idea that aloha personifies a "cultural essence of Hawaiianness."[41] It is this political relationship of power that then transformed aloha into an ideology for the development of tourism. The production and dissemination of such performances of "aloha" and imagery to promote tourism thus became deeply intertwined with what gets defined as "Hawaiian" by Kānaka Maoli and settlers alike.

Throughout the territorial and post-statehood period, aloha had to be nurtured and preserved for tourism. In these instances, aloha performs and is performed, constituting its own discursive formation, disciplining those who deviate from the meaning of aloha as "un-Hawaiian" because aloha has "taken on the semblance of a Hawaiian origin or interiority that seems native."[42] Hawai'i's so-called primary resource and export—the aloha spirit— is thus exploited by the tourism industry to capitalize on ideas about Hawai'i that its residents internalize in a way that makes tourism appear to be the only way that Hawai'i can sustain its economy. In the 1980s, there was a heightened emphasis on aloha's so-called natural presence in the islands, but through the changes taking place—urban development, increased commercialization, and an influx of tourists—people began to express anxiety in newspaper articles and editorials, calling for the need to "save aloha" and rhetorically posing the question, Is aloha dead?[43] In letters to the editor, aloha is marked as necessary to the promotion of tourism, emphasizing that aloha is what makes Hawai'i distinct from other tropical destinations.[44] Letters from residents also bemoan the recession of aloha from the quotidian, posing questions about aloha's diminished significance, expressing a nostalgia for a rural and simpler time, when aloha was expressed among residents in a supposedly more "authentic" form, away from the machinations of mass tourism. These two perspectives on aloha—the need to save it *for* tourism and the need to save its authenticity from commodification *by* tourism—exemplify aloha's discursive status, whereby it is actively reiterated and policed. The success of mass tourism caused aloha to evolve from its previous manifestations in multiculturalism to become the so-called spirit of the islands that is available to Kānaka Maoli, settlers, and potential tourists.

The naming of the state in this manner solidified institutional support of aloha, and the statist imperative to perform aloha implored citizens or subjects to perform aloha as a requirement of multicultural civic participation and to function within a capitalist system focused on selling Hawaiian culture. The Christian demands of aloha might allow a delay in its consequences—so to speak—but not being friendly to tourists might result in losing your job, not being authentically "Hawaiian," and not being seen as a member of a community. Later, as tensions mounted in the 1970s around issues of Hawaiian sovereignty, the local government felt the need to pass what is known as the Aloha Spirit Law.[45]

The Aloha Spirit Law

In 1986, Hawai'i passed the Aloha Spirit Law, which encourages people to emote good feelings to each other, especially in government dealings.[46] The passing of the Aloha Spirit Law occurred in the wake of the Hawaiian Renaissance and several years of unrest within the local government. In the late 1970s, Hawaiian groups agitated for an acknowledgment of the injustices done to Kānaka Maoli, precipitating the creation of the Office of Hawaiian Affairs (OHA), an end to the U.S. military target practice bombing on Kaho'olawe, and the emergence of a Hawaiian sovereignty movement. Such tensions influenced the need to codify Hawai'i's most prized essence in law. The Aloha Spirit Law states:

> These are traits of character that express the charm, warmth and
> sincerity of Hawai'i's people. It [Aloha] was the working philosophy
> of native Hawaiians and was presented as a gift to the people of
> Hawai'i. "Aloha" is more than a word of greeting or farewell or a
> salutation. "Aloha" means mutual regard and affection and extends
> warmth in caring with no obligation in return. "Aloha" is the essence

of relationships in which each person is important to every other person for collective existence. "Aloha" means to hear what is not said, to see what cannot be seen and to know the unknowable.[47]

Early discussion of the bill included legislators questioning what it means to define aloha and if such an act was necessary. Similarly, the testimony included discussion on whether it was the place of the state to define the Hawaiian term. Richard Pomaikaiokalani Kinney of the Hawaiian Political Action Council testified against the bill, saying that the measure "interferes with religious freedom" of Native Hawaiians and would "become the one and only legal interpretation of Aloha Spirit."[48] Additionally, there were fears that the passing of "aloha" as a law would cause criminals to go unprosecuted if people were legally obligated to treat one another with kindness. Kinaʻu Kamaliʻi, who initially supported the bill, later objected to it on philosophical grounds, stating, "It seems to me that if we have to statutorily define and remind ourselves and others to act with aloha, then we are implicitly acknowledging that we are losing that spirit."[49] Kamaliʻi makes a critical point that the need for the law points to anxieties about losing aloha and questions what the aloha spirit is to begin with.

This law is relatively unknown among the residents of Hawaiʻi, which speaks to its insidious nature as well as to the power of aloha to pervade the public sphere going unnoticed. It signals the extent to which aloha functions like a state ideology. As Jonathan Osorio explains, the law allows competing groups in a society to coexist because it requires that people place their faith in the law.[50] In other words, the Aloha Spirit Law represents the state's desire and need to codify aloha in order to compensate for the apparently increasing lack of aloha within Hawaiian society at the time. The law itself is rarely invoked in public discourse, but when it is, its purpose is usually to unite Hawaiʻi's people under a banner of peaceful coexistence, coming together, and belonging. One example of this occurred in 2013 when Hawaiʻi governor Neil Abercrombie invoked the Aloha Spirit Law in a speech prior to signing a marriage equality bill (SB1) that divided many local communities.[51] This example of "equality," one that many progressives would celebrate, is actually emblematic of the way that aloha—through its ideological feel-good impulses—silences critiques that can come from varying political inclinations. In particular, the critique that aloha glossed as "love" functions to support a homonormative political agenda or that invoking Hawaiian culture to justify an institution such as marriage, which is rooted in heteropatriarchal and juridical forms of property and ownership, is yet another instance of colonial imposition that constrains performances of gender and Indigenous sovereignty as they are lived daily.

Resisting the Discourse of Aloha

These brief examples exhibit just some of the ways that aloha functions with ISAs in Hawai'i to reproduce and discipline subjects. This has created what Lori Pierce has called a "discourse of aloha."[52] This discourse of aloha structures what is possible, and what is possible is sustained by the state's use of aloha as an ideological force. The "discourse of aloha" in Hawai'i was created as a strategy to ignore institutional racism and to turn a blind eye to the injustices suffered by Kānaka Maoli and the subjugation of Asian laborers on plantations. Achieved through civic celebrations that featured ethnically diverse people living together in harmony, the "discourse of aloha" made it appear that America's mythical melting pot had succeeded in Hawai'i, in spite of ongoing racial tensions. Most importantly, the celebration of ethnic diversity did not threaten haole hegemony.[53] Heather Diamond explains in *American Aloha* that the state approves and supports performances that promote an apolitical, domesticated, nonthreatening, multiethnic "local" culture that caters to tourist desires.[54] In today's liberal multicultural climate, then, culture can be celebrated in a manner that detaches cultural difference from political ideologies that challenge the interests of those in power.[55]

Aloha may work in ways that uphold haole hegemony, but the ideological hold of haole hegemony is never a done deal, and most certainly not in Hawai'i. Kānaka Maoli have always resisted colonization, for throughout the late nineteenth and early twentieth centuries, Kānaka Maoli expressed agency against colonial forces, as exemplified notably by the Wilcox Rebellion (1889), the Kū'ē Petitions (1897–98), opposition to statehood (1950s), the Hawaiian Renaissance in the 1970s, and, in the 1990s, the rise of Hawaiian sovereignty movements that continue today. Hawaiian groups have always found inventive ways to use aloha. In the 1970s, Aboriginal Lands of Hawaiian Ancestry (ALOHA) was a well-known Hawaiian activist group that called for reparations for Kānaka Maoli. Protect Kaho'olawe 'Ohana (PKO), one of the more prominent activist groups in the 1970s, was known for its motto, "Aloha 'āina." PKO made multiple trips to the island of Kaho'olawe to protest ongoing U.S. military bombing. During PKO's landings, they would give offerings, replant vegetation, and identify sacred sites, all while the island was being actively used for target practice. One of its founders, the activist and musician George Helm, gave his life in 1977, along with another activist, Kimo Mitchell, who were both lost at sea. Helm encouraged the people of Hawai'i, and Kānaka Maoli especially, to take up the cause of aloha 'āina, reminding everyone that the culture cannot exist without the land.[56] This call for aloha 'āina in the 1970s was not just a call to care for the land; it held historical symbolism because it was also the name of the liberal Hawaiian-language newspaper *Ke Aloha Aina* in the late twentieth century. The newspaper was run by the Hawaiian lawyer, legislator, and patriot Joseph Nāwahī and was known for its "biting criticism of the haole elite."[57] Aloha 'āina continues to be an organizing principle for Kānaka Maoli who seek to live sustainably with the land. All of these varied political perspectives and movements challenge U.S. hegemony but unsettle the articulation of aloha solely with the state apparatus, tourism, and multiculturalism. This is why the state needs to promote its own brand of aloha post-statehood and why in the 1980s the crisis of aloha prompted the passage of the Aloha Spirit Law.

These public displays of resistance work to exacerbate racial tensions between Kānaka Maoli and settlers. Hawai'i's multiethnic population, a legacy of multiple generations with roots in plantation labor immigration primarily from Asia, overlaps with Kanaka Maoli culture in precarious ways. The term "local" is used in Hawai'i to differentiate between Hawai'i-born residents and newcomers; the latter are commonly imagined to be white or haole, although not always. "Local" is politically linked to the legacy of land dispossession and ownership in the islands, where the history of these processes were played out first in the plantation economy and continues today through tourism.[58] Scholarship theorizes local Asians as "settlers" who in their aspirations for equality and citizenship colluded with the state of Hawai'i and are also to blame for the disempowerment and displacement of the Kanaka Maoli people.[59] Hawaiian sovereignty operates as an "ethnic pressure point" that, as Jonathan Okamura explains, continues to be perceived as a threat to other ethnic groups.[60] In turn, the ethnic identities of certain groups, namely, Asian settlers, are destabilized because Hawaiian sovereignty questions the very underpinnings of the settler state and works to illuminate discrepancies in power, privilege, and status in contemporary ethnic relations.[61]

Indigenous peoples have a relationship to the nation-state that differs considerably from that of settler groups. Rather than seeking equal treatment via civil rights, Indigenous peoples must grapple with issues concerning territory, sovereignty, nationhood, treaties, land claims, and even radically different epistemologies and ontologies or cosmologies.[62] When Kānaka Maoli pursue formal sovereignty claims, they issue a warning to the Aloha State—a challenge to the very legitimacy of the American political infrastructure in Hawai'i. In government, economy, law, and education, Hawaiian indigeneity pervades the public sphere in Hawai'i.[63] The ongoing agitations of Hawaiian sovereignty activists thus burn holes in the idyllic multicultural quilt that has been woven around Hawai'i's past. This is why the state is so deeply invested in retaining its hold over aloha.

Given this threat, Kanaka Maoli sovereignty activists are framed as racist separatists who betray aloha in their aspirations for Hawaiian sovereignty or independence.[64] The most salient iteration of aloha's power is when it is used against the very people (Kānaka Maoli) from whom aloha originates.[65] Examples of this can be seen in the U.S. Department of the Interior (DOI) hearings held in Hawai'i in the summer of 2014. The DOI meetings were held to solicit "feedback" from the Kanaka Maoli community about the United States' role in "helping" to "organize" a Hawaiian governing entity. During these meetings, Kānaka Maoli actively called one another out for not having "aloha" for the DOI panelists and one another. Perhaps noncoincidentally, the DOI meetings were announced shortly after OHA CEO Kamana'opono Crabbe wrote a letter to Secretary of State John Kerry inquiring about the status of the Hawaiian Kingdom under international law.[66] In a very public conflict between Crabbe and the other OHA trustees, Crabbe was accused of a "breach of aloha." OHA trustee Collette Machado invoked our beloved Hawaiian value, aloha, to accuse Crabbe of wrongdoing and, worse, of displaying "un-Hawaiian" behavior. These internal conflicts were a repeat of previous struggles over the articulation of aloha with an accommodating and docile form of Hawaiianness that is not supposed to question the Aloha State apparatus. These internal conflicts were a repeat of previous struggles from the 1990s when advocates for Hawaiian sovereignty became particularly vocal.

The fervent backlash against activists was a result of friction between Kānaka Maoli and settlers in Hawai'i, exacerbated by the growing power of the Hawaiian sovereignty movement. These backlashes represented Kānaka Maoli as having forfeited their authentic "Hawaiianness" on account of their lack of aloha, as evidenced by their political agitation and criticism. Thus, these backlashes framed Kanaka Maoli activists as betrayers of aloha and their betrayals as much more dangerous than when committed by members of other ethnic groups. When Kānaka Maoli betray or resist aloha, they defy their subject positions as the embodiment of aloha, which is crucial to Hawai'i's image.[67] Even worse, when Kānaka Maoli betray aloha, they become no longer "Hawaiian," and to no longer be "Hawaiian" is to no longer have a place in Hawai'i. This helps explain why social protest in Hawai'i is often devalued, because it is considered a violation of the aloha spirit. Violating the aloha spirit is blasphemy in Hawai'i; betraying aloha is akin to losing your "local" status; in a sense, betraying aloha is grounds for excommunication. The potential for ostracism or excommunication exhibits the ways that aloha disciplines behavior in Hawai'i and polices Kānaka Maoli specifically, whose social identities hinge on embodying aloha.

Rethinking Our Gift to the World

Aloha has been called Hawai'i's "gift to the world." So has surfing; so has the 'ukulele; so has the slack-key guitar; and so has Hawaiian Host Chocolates, a famous locally owned company known for its macadamia nuts and other goodies. Aloha, especially, has been posited as the essence of Hawaiian identity that represents our humanity and value in the global marketplace. Aloha, when used in public and in tourist settings, performs a depoliticized, decontextualized Hawaiianness that enables everyone to be Hawaiian if only while they are on vacation, visitors at Paradise Cove, or at any number of shows held throughout the islands. As a floating signifier waiting to be filled by the desires of tourists, aloha can be experienced, performed, and embodied by anybody. One of the significant ways that the invocation of Hawaiian culture can be oppressive for Kānaka Maoli is in how it is represented as exceptional or special in what it can teach and offer the world. It is in the combination of culture as the basis of specific identity as well as culture as having intrinsic value for everybody that Hawaiian culture and identity can be so easily commodified and appropriated. This is why everybody wants to be or can be Hawaiian or at the very least "Hawaiian at heart."[68] It is a potent discourse of difference that performances of aloha personify. One can experience aloha and even be changed, but an understanding of the political implications of aloha's appropriation is not necessary. This allows us to enjoy the culture of "the other" without forcing us to be transformed by it.[69]

The constant celebration of aloha as the Hawaiian gift to the world is representative of the convergence of neoliberal market forces that acknowledge and accept cultural, ethnic, racial, and gender difference as well as calls for minoritized populations to "speak their truth" in order to be included in a history that has excluded them. In other words, the neoliberal embracing of "cultural difference"—because it now has economic value—is just another project of political and economic assimilation and incorporation. The emphasis on learning and sharing aspects of culture—notably through cultural performances that the state authorizes—stands in for a kind of "truth" that can be remembered, shared, and used to police Hawaiian indigeneity. Thus, while it might appear that the cultures of "the other" are now being accepted and celebrated (that is, that our culture, our aloha, is valued), it often happens through a frame of liberal multiculturalism that depoliticizes and aestheticizes difference by emphasizing a surface-level or shallow celebration of cultural diversity that does not fully engage a transformative struggle against racism and white supremacy. This kind of celebration is dangerous because the recognition of cultural or ethnic difference can actually culturally bind the subaltern subject.[70] Indigenous peoples, especially, must be cautious of this kind of incorporation or recognition, as Native studies scholars have warned. Native "truth" as it is linked to cultural knowledges that have cultural and economic value in the eyes of the state or neoliberal forces is adjudicated and authenticated only if it has something to offer universal humanity. As a form of governmental and cultural recognition, Natives must always prove our "truth," perform our culture, as a way to prove our humanity.

Aloha has been marked as an indicator of Hawaiian culture's utility for universal humanity. It is, after all, our gift to the world, but we must be suspicious of these ongoing practices of incorporation through apolitical celebrations that are endemic to neoliberal multiculturalism. Such articulations and performances of culture certainly challenge the canons of mainstream knowledge, but these cultural products might also be consumed in ways that reproduce prevailing structures of power.[71] Embracing "the other" comes through rewriting history and supporting neoliberalism, but not by rewriting policy or not in a matter that questions white supremacy, heteropatriarchy, capitalism, and the legitimacy of the settler-colonial state itself. Celebrations of multiculturalism often require a liberal emphasis on unencumbered freedoms, which means that access to power is achieved through market participation. The free market desires the recognition and integration of difference because it continues to be a source of brand value that can be celebrated and marketed as diversity, as love.[72] Thus, access to the cultures of "the other" is always a global good. This then affirms a neoliberal marketplace that desires more than just the cultures of "the other" for dominant consumption; it also wants "the other" to believe that their liberation is wrapped up in these spheres of representation.[73] Put another way, settler cultures endeavored at first to extinguish indigeneity completely, but they later mined it, appropriated it, and claimed it as their own through celebrations of diversity. And certain identifiable discourses of culture and especially of aloha—both deploying and deployed by Kānaka Maoli and non-Kanaka alike—become the modes by which Kānaka Maoli may seek emancipation but nevertheless find ourselves colonized once again, albeit in new cultural forms.

This isn't just about us, Kānaka Maoli. Aloha, as a signifier of Hawaiʻi and Kānaka Maoli, not only flattens Kanaka Maoli differences but also insidiously operates as a stand-in for all Pacific Islanders and our varied cultures, undermining our differences and dynamic connections. The cadre of imagery associated with aloha and Hawaiʻi continues to be propagated by Hollywood, as recently displayed in the film *Aloha* (2015), which met considerable criticism because of its casting choices as well as its usage of "aloha" as a kind of branding that evacuates aloha of its spiritual significance. As explained by the collective Hinemoana of Turtle Island (which I am a member of), the film ultimately recycles cinematic tropes about Hawaiʻi that center white fantasies which lay claim to Hawaiʻi and Hawaiian culture, thus supporting settler colonialism and U.S. military interests across the Indigenous Pacific.[74] Films like this one continue the long tradition of imposing Hawaiian iconography on all Pacific Islanders. Pacific Islanders have multiple political statuses within the United States, and the designation "Pacific Islander" as a whole doesn't account for the diversities within the category. Further, while the love of Hawaiians might be sincere, it never manifests in love of other islanders.[75] The uncritical celebration of aloha impacts all Pacific Islanders, for aloha's deployment in a number of discourses undergirds the ongoing military occupation of the Pacific, the cultural exploitation of our cultures, and the attendant environmental degradation across our sea of islands. Still, I am compelled to defend aloha in spite of its internal conflicts and the contradictions that reform and reproduce its power. Aloha is promoted as what is "Hawaiian" and the thing that binds us, and it does. Aloha shields violence and encourages inclusion, supposedly producing good feelings for all of humanity. As the previous section explained at length, aloha is promoted as the essence of Kānaka Maoli and, by extension, the islands. This is the story Hawaiʻi tells itself and the world; I would be lying if I said I didn't believe in aloha too.

"Aloha" Refused

Aloha is the intelligence with which we meet life.

—KUMU HULA OLANA AI

Kānaka Maoli, Hawai'i residents, and anyone else who might have emotional stakes in aloha must acknowledge that aloha has been commercialized and continues to be a justification for the ostensible dispossession of Hawaiian lands and culture. Yet I still believe in aloha and feel that it is real. I am not sure why. Maybe it is real because we believe in it, even when we know that aloha can be a violent hailing force. Maybe we believe in it because our kupuna or elders did, and by believing in aloha we are somehow honoring them. The epigraph by kumu hula (hula master/teacher) Olana Ai forces me to *feel* the Kanaka Maoli investment in aloha. Ai's words articulate Hawaiian philosophy and ways of knowing with inherent value on their own terms.[76] The words are so simple and beautiful that they put me in diasporic tears, ironically after I write page after page about aloha's exploitative impacts. It is this response that personifies aloha's power for Kānaka Maoli. Aloha is thus embodied by Kānaka Maoli in these moments of affect that depend on the very performance of aloha. Notice that I am even performing aloha throughout this book. This is the measure and extent to which even in my criticism I am still accountable and beholden to aloha because it is inextricably tied to my sense of indigeneity.

Curiously, other contemporary Kanaka Maoli scholars or specialists do not engage aloha in their knowledge production.[77] In many respects, it's not that aloha is being dismissed; it just isn't publicly spoken about or written about in Kanaka Maoli academic discourse—at least not without being attached to aloha 'āina or, more recently, Kapu Aloha. In fact, as documented by Ohnuma, the most-cited works in Hawaiian studies, notably Kame'eleihiwa and Osorio, make no mention of aloha at all. Noenoe Silva's game-changing book *Aloha Betrayed*, while not about aloha per se, boasts a provocative title that gestures toward the idea that there is this thing called "aloha" and that the colonial conspirators who overthrew the Hawaiian Kingdom betrayed that aloha. And of course Trask's work openly analyzed aloha's exploitation and its consequences. It follows, then, that aloha's hypercommodified and arguably overdetermined status almost requires a gutting of the term or in some cases a total avoidance of it. *Fuck you Aloha, I love you.* This phrase seems to embody the tensions at the heart of aloha. Aloha has been so commercialized that I bemoan it. I roll my eyes whenever I see it invoked in non-Hawaiian contexts. It is deeper than being upset about appropriation because I know that without it, Kānaka Maoli would have a hard time *being who we are*, so we perform aloha and inhabit a contradictory space of believing in aloha. I am frequently tortured by the "why." Each time I think I can turn away from aloha, something continues to call me back.

To answer this question of why I come back to aloha, I reconsider how "the call" is impossible to turn away from. When the subject turns toward the voice of authority in an act of interpellation, it is a moment of self-recognition because we want to become its subject, because it provides us with an identity and security, even if that security is temporary. As James Clifford has elaborated, "Interpellation is a reminder that what we wish to be, what makes us feel authentic and completed, are social performances significantly structured by power. We adopt available roles, rising to occasions that are not of our choosing."[78] Thus, we hold onto aloha because we are told it is what makes us worthy; it shows the value of our culture on several levels, from a Hawaiian perspective, but also through the state, and under Western capitalism and the Western world that we have all been interpellated into. In effect, and paradoxically, these attachments produce the possibilities and limits of who we are.[79] This theorization of Kanaka Maoli interpellation through aloha can certainly be paralyzing, but as Clifford has also explained, "Interpellation is not simply coercive: it is energizing and fulfilling."[80] We must therefore return to the scene of interpellation, armed with theories of articulation and performativity, to recuperate the subject's agency in hopes of providing a surprisingly hopeful perspective of why Kanaka Maoli subjects still answer the call of aloha.

In *The Sublime Object of Ideology* (1989), Slavoj Žižek formulates a different theory of how we become subjects of ideology. According to Žižek, interpellation cannot be explained; it is an irrational act that the subject engages in. Through interpellation, we take a leap of faith that allows ideology to patch over the fissure or fill the gap between ideology and the subject, pulling together the subject and the ideology into which the subject is hailed. We take a leap of faith as a result of a traumatic kernel that itself cannot be interpellated by the law.[81] This "traumatic" kernel is the leftover or remainder that cannot be interpellated, what cultural nationalism cannot resolve.[82] The kernel is the motor of ideological structure because ideology promises a refuge from it. The kernel is the traumatic unknown; it is the chaos within us. Ideology is supposed to provide a refuge from this kernel—a cover—but ideology is always insufficient because the kernel cannot be fully covered or integrated; otherwise, ideology would be un-necessary.[83] This unknowable thing is always with us. To not answer "the call" is to resist an open field of association and to engage the traumatic kernel, the unknown. So when the subject answers the call, the subject af-firms itself by resisting a "radically open field of significatory possibilities" and the *terror of complete freedom*, rather than resisting institutionalization.[84] Whereas other theories construct a resistant subject that is able to with-stand the temptation of the call, Žižek flips it and focuses on the resistance to the unknown. The resistance is, then, against ontological terror.

Chow's interpretations are fruitful for my analysis of why Kānaka Maoli answer the call of aloha. Chow builds on Žižek's theory to explain that the leap of faith is unconscious and senseless and that interpellation succeeds precisely because of it.[85] For Kānaka Maoli this means submitting to the state's ideology, an Aloha State apparatus that positions Kānaka Maoli as the natural repositories of aloha, destined to welcome visitors and perform our aloha for them. So why, then, would a Kanaka Maoli participate in this econ-omy of subjection? The Kanaka Maoli subject answers aloha's call when she or he takes this leap of faith (through the process of being interpellated) to affirm one's subjectivity as a Kanaka Maoli. Not answering the call would leave us lost in an ocean of associations, which can leave the Kanaka Maoli subject "lost at sea," lost in our own place.[86] Kānaka Maoli, in short, inter-nalize aloha to retain our identities and to resist the unknown.

Now, let me be clear: our belief or faith in aloha is not easily dismissed, nor is it a simple evasion of the unknown or the traumatic kernel that inter-pellation shields us from. The leap of faith is not senseless or irrational to Kānaka Maoli. Kānaka Maoli unconsciously (and as a form of automation) answer the call of aloha (by performing aloha and believing in it) because it is necessary for us to participate rationally in the modern world. In other words, it is an act that we are accustomed to, that rises out of a survival instinct, to secure our social life through the law, to guarantee our exis-tence. Because what happens when Kānaka Maoli give up aloha? What happens when we don't answer its call? In our leap of faith (to believe in aloha, and in turn to be Kanaka Maoli), we retain what it is that we imag-ine makes us Kānaka Maoli, and this gives our identities legitimacy and se-curity as well as a sense of "potentiality and empowerment."[87]

It is imperative, then, to mark how Kānaka Maoli articulate and perform aloha with other Hawaiian philosophies as a strategy to disarticulate aloha from its most commodified forms. Native Pacific cultural studies scholars have contributed greatly to articulation theory in this regard. Teresia Teaiwa's meditations in particular lead us to question the categorization of the Native and the ways that it is articulated with different things.[88] "Articulation" is a way of understanding how ideological elements come together within a discourse; it enables us to think about how an ideology sometimes empowers people while also locking them as subjects into a spot within a given oppressive discourse, but these meanings and articulations are never static. We must view Hawaiian indigeneity as part of a system of culture that is actively produced, contested, and articulated in specific contexts, at times to support the Aloha State apparatus or to encourage practices of aloha ʻāina. Articulation and performativity can work together productively to help us understand our indigeneity as always flexible and innovative over time.[89]

I am not advocating a total recuperation of aloha but instead a strategic performance that allows a simultaneous movement between recalling the cultural significance of aloha, questioning where aloha's performance and varied articulations have gotten us, and, finally, reimagining where we want the performance of aloha to take us. The naming of the Aloha State and the creation of the Aloha Spirit Law are two examples of aloha that require disarticulation. We must recall the definition of aloha put forth by Pukuʻi, that aloha is embodied in spaces where people gather to provide mutual helpfulness for collective benefit. Further, aloha functions alongside other Hawaiian values, such as ʻohana (family) and kōkua (help), which challenge articulations of aloha purely in the name of capitalism. Take, for instance, an apparent corporate effort by Coca-Cola to offer Hawaiʻi-specific products during their 2014 ad campaign that emphasized the joys of sharing a Coke with a friend because your name is on the can or label. The creation of Coca-Cola soda cans with "aloha ʻāina" on them is a small example of the misuse of the term. Other examples are the growing frequency with which "aloha ʻāina" appears in state of Hawaiʻi governing documents; real estate developers selling the phrase to emphasize "green" practices; or even the U.S. military invoking it in environmental impact statements. While articulating this utopic revision of where we want it to take us, we should not forget that as much as people articulate aloha with aloha ʻāina, there is always a danger of aloha being articulated in the direction of tourist interests in search of an authentic feeling of "aloha," a form that many Kānaka Maoli believe also still exists. But a belief in aloha will survive only through its constant performance. All performances have the possibility of failure, so survival through performance is indeed precarious.

In the end, performing aloha keeps us alive; Kānaka Maoli answer aloha's call as an act of survival. Under capitalism, it is a form of automation, whereby performing aloha is no longer a choice we make; it is the way that we remain connected to Hawaiian indigeneity. Not answering aloha's call becomes a kind of social death with material (lack of capital) and psychological (lack of identity) effects. If we deny aloha too much, we run the risk of full erasure or Native absence. We run the risk of no longer being Kanaka Maoli. Aloha is how we remain connected to the tree, to our roots, to our kupuna. Aloha is the crux of Kanaka Maoli potential, empowerment, and survival, even if it has also become the means of disempowering us.

And it is this latter point that gets at the tensions existing at the heart of Hawaiianness: we fight with ourselves. We want to believe in aloha because, deep down, we believe it connects us to our ancestors, to who we are. So we choose to retain aloha because it affirms us, even in its contradictions.[90] As Butler explains, "Only by occupying—being occupied by—that injurious term can I resist and oppose it, recasting the power that constitutes me as the power I oppose."[91] We are attached to this kind of subjection because it is our resource and because it conditions the environment in which the resignifying of interpellation becomes possible. These contradictions manifest in cultural representations, specifically in the performance of the ethnic self.[92] I therefore must surrender to this necessary contradiction—to get paid, to be recognized and identified as Kanaka Maoli—to live.

Rather than pretending that we need to go beyond aloha or get back to aloha's real meaning, the remainder of this book shows how performers negotiate aloha and perform it in defiant and divergent ways. Resignificatory possibilities of any performance always rework and unsettle subjects' passionate attachment to subjection and thus provide ways to rethink subject formation and reformation through performance.[93] In chapters 2 and 3 I show that Krystilez refuses aloha altogether through performances of defiant Kanaka indigeneity that upset multicultural fantasies of belonging in Hawai'i. Similarly, chapter 3 examines how Cocoa Chandelier performs aloha *in drag*—strategically hidden—at times to comment on something larger than the actual performance of aloha itself. Chapters 4 and 5 look at how staged performances also allow us to express aloha through mourning the Hawaiian Kingdom and what aloha looks like in the diaspora. These chapters engage how performers are grappling with aloha, but they also raise questions about the future of aloha, Hawai'i, and, of course, Kānaka Maoli.

While many Kānaka Maoli openly critique the way tourism and multiculturalism have bastardized aloha, you would be hard pressed to find a Kanaka Maoli who would utter the words "Fuck you, aloha" without extensively qualifying such a statement. Instead, we wax poetic—"Aloha is the intelligence with which we meet life." And it is true: aloha is very real for Kānaka Maoli today. Perhaps aloha is not the cultural concept we would choose to describe ourselves, given the way it's been used, but aloha is, for better or worse, tied to "Hawaiianness" and who we are. The presence of aloha reminds Kānaka Maoli that we still exist, that we existed, that we "meet life" with intelligence and will continue to, whether or not the Aloha State continues to exist or the Aloha Spirit Law is enforced. Kānaka Maoli performed aloha to survive and will always find ways to perform aloha to challenge its dominant ideologies. For this reason, this work looks closely at these performers and their performances of aloha in their very contradictory and yet productive spaces and moments. Despite aloha's contradictions, Kānaka Maoli are committed to it, to meeting life with intelligence, because even as we are told that aloha now belongs to the world and that we gave it away, we still know that, deep down, aloha belongs to us. We are hailed to retain aloha's dynamism and resilience, and this keeps us moving forward. It is in this space of contradiction that Kānaka Maoli find our thrust, our ingenuity, our indigeneity; it is in this place where things are "not right" but "yet still all is right." *Fuck you, Aloha, but I still love you.*

CHAPTER TWO

Bloodline Is All I Need and
Defiant Indigeneity on the West Side

I'm an angry local you cannot tell me what for do

I'm just your karma catching up with you

—KRYSTILEZ, "Karma"

On June 17, 2011, the *Honolulu Star-Advertiser* published a review of the Kanaka Maoli rapper Krystilez's release "Dear HARA" along with an image of him with a piece of duct tape over his mouth that read "ALOHA" in capital letters.[1] Exhibiting the tensions embodied in Hawaiian indigeneity and the pressures to perform touristic visions of aloha that have been internalized as a natural or proper form of Hawaiian expression, Krystilez shows how aloha operates as a force that silences him as a Kanaka Maoli man, throwing into relief the primary cultural referent through which Kānaka Maoli are identified in the global imagination. The previous chapter documented that aloha has become synonymous with Hawaiian indigeneity and Hawaiianness, possessing considerable cultural and commercial power that is mobilized to sell almost anything and everything, being spread around the globe through countless tourist advertisements, films, songs, and, of course, images of Hawaiian women dancing.

Krystilez stands in defiance of the latter. He is what many in Hawai'i would characterize as a typical local guy, a Hawaiian-Filipino man around six feet tall; he is muscular, wears a baseball cap most of the time, and usually sports a T-shirt from the We Are HI clothing collective, which he is a part of, representing the intersection of urban hip-hop and island cultures. Since I first started writing about Krystilez he has transformed from hometown rapper to local radio personality to entrepreneur. Krystilez has not been able to play his own music on the radio because of its lyrical content (which includes swearing) and its lack of mainstream record label backing. His songs talk about robbing tourists and seeking revenge for the overthrow of the Hawaiian Kingdom. By invoking the beloved Hawaiian value, aloha, which is crucial in the marketing of Hawaiian music worldwide, Krystilez conveys his investments in a defiant artistic practice, intelligent lyricism, and a fearless indictment of mainstream Hawaiian music institutions. As the

"Karma" lyrics display, Krystilez is an "angry local," which is also the name of his other music group. Juxtaposing this image of him being silenced by aloha and the lyrics that describe him in motion, catching up with an abstract "you" in the song, Krystilez infers that "you" represents the mainstream Hawaiian music industry and the political establishment in Hawaiʻi that stands on the backs of locals (inclusive of Kānaka Maoli and Asian settlers) who are angry and "catching up with you." "Karma" later likens the "you" in the song to the Committee of Safety, the haole annexationist group that conspired to overthrow the Hawaiian Kingdom in 1893. Catching up to the same colonial forces that are responsible for annexation as well as those that continue to confine Hawaiian indigeneity in Hawaiian music, the song's title is certainly fitting. Krystilez, a defiant voice who cannot be bought or contained by accommodating forms of indigeneity, also supports stereotypes of Hawaiian men as violent, savage, and criminal.

Initially, I was turned off by the capitalistic and heteropatriarchal tendencies I observed when Krystilez opened for the renowned black nationalist group Public Enemy in 2005. Krystilez's early performances existed at the nexus of desires for mainstream success articulated through misogynistic undertones alongside a profound need to represent himself and people like him—young, urban Hawaiians (and locals) who grew up experiencing the rougher side of Hawaiʻi, the Hawaiʻi that struggles with drug addiction and violence and is not seen in postcards. While much of the scholarship on Hawaiian hip-hop has focused on celebrating the mixing of Hawaiian music without hip-hop as a form of resistance, it is imperative to look closely at both the promise of these performances of urban Kanaka Maoli indigeneity and the circuits that influence their production, such as hip-hop's mainstream dominance, whereby capitalist accumulation and misogyny are the norm, alongside the possibilities of hip-hop, which provides hope and voice for marginalized populations who live in a world that is predicated on the failure of Indigenous and other people of color such as Krystilez and the homestead communities he represents. This chapter thus analyzes how Krystilez navigates these circuits and crafts performances that trouble conventional understandings of Kānaka Maoli, Hawaiian music, and aloha through a performance of defiant indigeneity.

Hip-hop came to Hawaiʻi as quickly as it spread across the continental United States. Since the 1980s (as hip-hop rose to prominence in mainstream American media), hip-hop films, music videos, television shows, and concerts by prominent performers all came to Hawaiʻi.[2] I have a vivid memory from 1988, when Run DMC performed at Aloha Stadium. I peered out the window of my family's third-floor apartment in Makalapa Manor public housing. I could only see lights in the distance as I listened to the bass-thumping emanating from Aloha Stadium. My experience mirrors that of many of those in my generation who grew up amid the globalization of mass media in the era of late capitalism, during a time when black-identified American popular culture proliferated all over the world. Hip-hop's mainstream prominence has produced the adoption and creation of hip-hop by disenfranchised youth around the world through what Halifu Osumare has referred to as "connective marginality," a social and historical context that informs youth participation in hip-hop outside the United States.[3] Youth in places like Palestine, Japan, Ireland, Cuba, and even Hawai'i share experiences of cultural displacement, a connection with black-identified culture, and the desire for self-representation.[4] Hip-hop, understood as the expression of marginalized brown youth struggling in deindustrializing cities, makes the paradisiacal fantasies of Hawai'i appear a world away. Such images, though, are increasingly challenged by the unruly and resistant culture of "digital Natives" who contest long-standing colonial and touristic visions of indigeneity broadly, and most recently in Hawai'i.

In the late twentieth century, indigeneity experienced a resurgence of activism, cultural revitalization, and cultural expressions that are informed by a global critique of settler colonialism. Seeking more than to be simply recognized by the state, Indigenous people all over the world have been articulating Indigenous nationalism through various cultural forms, embodying Gerald Vizenor's notion of survivance, asserting native presence over absence.[5] In Hawai'i, Kanaka Maoli visibility and self-representation—outside of the tourist visions—have increased considerably, producing a plethora of narratives that emphasize our rich cultural knowledges and our ongoing resistance to U.S. occupation. But, as evidenced by Krystilez and some of his contemporaries, the internalization of heteropatriarchy within these narratives is sometimes business as usual, and it reenacts Kanaka Maoli subjection in gendered and other problematic ways. To push back against commodified and feminized versions of Hawaiian culture, as Ty Kāwika Tengan has noted, the discursive performances of Kanaka Maoli men attempting to reaffirm Kanaka Maoli identity often occur through patriarchal discourse.[6] Scholarship in Pacific studies has been attentive to these gendered dynamics, analyzing representations that render Kanaka Maoli or Polynesian men as nothing more than hypermasculinized professional athletes or, in the case of those who enter military service, as modern-day "warriors." There is a lack of criticism of the masculinity within Hawaiian hip-hop, and a sophisticated gender analysis is nearly nonexistent.[7] This is also true within Native hip-hop scholarship in general. There is an almost exhausting focus on politically conscious nationalist articulations of hip-hop and Native identity. While I am a fan of this music and scholarship, they neglect to account for the cadre of imagery within Native hip-hop that often replicates the misogyny and decadent artifice of mainstream hip-hop—which, of course, I love. Still, we must engage these problematic representations because they reveal a great deal about the labor that needs to be done within our communities. Native feminist analyses of the intersections of heteropatriarchy, colonialism, and hypernationalism as they are expressed through masculinity makes legible how these performances of Kanaka Maoli identity can be both liberating and deeply contradictory. As the previous chapter detailed, Kānaka Maoli perform aloha in a double movement of ideological hailing and cultural survival. This chapter discusses how defiant indigeneity and cultural survival function via the performance of Hawaiian hip-hop. Specifically, I analyze how this works within the performances of a Kanaka Maoli and Filipino rapper, Krystilez.

When I first began writing about Krystilez in 2007, I focused on the material conditions of his emergence. The growth of global hip-hop via the consolidation of corporate media markets and Hawaiian political consciousness was embodied in the formation of Krystilez's public persona. I have truncated the discussion of these global forces here in the interest of providing more space to attend to the nuances of Krystilez's representations and to assess how they have transformed. Over a decade has passed since I first wrote about him and, indeed, we have both grown up in the process. I see Hawaiian performances as always in process, and my thoughts on Indigenous performativity (as outlined in the introduction) require this allowance of transformation, process, and movement. Krystilez's art has matured since 2005, when he released his first album. The relationship I have to the production of this work in general has political and personal stakes. As kuʻualoha hoʻomanawanui explains, for Maoli scholars, sometimes maintaining and honoring our political connections take precedence over the demands of academia.[8] I am very cautious of the way that I represent this person, who is Kanaka Maoli, like me, who is from the West Side, like me. I was at first taken aback by the sexism in Krystilez's music, but the closer I listened, I realized there is so much more to his music and representations. Perhaps I have softened as a Native feminist, so what you read here is an attempt to balance my critiques with the caveat that after discussing the issue with him, and after all the time that has passed, it almost seems unfair to hold someone accountable for something he or she wrote over a decade ago. As a former performer, and now as a "scholar," I know that we all might look back at our intellectual, political, and artistic choices and cringe in hindsight. Thus, I honor this process of writing and understanding that has come out of my analysis of Krystilez, acknowledging that I have made a choice to emphasize these narratives as transitory because I am accountable to Krystilez and the broader Hawaiian community. I have a kuleana to be critical but also to allow for growth and change among us. Decolonization requires faith in possibility and transformation. Again, I point this out to emphasize that cultural productions and the discourses they produce through performance are never final, and that Hawaiian performance, like the Kanaka Maoli people, is always in process, working toward our unending futurity.

Defiant Indigeneity

Krystilez ("legally" known as Kris Ancheta) is a respected MC and Cadio personality in Hawai'i. In 2006, his first release, *The Greatest HI*, won the Hawai'i Music Award for Best Hip Hop Album, and in 2007 *The "O"* was nominated for a Nā Hoku Hanohano Award for Best Hip Hop/R&B Album. He is also known for his presence in the rap group Angry Locals. In addition to his musical career, Krystilez is a disc jockey on a popular local radio station (owned by the media conglomerate Clear Channel) and is also recognized on the underground hip-hop freestyle circuit. He is also part of the We Are HI clothing collective, which in 2016 opened its first storefront, Makau Market, dedicated to representing urban island culture in Hawai'i.

The primary themes within Krystilez's representations are focused on showing a harsher side of Hawai'i, narrating the lived realities of local people, and insisting on his own authenticity. Representing the latter is complicated, but beneath his assertions of "truth" and Indigenous authenticity are the processes of Indigenous performativity. As the process by which Indigenous bodies generate social meaning, Indigenous performativity centers Indigenous articulations of culture, outsider perceptions of such, and the constant interplay between them. This is a strategy that secures the ongoing expression of different modes of Hawaiian life. This is what many of Krystilez's songs are fundamentally attempting to celebrate—the real story and the life of people like him, people in his community, the urban and country Hawaiians from the West Side of the island of O'ahu, a place that is known for its substantial Kanaka Maoli population and is commonly represented as crime-ridden. Later in this chapter I discuss how Krystilez departs from and regenerates such stereotypes in his song "West Side" and how those ideas are contested in online commenting spaces.

As explained in the introduction, defiant indigeneity is an amorphous performance of Indigenous refusal and defiance, a purposeful performance that sometimes articulates heteropatriarchy, colonialism, and even antiblackness, but it also affirms Indigenous strength and pride in your ancestors. Defiant indigeneity might garner a negative response from elders, or it might be questioned for its futility in advancing the lāhui. Still, defiant indigeneity is a performance that is about a love for where you come from. Krystilez's performances exhibit how Kānaka Maoli perform defiance as an act of aloha. Aloha can be defiant and refused and still be used to convey a profound connection, to express our aloha for Hawaiian culture and our commitment to survival as a people. Krystilez's performances assert a Kanaka Maoli identity that refuses to be compromised or subdued by colonization, as his performances work to unsettle discourses about land, blood, and authenticity in the face of settler-colonial forces working to dispossess Kānaka Maoli of cultural claims, autonomy, and, preeminently, our lands. In a performance of defiant indigeneity, Krystilez performs aggression, stakes territory, and polices membership throughout his self-representation in photographs, videos, and music. This defiance constitutes the opposite of what "aloha" has come to signify in the popular imagination. Through carefully crafted narratives of Kanaka Maoli resilience on Hawaiian lands, these songs affirm Kanaka Maoli presence on these lands and a protection of those lands against outsiders. In this way, Krystilez's music is explicitly against what many have defined as the essence of aloha—inclusion. But simultaneously, because of Krystilez's indigeneity, he can claim a relationship to the land and perform his aloha for that land in ways that are unquestionably about aloha. This simultaneous performance and refusal of aloha confound conventional discourses of aloha, which discourage dissent and maintain the status quo. Through defiant indigeneity, Krystilez presents an alternative formation of aloha, one that is exclusively for Kānaka Maoli.

Krystilez is a performer invested in defying the boundaries of the music industry in Hawai'i. His second album, The "O," features fourteen original tracks of high-quality recording, slick promotional materials, and impressive lyrical content. In interviews he is noted for both his humble beginnings on a Hawaiian homestead and his desire to put Hawai'i on the hip-hop map.[9] In this chapter, I attend to the particularities of the narrative crafted by Krystilez throughout *The "O"* and his performance of defiant indigeneity. I also analyze the song, "West Side," which was released in 2011. I pay specific attention to the sounds invoked in various tracks to analyze how the music itself draws upon Hawaiian music iconography to complicate the representation of Hawai'i and Kānaka Maoli.

Influenced by the popularity of gangsta rap during the 1990s and the material realities of life on the homestead, Krystilez's performance as a "thug" in his early productions pervaded his lyrics and visual representations. To publicize the release of *The "O,"* Krystilez hung "wanted" posters of himself around O'ahu in the fall of 2006. The posters read "Krystilez, Wanted for Blowing Up Hawai'i/the 'O' in Stores Now." In these posters Krystilez represents himself as a figure who is "wanted." Alluding to the "wanted" outlaw posters made famous by the western film genre, Krystilez positions himself as inescapably criminal. This criminality references the western outlaw who is bound up in assertions of American masculinity and the conquering of the western frontier. What does Krystilez blow up? His homeland. This begs the question, Why would a Kanaka Maoli want to blow up Hawai'i, his or her homeland?

The phrase "Blowing Up Hawai'i" is derived from the expression "to blow up," a common hip-hop phrase that usually suggests that someone is rising to stardom or the idea of "blowing up someone's spot," that is, revealing a secret. The wording also denotes a criminal act of breaking something open through an explosion. This play on words is taken further in YouTube videos of Krystilez claiming to "blow up Hawai'i one way or another" and laughing while saying it.[10] In these videos, Krystilez addresses an abstract audience of YouTube users—some are fans and others are part of a wider imagined audience.[11] Even if the viewer recognizes that Krystilez is just a performer, the specter of Kanaka Maoli criminality, fears about terrorism, and imagery of Kanaka Maoli activists occupying space ('Iolani Palace, for example) undoubtedly come into play. By invoking this trope, Krystilez pushes against dominant representations of Kānaka Maoli as welcoming, docile, and lazy, supporting the perception that Kanaka Maoli men are unable to survive in the modern world because they are trapped in a cycle of violence, drug abuse, and criminal behavior. This is clearly illustrated in the video *Tiki's Taking It to the Streets*, where Krystilez is shown in Waikīkī selling CDs in the very space where Hawaiian cultural exploitation is most obscene. Krystilez is accompanied by Spookahuna, one of the producers of *The "O,"* and he is gathering a small crowd by freestyling live (with a microphone) about people walking by. Toward the end of the video, Krystilez is approached by a police officer and told to turn down the music, and the video cuts and shows Krystilez later receiving a ticket from the police officer, conceivably for disturbing the peace. Krystilez and Spookahuna tell the video audience that even when they are just trying to make an honest living, they are policed as Kānaka Maoli, as brown men taking up space in Waikīkī. The crime here is that Krystilez is taking up public space in a performance genre (hip-hop) that is decidedly outside the norm for Kanaka Maoli men in Waikīkī, where they are supposed to be nothing more than happy surfer boys, smiling Hawaiian musicians, or stoic hula dancers.[12] As I discuss later, reclaiming and creating performance spaces in Hawaiʻi is necessary for the dialogues and support that Krystilez hopes to create.

In the actual album *The "O,"* Krystilez features the descriptive tales of this reality layered over heavy bass aggressive beats, which fits well with his overall persona. He does want to "blow up" Hawaiʻi, after all. His performance of criminality and braggadocio operates as an oppositional strategy that bucks social conventions by ostensibly embracing them: Krystilez becomes the very "thug" that society tells him (or other Kānaka Maoli) that he should be. So when Krystilez claims he is going to "blow up Hawaiʻi," he is drawing on hip-hop slang and speaking about how he is going to achieve fame through hip-hop, even as he is also commenting on the need to reevaluate the conditions that exist in Hawaiʻi, to enlarge them for scrutiny in the public eye. His insistence on "supporting locals," which is spoken repeatedly in *The "O"* and in advertisements, is a veiled criticism of the corporatized music industry as well as state-level politics that favor the perceived desires of tourists, the military, and other economic imperatives rather than the needs of locals in Hawaiʻi.[13] The next section looks more closely at the defiant indigeneity in Krystilez's lyrics and overall representations, first in *The "O"* as a whole album and then specifically in the song "Bloodline."

> Where the palm trees is where you want to be
> but paradise is not what it seems
> This is the O!
> Where you get hustled
> tourists get mobbed
> and if you start a fight
> bitch you'll get mobbed
> —Krystilez, "The 'O'"

FIGURE 1 Krystilez next to a poster of himself. Photo by George F. Lee, originally published in the *Honolulu Advertiser*, January 26, 2007.

In figure 1, originally published with an interview in the *Honolulu Advertiser*, Krystilez is decidedly laid back, the top of his head and eyes covered with a hood, leaning against a wire fence. The smile and the image of reclining against the fence convey the sense of chillin' next to this "wanted" image of himself, which could be interpreted in a number of competing or complementary ways: the smile might be a mischievous acknowledgment of his bad boy reputation or what it serves to accomplish; he might be tired or bored of having to play the wanted criminal; or maybe he is smirking at the inside joke—that his entire persona is a fabrication and not "real" within a genre that emphasizes the need to keep things real. Whichever it is, this image captures for me the double nature of Kanaka Maoli existence, especially for performers, who work to produce specific types of representations to confront social expectations of themselves in a context that forces them to perform in particular ways to be recognized as "Hawaiian." As a Kanaka Maoli, he contends with constant representations of who and what he should be. This context raises another possible reading of the image, one of contemplation: leaning back, Krystilez may also well be in the middle of a deep sigh, thinking to himself, "(sigh) Bloodline is all I need."

For a stronger sense of what he is thinking, we can turn to a series of videos posted on Tiki Entertainment's YouTube page. Here, we get a strong glimpse into his vision of and for *The "O."* To generate hype, Krystilez recorded videos of himself counting down the days before the release of the album. After its release, Tiki Entertainment, the company that released the album, claimed that *The "O"* sold out of stores on the first day and that it was the greatest Hawai'i hip-hop album to date. The braggadocio and hype aside, it manages to rise above the violent and misogynist commentary to present a rich tale about contemporary Hawai'i. While Krystilez in many ways ascribes to the rampant sexism, endorsement of illegal activity, and glorification of violence (particularly on the tracks "Shake," "How Bad Do You Want It," and "The Way It Is") that mainstream U.S. hip-hop is known for, he also presents a narrative of life in Hawai'i that is conveniently ignored or dismissed in Hawai'i's dominant discourses of "local" culture. Tracks like "The 'O,'" "Diamonds," and "Bloodline" present glaring counternarratives to the mythic representation of Hawai'i as paradise.

The album's title track—"The 'O'"—is an homage to O'ahu and the island's lifestyle, which differs considerably from the one in the popular imagination. "The 'O'" begins with a half note played on a synthesizer. Then the beat drops as the voice of a chanting woman fades in. The sound conjures the mental and (for the Hawai'i audience) familiar image of a kumu hula (hula master) in the process of commanding her hālau (troupe) to take the stage. But Krystilez suddenly and forcefully interjects, "Where the palm trees is where you want to be/ but paradise is not what it seems." Still, the chant or, more precisely, an oli (chant) performed in the ho'āeae[14] style, remains audible throughout the aggressive rapping style that ensues.[15] With its signature unmetered style, this oli actually loops throughout the song, and though it fades into the background, it continues to function nonetheless as an important foil or counterpoint to Krystilez's often-brutal rhymes.

The feminized sound is meant to be the island of O'ahu. As the oli is repeated, Krystilez's rhymes can be read as performing an ode to her. In this case, the oli narrates her current condition under colonial rule or occupation (somewhat like an oli ho'ouweuwē[16], characterized by funerary wailing). "This is the O!" is repeated over her authoritative voice of tradition as Krystilez vamps into each chorus. In this song, however, the voice of tradition is not simply relegated to the background and is not monotone. As Krystilez leads into each chorus, the chant rises in prominence to augment rather than counter a slew of charges or indictments that make up the chorus lines. In one chorus, it is "Where the locals run the whole show." In the next, it's "Where the sex lingers is the best place, where the best bitches are to get laid." Another: "Where the boys hustle because the crime pays no other road this is the HI-way." Subsequent lines refer to "making hits," "hustling," and so on, all of which signify life in urban Honolulu, but especially in a locale identified specifically as "the West." This "West" refers to the west side of Oʻahu, to places such as Nānākuli and Waiʻanae, which have large concentrations of Kānaka Maoli and which are typically perceived to be the "bad" part of the island of Oʻahu. Here, the narrative addresses the tourist: "Where you're told not to go when you come off the plane. At the beaches proceed with caution."

These lyrics invoke a profound and enduring Hawaiian cultural value of reckoning one's identity and genealogy in specific relation to and responsibility to it. This idea is captured in the concept of kuleana, which simultaneously refers to one's responsibility, one's relations, and one's land. The same ideas are captured in other key cultural concepts and practices—such as aloha ʻāina, which expresses deep relations of intense love and affection and stewardship to land as a manifestation of one's reciprocal relations to ancestors and descendants. As described by Katrina-Ann R. Kapāʻanaokalāokeola Nākoa Oliveira, in ancestral times Kānaka Maoli engaged in "performance cartographies" to reference their places, affirm their existence, and continue their legacies. These forms included mele (songs), hula (dance), moʻolelo (historical accounts), moʻokūʻauhau (genealogies), and ʻōlelo noʻeau (proverbs), among other cartographic representations.[17] These are practices that continue today in various forms, and Hawaiian hip-hop can be seen as a very modern manifestation of such practices. In keeping with Hawaiian music traditions, but also hip-hop traditions, of representing where you come from, Krystilez firmly locates himself in his hometown, Nānākuli homestead. By "mixing" forms, Krystilez can be appreciated as not simply continuing Indigenous traditions in new forms, but also actually widening the reach of Kanaka Maoli indigeneity through the invocation of the oli and the song's lyrical content of the specificities of genealogies of relations to a specific place. In what follows, I examine these expansive lyrics and accompanying visuals, which are rooted in these places.

Lyrically, The "O" is filled with sensationalistic imagery that narrates the positions of power—party promoter, bouncer, rapper, drug dealer, DJ, pimp—performed by Krystilez and his friends. The combined video for the songs "The 'O'" and "Won," originally posted on YouTube, presents visuals that, somewhat like the voice of the hula chanter, offers interesting moments of countering and augmenting the song's lyrical content.[18] The video begins with "Won," and with Krystilez's voice, intercut with a beat. Early on, we hear the words "Tiki Entertainment" spoken and looped across the track. The first visual we see is of Krystilez amid palm trees. The scene cuts to Krystilez in front of a raised SUV, with the iconic Ko'olau mountain range, green and lush, in the background. The SUV itself sports an advertisement for The "O" and for Krystilez, and it is also painted green (and blue). In a series of spins, Krystilez and his crew are shown in various positions relative to the SUV: sometimes they are inside, sometimes standing next to it, sometimes hanging out of the side or off the back. One character here is IZ Real, whose name plays off of the wildly popular and beloved Hawaiian vocalist, the late Israel Kamakawiwo'ole (Krystilez's idol). IZ Real also appears as Krystilez's sidekick in the "Bloodline" video. Notably, in this video, IZ Real is shirtless and is shown kneeling on top of the truck's roof, singing and punching the air, jerking and snapping his head toward the sky. The truck is driving slowly as "Won" starts. The song has a decidedly more critical tone than the others, expressing the problems in the "melting pot," in which cultures are supposed to blend but are instead continuously in conflict. At one point in the song, Krystilez says that being raised in Hawai'i means being "raised in the middle of racism." The song concludes lyrically by calling for peace in the islands because "you only have one home." Visually, however, "Won" is abbreviated and choppy, and this fast-cutting style also restructures the song's chorus, in which Krystilez repeatedly sings "Number one" ("Won") in such a way as to morph suddenly into the phrase "This is the O!" At this point, a Hawaiian flag fills the screen, and the video transitions to the song "The 'O.'" Moving from the "number one" ("Won") to "The 'O,'" the camera pans back to the opening shot of the SUV in front of the Ko'olau mountain range, to where a man in green and brown baggy fatigues holds a Hawaiian flag in the air. Then the camera cuts to Krystilez, who now raps the first few lines of "The 'O.'" The screen suddenly goes blank except for the teaser, "to be continued." If "The 'O'" mixed Hawaiian and hip-hop traditions of "repping" identity, this combined teaser for "Won" and "The 'O'" also blends (or blurs) the enduring nature of Hawai'i through the imagery of the Ko'olau mountain range with iconographic imagery of hip-hop and street culture in the SUV, through the natural colors of the advertisement and the camouflaged military garb, which themselves get displaced by (or which set up for transition into) the Hawaiian flag as the central icon of the struggle to fight for and restore the Hawaiian nation, or at the very least to convey Hawaiian pride.[19] These are not simply expressions of Indigenous masculinity that have become common. In this visual narrative, the figure of the shirtless IZ Real atop the SUV signifies success and prosperity in hip-hop culture in the face of settler colonialism, occupation, and statecraft that attempt to manage the various articulations of Indigenous resistance that IZ Real and Krystilez put forth via hip-hop music. It is also noteworthy that these videos are no longer available, as they were removed from Tiki Entertainment and Krystilez's YouTube page sometime in 2011.

To be sure, the SUV and the shirtless imagery clearly denote the bad boy image of defiant urban and street culture that informs and saturates hip-hop, just as "The 'O,'" "Bloodline," and "Won" signify Hawaiian hip-hop's referencing to other Kanaka Maoli locales, places, and peoples who are commonly associated with criminality. Indeed, other songs on the album reference drug use and trafficking, with Krystilez implying his participation in such activities. In "Diamonds" and "The Way It Is," Krystilez takes a pensive approach by referencing illicit economies that exist in Hawai'i, calling it the "meth capital" (in "Won") and affirming that "hardcore crime pays" (in "The 'O'"). In "Diamonds," Krystilez laments one man's crystal meth addiction and his subsequent murder. But in "Won" the rapper's demeanor is playful and mischievous: "Hawai'i has the best sex, these prostitutes are taxing you." This is in fact one of several recurring moments in this album when Krystilez self-identifies as a gangbanger ("a banger"). Even lighter in tone are songs such as "Shake" and "How Bad Do You Want It," which are bass-thumping and soul-infused, seemingly intended to be club hits. These songs feature formulaic mainstream hip-hop lyrical content about Krystilez's sexual prowess and getting drunk or high, and are usually set inside nightclubs ("Shake" and "Tha Word").[20] "Shake," especially, mimics mainstream hip-hop videos in which the primary MC is shown rhyming in the back of the club, surrounded by women who serve as adornments to his actual physical space as well as to the rest of the club. Everyone in the scene appears to be his friend, as he shouts them out at various moments. Though set in an urban environment and saturated with hypersexist sentiment, these songs are also quintessentially about pride and about supporting one's own community (however broadly construed it may be). Here, Krystilez uses Hawaiian hip-hop to carve out a space not meant for tourists, a place and space for Kanaka Maoli (or "local") performers. Moreover, he reminds us that indigeneity is not to be incarcerated in the space of "nature" even if nature continues to be an enduring space for indigeneity.

> Seein through a thug's eyes
> We ride all night till sunlight
> All because I love my muthafuckin bloodline.
> I rather die on my feet than ever live on my knees
> till I face defeat bloodline is all I need.
> —Krystilez, "Bloodline"

"Bloodline" was originally conceived as a fighting anthem. Its circulation on YouTube and its performance live have given the song new life. As a way to represent Kanaka Maoli presence in modern Hawai'i as well as in the Hawaiian diaspora, "Bloodline" performs a tribute to Hawaiian homesteads, remaking homestead space through listener identification with bloodlines in order to traverse the colonial taxonomies that demarcate homestead space. By shouting out multiple homestead names and referring to them as bloodlines, Krystilez invites Kānaka Maoli to "rep your bloodline." Even if listeners are not from the homestead, the innate connections remain. Krystilez's greatest defiance is that his narrative of Indigenous survival is based on the legacy of homestead legislation, which was intended to manage a declining Kanaka Maoli population.

In "Bloodline" Krystilez represents where he comes from, but he does so in a way that explicitly engages state logics of racialization: by crafting a narrative based on blood that operates with and against the Kanaka Maoli epistemological belief that we are genealogically descended from specific places. "Bloodline" articulates a cultural identification with homesteads in a manner that centers recognition in community rather than in state-based forms, even as Krystilez's invocation of the homestead itself is a product of the state. He performs this in what is an ode to Hawaiian homesteads and Kanaka Maoli endurance on these lands. Through a complex combination of nostalgia for a romanticized precolonial Hawaiian past and a tributary performance of community resilience, "Bloodline" lyrically and visually reiterates an old narrative about identity through place and pride in spite of nearly two centuries of attempted genocide. This is what we might now recognize as performative iteration of Krystilez's defiant indigeneity. It is also an extremely messy one, exhibiting his investments in heteropatriarchy, the glamorization of violence, and appropriations of hypercommodified blackness, all of which make him complicit with circuits of power that can be oppressive. In other words, defiant indigeneity contains contradictions of its own. It is not innocent, for instance, in its disturbing depictions of Kānaka Maoli as criminal, homophobic, sexist, and, as some might interpolate, unfit for self-government.

The video for "Bloodline," posted on YouTube, begins with Krystilez in front of a black background, singing, "I can't deny it I'm fucking Hawaiian none of y'all can't beef with me." As the lens pulls back, Krystilez also steps away from the camera, as a crowd walks up behind him. The effect is to distance himself from the viewer and to move the community into the foreground. In the meantime, he continues, maintaining the centrality of his position or persona, but in the appropriate locale or context: "Muthafucka got the streets with me, so you best believe in me."[21] The video is set in the evening, and the predominantly male crowd members—for the most part, the community is male—behind him are holding shirts that say "Made in Nānākuli." Others wear 3RD shirts, in reference to Nānākuli Third Road homestead housing, and make a W with their hands to represent the west side of Oʻahu as well as the number three, for their homestead road. As the video continues, Krystilez (and the others in the video) look directly at the viewer, sporadically punching the air and pointing at the camera.

Throughout the video, the crowd makes visible the community that Krystilez is representing. The crowd sings along with him, and IZ Real, who is particularly aggressive in his rapping style, frequently steps forward, using his hands to articulate his lyricism. IZ Real is shown during the daytime in the parking lot of what appears to be a warehouse setting, behind a chain-link fence. He is remarkably smaller in stature than the other men in the video (in "Bloodline" he mentions being 5'6"), wearing long shorts and a black Kamehameha the Great shirt[22] that many of the other people in the video are also wearing. In his verse he explains how he is trying to leave beefing (fighting) behind, but people keep calling him out, and he has no choice but to assault them. He is shown always moving, shaking his head back and forth, bulging his eyes, performing a sort of mental instability. The video ends with Krystilez and IZ Real in a boxing ring, as a thin brown woman in tiny black shorts, tube top, and platform stilettos—and whose face is never shown—circles the ring holding a sign in the air that says "bangers 4 bangers." As the camera fades out, Krystilez and IZ Real jump around the ring, shouting, "Nānākuli Bloodline," "Waiʻanae Bloodline," and "Waimānalo Bloodline" in reference to some of the more well-known homesteads.

The 1921 Hawaiian Homes Commission Act (HHCA) affirmed the special relationship between the United States and Kānaka Maoli by setting aside 200,000 acres of Hawaiian homestead land—lands that belonged to the Hawaiian Kingdom before it was illegally overthrown in 1893. Passed by the U.S. Congress in 1921, when Hawaiʻi was a territory, the HHCA conferred the responsibility of administering the homestead lands to the state of Hawaiʻi when it was admitted to the Union in 1959. In 1978 responsibility for homestead lands was transferred to the newly created Office of Hawaiian Affairs (OHA), a semi-autonomous state agency that manages Hawaiian entitlements.[23] Annual lease rent for a residential, agricultural, or pastoral lot is $1 per year with a ninety-nine-year lease term that can be extended for an additional hundred years. As of 2013 there were 43,080 applicants across the islands for a lot. Of those applicants, 21,929 are on a waiting list for a residential lot, where they may stay for years.[24] According to a 2014 report, 31 percent of homesteaders waited between twenty-one and thirty years before they were awarded their plot.[25] The administration of these lands has come under considerable scrutiny because of the 50 percent blood quantum requirement or the requirement to be the descendant of someone on the waiting list, which prevents many Kānaka Maoli from qualifying for lands.[26] In addition to this requirement, because obtaining the necessary documents and making a formal claim are mired in various levels of bureaucracy, many Kānaka Maoli have difficulty qualifying for these lands. They are further deterred from the application process as they see how many people, spanning several generations, remain on the waiting list. Another obstacle is the fact that one might be awarded a homestead plot located in an unfavorable site, for example, far away from one's workplace. Some awards have even been located on an island different from where the awardee currently resides.

J. Kēhaulani Kauanui has argued that the blood quantum requirement for Hawaiian homesteads was created because the U.S. government thought that high rates of intermarriage would eventually cause the number of Kānaka Maoli who could qualify for lands to dwindle (and it did). Within this logic was the hope that the "pure" or "real" Kānaka Maoli would eventually disappear. The elite Kānaka Maoli who supported the act underscored the connection between access to land and the U.S. government's moral obligation to the Kanaka Maoli people.[27] The language used at this time was that of "rehabilitation." Kānaka Maoli were encouraged to return to the land, participate in agriculture, and re-embody their "natural" state rather than navigate the worlds of technology and industry.[28] Framed in such a manner, Kānaka Maoli were (and continue to be) viewed as welfare recipients, not as genealogical descendants of the lands in question or as citizens of the Hawaiian Kingdom seeking redress from an illegal occupier.[29] Advocates of the HHCA did not question U.S. annexation itself, and such an oversight contributed to the layered contradictions that continue to plague homestead administration. The latter continues to be debated in legal cases specific to the HHCA and many others that attack Hawaiian entitlement programs as being racially discriminatory against settlers in the islands. Further, Kānaka Maoli themselves have adopted the heteropatriarchal and colonialist perspective that the 50 percent blood quantum rule is necessary to protect Hawaiian authenticity, and most recently the Department of Hawaiian Homelands has begun to accept DNA testing to verify ancestry.[30]

The narrative Krystilez presents in "Bloodline" walks a fine line by basing itself on an identity claim, predicated on land claims, rooted in scientific discourses embedded in settler-colonial processes aimed at displacing Indigenous peoples. The blood quantum regulations built into the HHCA are damaging for Kānaka Maoli because, in contrast to U.S. policies and understandings about race and blood, it is genealogy that connects us to each other, to place, and to land.[31] Just as Christian morality became law in nineteenth-century Hawaiʻi, the early twentieth century saw the adoption of so-called truth in the science and technologies of the body, which influenced the blood quantum laws that were deployed to racialize Kānaka Maoli. Laws, in combination with a slew of new regulations, intended to modernize the Hawaiian Kingdom included huge shifts in land tenure, relegating Kanaka Maoli bodies to particular lands, places, and spaces. The original intentions of the HHCA came from elite Hawaiians seeking to rehabilitate "common" Kānaka Maoli who were suffering from the material realities of colonization that Indigenous people often face, such as poverty, poor health, high mortality rates, and homelessness, issues that persist today.[32]

Articulating these historical claims within the confines of U.S. law, citizenship, and racial categories proved difficult for Jonah Kuhio Kalanianaʻole, the Hawaiian congressional delegate, who was in line for the throne if the Hawaiian Kingdom had not been overthrown.[33] The HHCA thus imposed a quantification of Kanaka Maoli identity through blood quantum rather than through Kanaka Maoli cultural affiliations and genealogy, which worked to exacerbate land dispossession and the devaluation of Kanaka Maoli epistemologies. Situated in the discourse about blood and authenticity that permeated the late nineteenth and early twentieth centuries, the blood quantum restrictions imposed on Kānaka Maoli were similar to the "one-drop rule" imposed on African Americans and the blood quantum requirements exercised by many Indigenous tribes in the United States today. Despite this troubled history around blood quantum, many Indigenous groups still use blood to claim identity. My intent is not to criticize how other Indigenous people use blood quantum, but I seek to acknowledge its problematic origins in colonial discourses even as I acknowledge the dilemmas that blood quantum poses for contemporary Natives who are defined according to its criteria. Part of this dilemma has to do with the need (and the right) to regulate membership and to protect diminishing resources and claims that belong to members. Nevertheless, it is also clear that Native groups have not blindly internalized externally imposed racialized or blood-based definitions of identity. In Hawai'i's case, as Kauanui has explained, Hawaiian concepts of genealogy do not automatically or necessarily preclude the metaphorical uses of blood and genealogy for the purposes of collective self-identification.

Krystilez's narrative provides a prime example of this blood-based self-identification when he raps, "What's the color of my skin? What's the color of your blood?" to mock reductive racialized logics.[34] Throughout "Bloodline," Krystilez challenges the politics of recognition that are based on race and blood even as he claims and defends a "bloodline." The call-and-response at the end of "Bloodline" combats this. When IZ Real shouts, "Rep your bloodline! Nānākuli Bloodline!" a cacophony of voices replies, "Nānākuli get!" The song slowly fades out as a long list of places on O'ahu—all communities with large Kanaka Maoli populations—are called out and the appropriate response repeated.[35] Notably, after the actual places are shouted out in "Bloodline," the last few shouts are "H-I Bloodline" and "Tiki Bloodline" in reference to Hawai'i and Tiki Entertainment. This can be interpreted in several ways. On the one hand, they are merely representing the record label, but on a deeper level they could be interpreted as shout-out to the label and the sense of community it provides for them and for possible listeners who may have a different relationship to the places shouted out (that is, being in the Hawaiian diaspora and not being familiar with actual homesteads).

Kanaka Maoli relationship to homesteads, the blood quantum rule, and the resulting identifications with "place" have a lasting impact on contemporary Kanaka Maoli claims to self-determination, particularly in a climate where questions of Hawaiian self-governance are gaining federal deliberation. Krystilez's visual and sonic recreation of homestead space in

"Bloodline" allows Kānaka Maoli to identify with homesteads through song, and more importantly, it encourages Kānaka Maoli to claim homesteads as their own—even if they cannot qualify for a homestead plot. "Bloodline" returns the homestead to Kānaka Maoli, to all Kānaka Maoli. Returning the homestead to Kānaka Maoli through song marks events, memories and emotions for listeners, connecting them to homesteads, to Hawai'i, to each other. "Bloodline" expresses a long-standing tradition of Kanaka Maoli connectivity to place. This rearticulated connection is all the more crucial in an era in which many Kānaka Maoli, wherever they live, may no longer meet the stringent blood quantum requirements. By shouting out these places, "Bloodline" makes visible an affirmation of pride in the homestead that viewers can experience in spite of the tension that exists between the Kānaka Maoli who can make claims to homestead land and those who cannot. Still, the response in "Bloodline" is for all Kānaka Maoli to step up and "rep your bloodline," to show your aloha for that place. Hawaiian homesteads continue to serve as sites of cultural ownership and pride, even if these sentiments are experienced alongside highly charged political debates, including those that seek to quantify indigeneity through blood quantum.

While Krystilez emphasizes his homestead upbringing, another prominent element of his pride is his Filipino background. References to his being Filipino are frequent, as explicitly stated in the song "Who I Am." He raps:

I'm Filipino.
I'm Hawaiian.
Who are you to judge what the fuck I am?
This is what I am. Defiant.[36]

As a similarly racialized and colonized group, Filipinos are often politically and economically marginalized in Hawai'i. Stemming from a wealth of stereotypes of Filipinos as uneducated and poor, as uncivilized dog eaters, and as sexual predators, which date back to plantation-era racial stratification, Filipinos are the butt of many jokes that contribute to their ongoing subjugation locally and globally.[37] Filipino presence in hip-hop, however, has been significant, especially among dancers and DJs. Recent scholarship has documented this history. Krystilez contributed a piece to the anthology *Empires of Funk* (2013) about Filipino American presence in hip-hop. His piece, "Homesteady," discusses his coming of age story through hip-hop and how he has shifted his approach over time.[38] In Krystilez's later releases, such as "Karma" and "Dear HARA," he explains that he is an artist, not a rapper aspiring for mainstream success. Older and wiser, he places an emphasis on helping to grow and build the local hip-hop community, especially in an environment that has shown little love for locally based artists who cannot get played on the radio because they lack corporate sponsorship and because they are outside of the "Hawaiian" music genre. In the song "Dear HARA," Krystilez critiques Hawaiian music institutions such as the Hawai'i Academy of Recording Arts and the forces behind the Nā Hoku Hanohano Awards. These organizations serve as watchdogs and launching pads for many Hawaiian performers. The presence of non-Hawaiian genres within the organization has been contentious and contested, especially the hybrid rap/hip-hop category that Krystilez critiques in "Karma," inferring that the Nā Hoku Hanohano Award category is rigged by people in the music industry.[39] Further, he explains that existing outside of the formal legible or recognizable forms of Hawaiian music makes it difficult for his music to get acknowledged. In "Dear HARA" he raps, "I may not know all the words in the Hawaiian language, but I am fluent in speaking aloha through my actions." The divisions within the Hawaiian music industry are a mirror to the Hawaiian community at large. While Hawaiian has been adopted as the official language of Hawai'i alongside English, and while the success of Hawaiian-language immersion schools has been considerable, recent estimates reflect that only 5 percent of the Hawaiian population can actually speak Hawaiian.[40] Krystilez highlights this in these lyrics, which lay bare the dramatic differences and realities of access to and engagement with the Hawaiian language and so-called Hawaiian forms of music and culture.

Keeping It Maoli

Wanting to be seen, acknowledged, or recognized for who they are is a reaction to the constant misrepresentation of Kanaka Maoli people, as presented in the introduction. In sharing his experience, Krystilez explains: "It's about respect, to be proud of where you're from. I feel that way about us locals. It's not just about being agro [aggressive]. We just want respect."[41] Krystilez's desire for respect speaks to a need among Kānaka Maoli, one that seeks to move beyond stereotypes and one that acknowledges our varied articulations. The tourism industry prefers Kānaka Maoli as happy natives, while the "justice" system and other state authorities continue to displace homeless Hawaiians.[42]

As a reaction to disempowerment, Kānaka Maoli (youth) have turned to the Internet and social media to create their own spaces. With the exception of Hawaiian music radio stations (which played the Hawaiian hip-hop group Sudden Rush in the 1990s) and the college radio station KTUH (at the University of Hawai'i), it is rare that a local hip-hop artist would be played on the radio—no matter who they are. Krystilez attempted to have a "local hip-hop" radio hour on the radio station he works for, but after a few weeks the show was discontinued. Despite not being played on the radio or performed regularly in live-music venues in Hawai'i, Hawaiian hip-hop continues to grow through digital social networking sites where users can create their own spaces to represent themselves. In fact, while OHA, politicians, scholars, and activists are arguing over federal recognition, nation-building, and occupation, Kanaka Maoli youth who participate in the local hip-hop scene are not waiting for the government to recognize them or to define who they are. "Bloodline" provides a good case in point, as it presents an example of the ways that Kanaka Maoli youth are asserting their identities on their own terms. As Robin Kelley has argued, cultural productions (and rap in particular) are sites of political consciousness raising and contestation, but they are not pure, nor are they to be understood as a substitute for state-sanctioned political activity.[43] On the contrary, they provide a training ground and a learning process that disenfranchised youth can use to negotiate their political views and to feel that they are actually heard. At the same time, the representations created are just that—representations—they are not "truth" or always real or authentic.

In 2006, when Krystilez was initially promoting The "O," he asserted an unapologetic "thug" persona, which at its core was and continues to be an assertion of Indigenous authenticity. Throughout Krystilez's performances there are overt references to representations of "reality" and "truth," as Krystilez proclaims, "This is reality, this is not a movie!" and "That's the truth, please try us, we'll fight to the end." Krystilez and other Kānaka Maoli must always contend with fantasies about Hawai'i, and it is this context that in many ways forces Krystilez to insist upon his authenticity when he raps, "Is he real? Yes, he is. Fucka!" ("The 'O'"). The goal in many ways is about putting Hawai'i on the map, through the homesteads and on the streets, getting it recognized, letting its voice be heard. Conveying social realism may be central to hip-hop, but let's be *real*: this also presents troubling portrayals. The video for "Bloodline" features misogynistic and aggressive imagery throughout.[44] Looking at this video (and his videos for "Won" and "Shake") within the larger genre of Hawaiian hip-hop, it is striking that most of the older Hawaiian hip-hop groups or performers have barely mentioned women at all, whereas the later crop of Hawaiian hip-hop performers (I.A., Big Teeze, Parc Cyde) explicitly talk about women, sometimes honoring them and at other times—in the hip-hop tradition—reducing them to the perks of "success." As such, violence is explained as being part of the "game." It behooves us to remember how "keeping it real" is frequently used as a justification for voyeuristic fantasies that position women as objects and glamorize violence.[45] Also, as Murray Forman describes, "the real" is an example of racist ideas about authenticity that relegate youth of color to inner-city or ghetto environments to segregate them from the social mainstream.[46] Authenticity is also a trope manipulated for cultural capital, a phenomenon that can clearly be applied to the Hawaiian case.[47] "Keeping it real" should be understood as an effect of media mergers in the marketplace, where representations of hip-hop allow privileged identities to perpetuate stereotypes about black people and degrade women under the auspices of "realness." I wonder, how then, is this "real" a type of resistance?

Krystilez's performance of the "savage" or criminal native man can be read as counterhegemonic in contrast to the "happy native"; or this might be a retelling of the realities surrounding him; or the "savage" is actually aware of the representation he is presenting. This still can be read as a very savvy political move on Krystilez's part, but it can also reproduce negative stereotypes that unwittingly support Kanaka Maoli dispossession. To work through the colonial processes at play within these counterhegemonic representations can feel like chasing one's tail, but what these representational moves do show us is that there exists a system that both normalizes these representations and limits other more-nuanced expressions. It is this system that needs explicating. Reconciling these conflicts or finding the "truth" of Krystilez's narrative is beside the point; understanding that once a performer enters the circuits of power through which these representations move, we need to assess the terms of their agency and how they become complicit with the forms of power that are at work. At the same time, we must look at the larger social conditions under which artists claim their histories and contest despair and dispossession to generate cultural resistance. The critical project here, moreover, is, again, tricky, because, as critics have noted, hip-hop thrives because it offers something real or authentic in a materialistic world. Hip-hop's magic is its ability to connect with the powerless and give them a voice in a world that sees little, if any, value in them.[48]

Indigenous authenticity is a slippery slope littered with preconceived notions of how Natives are supposed to act, perceptions Krystilez upsets in various ways through his performances of defiant indigeneity. Krystilez openly engages with stereotypes in his lyrics, in many respects because he has to. This is necessary to set a reference point for those not familiar with the issues he is talking about and for listeners who identify with homesteads and the articulations of sovereignty that he is putting forth. Krystilez's Indigenous authenticity is representative of E. Patrick Johnson's theory about the lived experience of blackness. Building off Patricia Williams's 1997 book *Seeing through a Color-Blind Future*, Johnson has written that blackness becomes a material way of knowing, one that combines the theatrical fantasy of blackness in the white imaginary that is projected onto black bodies, as well as the lived racial experience of black people.[49] Indigeneity operates in a similar way: Kānaka Maoli must also constantly balance social expectations and cultural identity amid the legacies of the colonial imagination that frequently mark Kānaka Maoli as nothing more than carefree surfers and hula maidens.

Hip-hop is predicated on representing some kind of real or authentic street (hood) experience, and those conditions are not thought to exist in Hawai'i. Hawaiian hip-hop is easily dismissed as an inauthentic expression of hip-hop (and Hawaiianness). Hawaiian hip-hop performers like Krystilez are often criticized for trying to "act Black." At the same time, it has been proposed that "Blackness has become contingent, while the ghetto has become necessary."[50] Put another way, race may no longer be a hip-hop prerequisite, but a relationship to the "ghetto" or some kind of lived struggle is. Hawai'i seems like a far cry from the "ghetto" or "the street," and such sentiments are even expressed by Kānaka Maoli, particularly older generations who take issue with young Kānaka Maoli who, according to them, don't know who they "really are."[51] Behind such criticism of Hawaiian hip-hop, especially when expressed by Kānaka Maoli, is a psychic evasion of the material realities that frequently limit Kanaka Maoli lives. Indeed, centering a Kanaka Maoli "struggle" is not difficult. Sugar and pineapple plantations were transformed into tourist-driven economies, as plantation holdings became hotels, resorts, golf courses, shopping malls, and suburbs in the late twentieth century. This kind of unchecked real estate development has resulted in Hawai'i's astronomical cost of living—the second highest in the United States.[52] Krystilez and his contemporaries express in song these harsh economic realities, commonly referred to as "the price of paradise," that accompany life in Hawai'i. Kānaka Maoli, like many Native populations across the United States, experience the brunt of this economic tyranny, with median incomes far below state and national averages, high unemployment, a lack of educational attainment, drug abuse, and increasing risk of homelessness or unstable living conditions.[53] Such conditions compromise a general quality of life. Hawaiian hip-hop provides a crucial forum in which to talk about these realities but also to destabilize and unsettle old tropes about Hawaiian indigeneity to make space for new articulations that center Indigenous concerns—respect and love for the land that you come from. Songs such as "Bloodline" and (as I explore in the next section) "West Side" are forms of aloha ʻāina, which is a way that Kānaka Maoli perform and experience their love for their culture and Hawaiʻi, but in this case expressing, through song, the aloha we have and its many facets because it is an ongoing reminder that we have survived.

"West Side" and Aloha ʻĀina

Six years after the release of *The "O,"* Krystilez released the video for "West Side." Whereas "Bloodline" was about fighting and representing specific homesteads, "West Side" is a calmer, reggae-infused song where representation of place overrides the visual references to violence that come at the end of the video.[54] The song and the video signal a more pensive and grownup aesthetic and perspective on the part of Krystilez. While the video actively represents Krystilez (and the West Side) as a place where people are ready to fight at any moment, what comes through is, again, pride about place and the aloha the people have for that place—necessary because of the challenges that are faced there. The constant affirmation of the West Side signals that there are many forces that do not affirm it as a place and a way of life to be proud of.

"West Side," like "Bloodline," is a form of aloha ʻāina. As people of the land, Kānaka Maoli bear the privilege and responsibility of caring for the ʻāina. "ʻĀina" means "that which feeds"; the ʻāina is a source of nourishment and sustenance. As noted by Lilikalā Kameʻeleihiwa, communal access to land, sharing of food, and the collective responsibilities among the people, as well as the land and sea, were all connected to the ʻāina.[55] Caring for the ʻāina was about relationships with all that was around you—the aliʻi (chiefs), the commoners, ancestors, the plants, the animals; ʻāina was never bought or sold. It is vibrant, something to be shared, cared for, and honored.[56] "West Side" honors the ʻāina in such a way—it is a Hawaiian hip-hop representation of cultural values such as kuleana, a genealogical relationship and a custodial relationship to the land, and to aloha ʻāina, the

Hawaiian philosophy of loving and caring for the land. Defending the land is also kuleana.

Aloha ʻāina is a Hawaiian epistemological perspective and political position that has endured since time immemorial. Like the meanings that undergird kuleana, aloha ʻāina speaks to the familial relationship Kānaka Maoli have to the land that gives life to the love of nation in Hawaiʻi.[57] As Noenoe Silva has documented, during the time of the overthrow, Kānaka Maoli mobilized politically to retain the sovereignty of lāhui through organizations such as the Hui Hawaiʻi Aloha ʻĀina, which worked to gather signatures on the anti-annexation petitions and offered testimony to U.S. Commissioner James Blount, who was investigating the overthrow of the monarchy in 1893.[58] Aloha ʻāina reemerged in the 1970s during the Hawaiian Renaissance when members of Protect Kahoʻolawe ʻOhana began protesting the ongoing U.S. military use of the island. Aloha ʻāina has thus survived as a vital part of Kanaka Maoli political consciousness, as an alternative practice of loving the land to oppose tourism development, military occupation, and suburban sprawl. As Haunani-Kay Trask poignantly asserted, "Our philosophy as nationalist Hawaiians must be aloha ʻāina, an alternative to tourism and militarism. It means a profound cultural belonging to the land as our ʻohana."[59] In this sense, aloha ʻāina works to "take back" aloha from capitalist exploitation and alienation and recenters it for Kānaka Maoli.[60] The imposition of colonialism and capitalism in Hawaiʻi has transformed how Kānaka Maoli are able to physically relate to the ʻāina. Hawaiian music and its numerous place songs are descendants and practices of aloha ʻāina. Krystilez provides a new soundtrack for aloha ʻāina, representing ka poʻe ke aloha o ka ʻāina (the people who love the land) now.

Expressing aloha ʻāina through music is not a stand-in for physically working on the land. But let's be real: many Kānaka Maoli who live in urban areas probably have never worked in a loʻi kalo (taro patch). Why would they? Who has time or energy, when you have been working all day, sitting in traffic for two hours to drive twenty-five miles just to get home? I assure you, my father and many of my Kanaka Maoli ʻohana have never set foot in a loʻi and likely won't in the near future. This is profoundly depressing—an urbanized reality, a product of Indigenous life under settler colonialism, which removed and detached Kānaka Maoli from our lands and continues to further alienate us by overworking our bodies in other industries or preoccupying us with other activities so that working in the loʻi is perceived as something only certain kinds of Kānaka Maoli participate in. Again, this illustrates the divisions within the Hawaiian community and in

FIGURE 2 Krystilez in "West Side" YouTube music video.

Hawai'i that position some Kānaka Maoli as being invested in cultural revitalization and typically "Hawaiian" activities in contradistinction to Kānaka Maoli who might be too busy or just plain uninterested in taro cultivation because on even a subconscious level it is perceived as antimodern and part of an Indigenous past that is not worth recovering. And yet they know all the words to numerous Hawaiian songs that express aloha 'āina. Thus, first in "Bloodline" and then in "West Side," Krystilez narrates again the ongoing relationship among 'āina, identity, and place (see figure 2). These songs have profound resonance with Hawaiian history, the politics of authenticity, and modern Kanaka Maoli identity.

The west side of the island of O'ahu is often called a "ghetto" because it is recognized as a profoundly Kanaka Maoli space and, by extension, is perceived as economically depressed and ridden with crime. Recall the line in "The 'O'": "Where you're told to not go when you come off the plane." In "West Side" there is a voice-over of a newscaster explaining, "O'ahu's West Side, a place of divided worlds. Sunny beaches, 'ohanas and jaded streets where life can turn hard." Rather than be bound by perceptions of the West Side like the one in the newscaster's voice-over, new meanings and relationships are enabled. As Cristina Bacchilega writes, Kānaka Maoli produce "nā wahi pana" or "storied places" that draw on cultural memory and activate history in the present moment and location.[61] Many places in Hawai'i possess stories about land, depicting the land as living entities. The localized, animated, specific, and emotionally charged narratives in "Bloodline" and "West Side" exemplify the backbone of Kanaka Maoli narrative traditions.[62] Moʻolelos are woven to narrate the history of these lands in a dialogue that enacts a transformative recognition of place.

As Kānaka Maoli negotiate the ways in which they have been dispossessed of their lands, they re-create spaces as well as the ways that they cultivate relationships within those spaces and on Hawaiian lands. Places and spaces are created through social relations to them. Physical spaces generate reality through the energies that are deployed within them.[63] Oliveira explains that through performance cartographies Kānaka Maoli utilized mele to map relationships to place, which was inspired by an intimate knowledge of the land and a commitment to place. Today, mele wahi pana (songs honoring storied places) venerate places, and composing a song about your kulāiwi (ancestral homeland) is one of the greatest honors a person can bestow on a place.[64] "West Side" honors place by producing new forms of cultural memory through Krystilez's narration of what the West Side means to himself and to other listeners as well. Rather than telling a story about economic decline, racial segregation, and criminal activity, hip-hop can explore the ways in which these spaces and places are made meaningful.[65] The stories Krystilez tells throughout his music draw on hip-hop's desire to represent place as well as contributing to nā wahi pana, which offers a narrative of the West Side that is not grim; it is, rather, one that asserts pride in Kanaka Maoli resilience, which is possible because of the boundaries that artists such as Krystilez are willing to cross.

Supporting Locals since Day One

Hawaiian music is an ever-shifting and evolving form. Unfortunately, because of a colonial legacy that associates and defines Nativeness in organic, pristine terms linked to nature, a Kanaka Maoli musical performer who deviates from that specific inheritance will be considered suspect as an "authentic" Native. This is why Kanaka Maoli performers who do not fit into "Hawaiian music" must create their own spaces and networks. In Hawaiʻi, there exist multiple levels of musical cultural production: a mainstream Hawaiian music scene that caters primarily to tourists (and residents or locals); a mainstream hip-hop scene that aspires to mainstream radio play and success (much like the hip-hop heard in the continental United States); and an underground hip-hop scene that focuses on hip-hop culture as a whole and celebrates all its elements of b-boy/b-girlin' (break dancing), graffiti, turntablism, and freestyling (rapping). Krystilez circulates in the latter two scenes. Moreover, in the broader musical scene, opportunities for live performers are limited, as many of the venues prefer Hawaiian music that caters to tourists and locals, military personnel, or others interested in genres such as American rock music. Spaces for the live performance of hip-hop are few and far between.

The lack of physical spaces in which to perform is compensated for by the proliferation of interactive digital spaces to foster a local underground scene. Videos of Krystilez on YouTube, Facebook, Instagram, and Twitter feature him speaking directly to the viewer, hence providing an opportunity for him to be in direct dialogue with his fans—whoever or wherever they may be. Often, participation in these online groups is organized with reference to geographical location, as a space to discuss pertinent local issues. The comments sections or posting walls of many of these online interfaces involve posts by fans who represent where they come from, praise Krystilez, call him out, critique him, and often post to promote their own agendas (albums, clothing lines, events).

On the comments page for "West Side" there is notable debate among the viewers. The majority of the comments are positive, with many users responding to the video by representing themselves. They point out scenes of commonality, such as the Manapua truck or the Pink Store Mini-Mart in Ma'ili, which anyone who is from there would know. The "black and yellow" and the "red and blue" are references to Wai'anae or Nānākuli High School colors, respectively. These recognitions of place matter to viewers and listeners. At the same time, there is a tension in these representations. For example, user isldsnow explains that the song and visuals were good except when the video showed guns: "In that context, the message seemed to be we gang bang, but we don't. would have made great sense though if it was a hunting context and someone was throwing a 150 pound bore [boar] on the hood of their trunk."[66] Additionally, user ryan sambueno writes: "Gottago you to we have the best bangas in Hawaii no need for gun you bitch we scrap if anyone talks shit boi or call us out you talk shit you better be ready to put your hands up you fuck." And PUNISHERx808 says, "I don't know what westside you reppin in dis vid but my westside no need guns we up and up scrap."[67] Both these comments express disapproval of imagery toward the end of the video that shows Krystilez standing between two masked men who are holding shotguns. Their comments challenge the level of violence on the West Side, noting that they don't "gang bang" or "no need guns," advocating instead for "scrapping" or fighting without guns as a more respectable form of fighting. Criticism of Krystilez's seeming celebration of violence is a common thread alongside critiques of what this representation overall does for Kanaka Maoli and Hawaiian culture.

Returning to "real" or "true" Hawaiian culture and ideas about aloha also figures into viewer opinions, as commented by Junior Boy. He asks: "What happened to 'aloha' spirit? Just like opihi, used to have before time, not anymore though. Nowadays, it's the 'I can scrap, carry guns, drink and turn into superman, knock out anyone that wasn't born on the same side of the island as me' mentality. I mean no disrespect. Just sad sometimes that true 'Hawaiian pride' is so hard to find. Seems like aloha only lies with the old timers. It seems to be dying off with them too."[68] His "What happened to 'aloha' spirit?" is a question that is constantly invoked, one that the commenter seems to be pushing Krystilez and many of his generation to consider what their assertions of masculinity and Kanaka Maoli identity lose in the process. The presence of guns and the lyrics about violence certainly display that there is perhaps a lack of aloha spirit on the West Side, but what is most interesting about this comment is the way that Junior Boy compares aloha to opihi. Opihi is a limpet that grows on lava rocks and that people gather for food. It is enjoyed by many Kānaka Maoli and other people in Hawai'i. In recent years, opihi has been overharvested and difficult to get unless you know the good picking spots. The user is inferring that, like opihi (which is scarce now), aloha is gone. According to this user, aloha is overharvested, just like opihi, and dying off with the original Hawaiians, who had "true Hawaiian pride." The comment makes aloha something that exists within nature, within Kānaka Maoli, who are supposed to be closer to an essence of aloha, a welcoming essence that old-timers had and the younger generation does not. The cause of this is overharvesting—when something is in demand and is then no longer available. Likening opihi to aloha and "real" Hawaiians is an astute critique of what has happened to aloha via tourism, exhibiting how the music of Krystilez and performances of defiant indigeneity translate to listeners who make these connections.

The critique by Junior Boy is really at the core of the antagonism some people feel toward Krystilez. As "Bloodline" and "West Side" exhibit, the lyrical and visual representation of Krystilez and others in his video "repping their bloodline" is coupled with imagery of young Hawaiian men advocating violence, often fighting, and in some instances holding shotguns. Krystilez has been criticized in the community and online for these violent images because they are "un-Hawaiian" or "against aloha." And even in my own writings about him, I have been critical of this violence. In an interview, I asked him about the violent imagery, and he shrugged it off, stating that his intention was not to offend anyone or even to advocate violence; rather, he wants to make people think. He knows that he should not be promoting violence in Hawaiian communities, but in his view, he is also struggling against images of domesticated and docile Hawaiians who are apolitical and support tourism. I asked Krystilez about the criticism he receives and how he deals with it. He explained that as a public figure within the hip-hop scene and in the radio industry in Hawai'i, being criticized is just part of the job; he just wants to produce art, and he can't help but be an extrovert. His personality is such that he just wants to put stuff out there and let people interpret it however they want, as long as people are doing something. During this interview on a Sunday afternoon at Zippy's on King Street in Makīkī, I listened intently as he shared his dreams and visions with me for a thriving local hip-hop scene. I was shocked at how thoughtful and pensive this man who talks about being a "thug" was. Krystilez dreams of a thriving and interactive Hawaiian hip-hop scene that supports local artists, fosters creativity, and produces dialogue among locals about issues that matter to them most.

The very same technology (and referent corporate controllers) that produces the conditions that disallow the mainstream circulation of Hawaiian hip-hop also possesses its radical promise. Because Krystilez does not get mainstream attention on local radio or television, and because there are a limited number of opportunities for him to perform, he has to promote himself in these spaces, both online and in the streets. In all of these instances, Krystilez's performance exhibits the different ways that the 'āina, the street, and performance spaces are manifested through Hawaiian hip-hop. Hawaiian music, surely, has always served the purpose of honoring place and the lāhui, as a form of aloha 'āina, a need that is amplified in the present as the Kanaka Maoli diaspora continues to grow. To feel a connection to a place, whether you have spent all or none of your life there, is increasingly negotiated through cultural production and the global digital media formats through which hip-hop circulates. In a capitalist economy that has pushed many Kānaka Maoli off-island out of economic necessity, this is crucial. Kanaka Maoli indigeneity, therefore, must allow this performative movement of indigeneity. As Kauanui has pointed out, one of the biggest problems facing the Kanaka Maoli diaspora is that Kānaka Maoli living off-island are invisible to each other and isolated from Kānaka Maoli living in Hawai'i.[69] Making this connection is an example of the ways that places are made meaningful through Hawaiian hip-hop, exhibiting these creative and interactive spaces, whether through online media or in a freestyle cipher. Krystilez's narrative thus presents an opportunity to examine the multilayered nature of Hawaiian hip-hop and, more importantly, contemporary Kanaka Maoli life everywhere, even if the song is representing only the West Side.

Looking closely at Krystilez's defiant indigeneity also requires an understanding of the ways that Kānaka Maoli are ignored and how performance spaces are remade through Kanaka Maoli assertions (for example, in songs like "Bloodline"). Responding to the call to "rep your bloodline," Kānaka Maoli affirm their ongoing presence on lands that were taken from them. It is the land as a material entity and as our ancestor that is the discursive terrain upon which current battles over land tenure are waged among Hawaiian nationalists, private landowners, the state of Hawai'i, and the federal government. *It was always about the land.* The call-and-response in "Bloodline" is about aloha 'āina, about the enduring connection to the land, and this is precisely when listeners respond to "rep your bloodline." When listeners respond with their bloodline, their homestead, or the place they are from, they are affirming their aloha for that place. When they respond, they place themselves, they become grounded, they sustain their Kanaka Maoli identity in a way that is, again, about community belonging and recognition. The emotive power of "repping your bloodline" exceeds the bounds of the state's gaze because this aloha is being performed through a refusal. In this sense, the refusal is in turning away from the state and returning to the 'āina, to the community, and to performing that aloha for your people, in a way that is connected to the past but is wholly modern and does not need the settler state. This connection can be both private and public; it can be done in the privacy of one's headphones, nodding quietly and screaming "Nānākuli get!" on the inside, or in a group, at a concert, defiantly representing who you are, "HI Bloodline!" This defiance is heard in Hawaiian place songs, seen on car decals, worn on T-shirts and in tattoos, held in our hearts. *Bloodline is all I need.* These performances of defiant indigeneity remind us of our ongoing refusal, of our aloha for Hawai'i and our fight to continue being Kanaka Maoli.

It is no coincidence that Krystilez's narrative emerges precisely when "debates" about federal recognition pervade public discourse. Since the early 2000s, OHA has been engaged in a process of so-called nation-building in attempts to lobby the state and federal governments for some form of recognition. The recognition drives of the organizations Kau Inoa and

Kanaʻiolowalu employ the rhetoric of Hawaiian disappearance. If you don't sign up for the roll, you will no longer be Kanaka Maoli. OHA uses scare tactics to make Kānaka Maoli believe that if you do not sign up for the roll, you will not be represented in the new lāhui. This process put forth by OHA has been justifiably criticized for the way it has divided the Hawaiian community, disenfranchising many Kānaka Maoli. Because OHA is a state agency, many Kānaka Maoli do not trust OHA, and it is a space that does not appeal to the youth, who may feel that the process is too formal and does not allow for dialogue or creative spaces to negotiate the lāhui-building process.

Krystilez turns away from recognition and demarcates his own boundaries, even as he employs state logics to found his identity claims. He does not need the state to recognize him—Krystilez makes no apologies for who he is, where he came from, and where he hopes to go. Krystilez's overall self-representation allows for a critique of colonialism that destabilizes stereotypical perceptions of Kanaka Maoli identity (for example, the hula girl, the beach boy, the Native warrior). But more than critiquing stereotypes, Krystilez performs on multiple planes of meaning-making and moves through multiple circuits of cultural production in Hawaiʻi, in ways that resignify both racialization discourses and Indigenous epistemologies. Thus, while Krystilez uses the logics of blood and is not averse to employing commercial circuits to root and route his indigeneity, his narrative also challenges the stereotypes of blood logic even as he asserts his connection to the homestead, while his connection to the homestead is set in motion in multiple media and performance circuits. Debunking stereotypes of happy and loving Natives, he also dismantles long-held notions about Indigenous groups as being unable to travel or change, inasmuch as Indigenous groups especially are expected to replicate popular preconceptions about themselves as "traditional" and unchanging. Krystilez's defiant indigeneity creates new cultural spaces out of old problematic ones, for himself and future generations. In one of the final moments in the video for "West Side," Krystilez is shown staring into the horizon as this image fades into a shot of the ocean before him. In this pensive scene he situates himself firmly in this place, looking contemplative, as though he is envisioning the unclear future in front of him.

Krystilez presents the possibilities that exist for Kānaka Maoli today, which get interrogated and invigorated through the performance of various types of cultural resistance that ironically make evident the legacies of racialized and gendered subjection while reconstituting them. In many ways, the defiant indigeneity personified by Krystilez narrates reality, asserting that Kanaka Maoli identity and cultural productions have no choice but to appropriate the discourse of authenticity in hopes of simultaneously undermining it. Krystilez's performances are evidence of the necessity of reclaiming places and spaces (including the discursive space of "the real") when there are laws and policies that prevent you from reclaiming lands. The sentiments expressed in Krystilez's music and videos speak to this sense of aloha for his home, an expression of aloha that is for the community that created it. In an unapologetic embodiment of Kanaka Maoli indigeneity, Krystilez makes visible and possible our ongoing refusal and defiance as we reclaim performance spaces in our homeland.

CHAPTER THREE

Aloha in Drag

No connectives are necessary: the imperial vision enables the
natives' life and death at the same time.

—EDWARD SAID, *Culture and Imperialism*

Cocoa Chandelier's Confessional

In an old Chinese restaurant converted into a hip loft nightclub that over-
looks North Hotel and Maunakea Street in Honolulu's Chinatown, Cocoa
Chandelier[1] staged a confessional. "Cocoa Chandelier's Confessional" (on
August 14, 2009, Madonna's forty-ninth birthday) featured Cocoa Chandelier and friends in an ode to the material girl. Blondes were granted free
entrance, and audience members were encouraged to donate money to confess.[2] Cocoa Chandelier performed a series of numbers from Madonna's
body of work, as did other performers. Numbers featured were "Erotica,"
"Justify My Love," "Cherish," "Hung Up," and many more.[3] Cocoa Chandelier's greatest costume feat of the evening was a blue and green mermaid
suit, mimicking Madonna's performance in the video for the song "Cherish," complete with bare-chested brown boys in towels who carried her onto
the stage, and a pink leotard and blonde wig for the song "Hung Up."

The loft space was adorned with candles and pillows. Audience members
sat on the floor, on pillows, or on small couches or stood around the periphery of the room. Throughout the room, red and white candle wax dripped
on the cool cement floor à la *Body of Evidence* (1993). Italian food (included
in the $10 presale ticket price) was laid out, but it seemed out of place in
the heart of Chinatown, where a variety of Asian cuisines are available to
satisfy your appetite. In Hawai'i these days, nothing is that cheap, but then
again, in Chinatown anything is possible. A few blocks away from Chinatown's then so-called revitalization, the area's backdoor economy still exists
to titillate the senses despite efforts to "weed" the area of drug trafficking,
homelessness, and prostitution. Stigmatized like most Chinatowns, Honolulu's Chinatown is known for its seediness, but in the early 2000s an arts
revival, in concert with increasing gentrification, turned these once-avoided
streets into a hotbed of artistic possibility.[4] These spaces of sanctuary for
makeshift communities living at the edges of Honolulu's skyrocketing

rents are precariously juxtaposed, with downtrodden youth and postado-lescents searching for space to see a good show. When I began this research, Chinatown was the locus of art and experimental performance and club spaces. This was a few years after the venues where I earned my chops as a punk singer had already closed to make way for upscale art and dinner venues appealing to an emergent business happy-hour crowd and tourists in search of a grittier side of Hawai'i. Alas, the venues that once hosted many art shows and performance events have moved on to the Kaka'ako area a few blocks away, where a local urban art scene is currently thriving. The cycles of urban renewal and redevelopment allowed this ethnography to initially take place, but as time went on, performance spaces like the Loft opened and then went out of business. These brief moments are emblematic of the instability of performance space in Hawai'i. The early 2000s to 2010 offered opportunities for artists to add new narratives to Chinatown's littered streets and histories lining Hotel, Bishop, Maunakea, and Pauahi Streets. With namesakes who ring prominently in Hawaiian history, these streets were obscured by "First Friday"[5] art gallery maps and bus schedules that high-lighted Hawai'i's booming multicultural arts scene.

I had been watching Cocoa Chandelier perform since the mid-1990s and was not accustomed to the crowd's tepid response to her call to confess. Dur-ing the "confessional," it was more than an opportunity for alliteration; Cocoa Chandelier asked people to confess, but not many did. Maybe it was the religious undertones that made everyone fearful. Confession is supposed to be private, I thought to myself—unlikely to happen in a room full of butchies and muffies afraid to talk for fear of public shaming by their peers who compose this tight-knit community.[6] Snickers helped to cut the tension in the room. You could not tell what was coming next. Musical numbers went from humorous to very serious. Cocoa Chandelier did not confess. An-other prominent drag queen, serving as the host of the evening, circled the room with a microphone and a shoebox and asked for confessions and do-nations, unnerving the audience. Most people made their comments or confessions from where they were seated on the floor or from the periphery of the space, preferring not to speak at the microphone to be heard by everyone. A prominent performer, Kaina Jacobs, walked to the front of the show, donated a handful of money, and walked away without confessing anything.[7] As the evening progressed, most people declined the call to con-fess, seemingly aware of the cost of their visibility in this small space. Given the seemingly intimate space inhabited by friends and family members, what was the justification for the silent response to Cocoa Chandelier's call to confess?

Cocoa Chandelier is a performer, choreographer, scholar, and educator working in urban Honolulu. At the time of this writing, she was a PhD candidate in theater at the University of Hawai'i. She engages in ambivalent and complicated performances that do not register as "Hawaiian performance." Cocoa Chandelier's body of work, in various groups and under various aliases, has dazzled (and baffled) audiences in venues ranging from the backdoor industrial warehouses of the mid-1990s rave culture, to the Waikīkī gay nightclub Fusions' Paper Doll Show Revue, to the Iona Pear dance company.[8] She is well known for her collaborative work with Giinko Marischino, an avant-garde troupe that performs in urban Honolulu and specializes in experimental butoh dance.[9] Cocoa Chandelier has also appeared in numerous stage productions around Honolulu and internationally, and has been an artist-in-residence at Leeward Community College theater, directing theater productions around Honolulu as well as teaching theater and performance workshops for youth.[10] In addition to her presence in the local drag community, Cocoa Chandelier regularly competes in local, national, and international drag competitions. She was crowned Universal ShowQueen in 2008, which I discuss at length later in this chapter. In addition, she has been Hawai'i's Top Entertainer of the Year (2015), Miss Gay USofA Sin City Classic (2011), Miss Hawai'i Continental (2009), Miss Venus (2007), and Diva of Polynesia (2006), and has held many other titles I am sure I am missing.

Within the local LGBTQ community, many know her from the stage, where she can be found hosting events at Fusions nightclub and Hulas Bar & Lei Stand. She was featured prominently in the film *Ke Kulana He Māhū* (2001), about the history of sexuality in Hawai'i and the role of māhūs[11] in modern-day Hawaiian culture. When she is introduced in the film, a montage of video footage is shown as Skeeter Mariah Crackseed's voice lists Cocoa Chandelier's various aliases. She is introduced as Samuel L. A. Akuna, Cocoa Chandelier, Paris France, Kinko Lush, and Sumir Lacroix. These aliases are indicative of Cocoa Chandelier's enigmatic performance persona. When asked in an interview about the origins of her drag name, she starts telling me a story, but I feel like she is making it up. I ask her again, "No, really, are you lying?" And she just laughs. In the midst of my incessant questioning and her laughing at me as a "researcher," I began to wonder, Why the evasiveness? Why the humor? I became suddenly aware of the role I am most reluctant to play, that of the researcher/ethnographer. Perhaps this aversion to tell me "the truth" was part of her performance strategy.

The first two chapters of this book explored the reasons Kānaka Maoli believe in aloha and the dynamic ways that we perform aloha to retain its cultural strength for ourselves and to be recognized as Kānaka Maoli. In Chapter 1, I argued that not answering aloha's call results in a kind of figurative death, as an act of erasure and absence. In short, Kānaka Maoli answer the call to survive and to secure social life. Chapter 2 examined Krystilez's refusal of aloha and his rejection of the performance modes that have been outlined for Kānaka Maoli. Still, I am nagged by several questions, What happens when Kanaka Maoli don't answer the call of aloha? What happens when Kānaka Maoli refuse to perform aloha in prescribed ways? More precisely, can we even really deny the call of aloha when aloha is such an integral and essential element of what it means to be Kanaka Maoli? This chapter analyzes how Cocoa Chandelier performs aloha *in drag*, as an evasive mode of performance that prioritizes Hawaiian forms of belonging and recognition, which get interrogated and affirmed in performance space. The push-pull interpellating force of aloha and its significance for Kānaka Maoli remind me of José Muñoz's theorization of *disidentifications*. Disidentification is a strategy that works on and against dominant ideology and is an example of when interpellation fails, thus making possible something else. Defiant indigeneity also pushes forward this possibility of *something else* that creates and reconfigures Kanaka Maoli life through performance.[12] Central to my methodological approach is a critique of the confession as a requirement for the performance of indigeneity. As a paradigmatic epistemological framework in ethnic studies and Native studies scholarship in particular, the confession supports an ethnographic framework that fetishizes the narratives of minorities, which at times especially binds Natives into one-dimensional receptacles of culture, instead of viewing Natives as agentic and innovative cultural theorists. Rather than focus on Hawaiian performance in typically identifiable "Hawaiian" forms, I explain how the constitution of those forms is always linked to how capitalism wants to "see" us and how we counteract these practices by performing aloha in drag as a defiant act of refusal.

This chapter provides close readings of performance scenes to map some of the ways that Cocoa Chandelier's material suggests a new approach to Hawaiian studies scholarship and knowledge production. Using drag as an analytic of performance, I examine how she queers the study of Hawaiian performance through two specific strategies—aloha in drag and Indigenous realness—to comment on the pressures put on minoritarian performers and to create alternate modes of Hawaiian indigeneity. This works ultimately because of the relationship the audience has to her as a performer, enabling a form of community recognition and belonging that is predicated on shared understandings of culture rather than commodified forms associated with Hawaiians (from tourism or popular culture) or even cultural influences that have been imported from colonialism (such as blood quantum or heteronormativity). Both strategies work to support a renewed sense of Kanaka Maoli indigeneity that is not overdetermined or inhibited by its widely circulated performances, while also illustrating the significance of these performances for the local LGBTQ community in Hawai'i.

Cocoa Chandelier partakes in a number of strategies to avert the colonial gaze. A theme that stretches across her performances is a refusal to engage in what Rey Chow calls "coercive mimeticism," a process by which marginal groups in Western culture—specifically, ethnics—are expected to replicate the preconceptions about themselves and objectify themselves according to dominant imaginings.[13] Hawaiian performance (and Hawaiian life) is thus queered when Cocoa Chandelier does not perform anything that can be identified as "Hawaiian."[14] What is considered "Hawaiian," as I have explained, is hypervisible in the American colonial imagination with attendant modern manifestations. In recent years, the stereotypical images of the past have been supplemented with images of Kanaka Maoli resistance (usually in Hawai'i), often in very public affirmations and protests by Kānaka Maoli themselves, which also contribute to this hypervisibility. Visibility, once perceived as the answer to misrepresentation and misrecognition, also has the ability to create restrictive norms and to limit alternatives. As Nicole Fleetwood explains, the visual sphere itself is also performative. It is a "doing"; it performs an action, producing a field of vision that renders racial marking.[15] The repetition of this field of vision is what maintains subjection for disciplined individuals.[16] Hawaiian performance, especially through the performance of aloha, can be appreciated or understood critically as a primary means through which Kānaka Maoli have become seen, "known," and disciplined. Power has been able to reproduce itself not just through disciplinary state institutions (federal and state laws and agencies; civic organizations), but also through how Kānaka Maoli ourselves have willingly performed subjectivities expected of us.

Kānaka Maoli have consistently performed *our aloha* because, as I argued in chapter 1, the performance of aloha, of "Hawaiianness," has become tied to how we understand and identify ourselves. Aloha has become our defining character trait—our "truth," our essence; it is who we are. This understanding of who we are became possible as a result of transformations to Hawaiian governance and political economies throughout the nineteenth century. Then, as now, performances of Hawaiian culture were subject to the colonialist gaze that structured Kanaka Maoli performances (because certain performances were more desired and thus worth more money). The gaze also enabled circulations of specific representations to become naturalized in discourse and internalized as norms among Kānaka Maoli. These representations are incomplete, and hegemony is of course always contested. Adding to the growing analysis on divergent and unexpected spaces of indigeneity, this chapter focuses on emergent performances of Hawaiian culture that exist beyond the gaze of the state, behind the curtain at the Kodak Hula Show (one example of many), and in the actual lived experiences of Kānaka Maoli. The latter have been notably overlooked when performances do not adhere to expectations of Hawaiian performance. Because Cocoa Chandelier is a performer who blatantly steps outside of the zones of Hawaiian respectability, it is imperative to outline how her strategies queer the study of Hawaiian indigeneity and performance.

Queering the Study of Hawaiian Performance

Queer studies have been profoundly lacking in Hawaiian studies. Sometimes it feels like there is such an intense urgency to rewrite Hawaiian history and revitalize our language to legitimate Hawaiian philosophies as rigorous knowledge and to support cultural nationalist efforts that people lose sight of how gender and all its relationships—notably the way our bodies relate to one another—inform the approach we take to securing formalized nationhood. The silence around gender and sexuality, however, has not been total, as several scholars have focused on the place of gender and sexuality in Hawaiian worlds.[17] Unlike in the continental United States, where "queer" is a term that was historically employed to degrade people performing modes of nonheteronormative behavior, or even in the recent reclamations of "queer" among the LGBTQ community, allies, and many others, "queer" is not often heard in Hawai'i.[18] In the Indigenous Pacific, "queer" is commonly coded as white despite the long presence of nonheteronormative communities. I flag nonheteronormative here because specific formations of gender and sexuality in various Pacific societies are not all the same, and they do not necessarily fit into Western categories of "homosexual," "transgender," or "transvestite."[19] Additionally, while the ongoing existence of these communities is not predicated solely on drag shows, they are fairly common across the Pacific, such as in Hawai'i, Aotearoa, Samoa, Guam, and the Cook Islands.

As explained by Niko Besnier and Kalissa Alexeyeff, these communities are deeply enmeshed with what many think of as "tradition," bringing new ways of thinking and being in the world; but while this might excite some, it produces negative attitudes as well. Thus, scholars have been attentive to the ways in which drag shows are spaces where gender transgression can be culturally acceptable because it is routed through indigeneity, even in light of Christian religious beliefs that might frown upon gender bending and its sexual undertones. Similarly, scholarship has explained that drag shows produce anxieties about Westernization and taste, but not necessarily about sexuality itself.[20] In this vein, historians and anthropologists have labored to situate the experiences of nonheterosexual or gender-transgressive individuals and their cultural significance throughout the Pacific. Historians have "found" through their analysis of early European accounts of islander sexual behavior that same-sex activities were common, and that observation of such sexualities influenced both European perceptions of islanders and the transformation of European sexuality itself. Perhaps most obviously, anthropologists have also documented this as they aimed to understand the cultural significance of these nonnormative sexual identities and performances.[21]

Bringing queer theory to Pacific studies is a tricky task, and my objective is to honor multiple identities without fetishizing them and relegating them to the indices of anthro-porn or making them available for misinterpretation and misappropriation in the service of (to borrow Scott Morgensen's term) settler homonationalism.[22] I am not really interested in telling you the life stories of the fa'afafine, the fakaleiti, or even the māhū—although such work is important.[23] I use "queer" here to mark how Cocoa Chandelier engages in antinormativity in regard to Hawaiian performance. As of late there has been a growing and very public queer movement across the Pacific, so while this is not the focus of this chapter, I want to flag that certain strains of queer theory, such as queer of color critique and queer Indigenous studies, bring forth useful critiques to problematize the imposition of heteropatriarchy and its impact on nonheteronormative relations in Native communities especially. In the groundbreaking anthology *Queer Indigenous Studies: Critical Interventions in Theory, Politics, and Literature* (2011), the place of LGBTQ2[24] Natives was highlighted in order to examine the long-term effects of heteropatriarchal colonial systems on Native peoples. The anthology focused on how Native LGBTQ2 people were excluded, and it began to trace a longer history of exclusion that queered Native peoples in the name of building a settler state. Driskill, Finley, Gilley, and Morgensen write, "Queer Indigenous critiques do not look for recognition from the nation-state for our pain and suffering because of identities, but seek to imagine other queer possibilities for emancipation and freedom for all peoples."[25] The latter points to the necessity of building forms of community recognition and belonging that highlight the love (and dare I say aloha) that exists within community and have allowed peoples who were meant to disappear actually to survive.

Although "queer" might not be a designation used in Hawaiʻi to denote sexual preference or gender presentation, queer Indigenous critiques enable a queering of categorizations that are common in Hawaiʻi. I focus on Cocoa Chandelier's drag performance not just to highlight gender performance, but to highlight that modes of performance and ways of being that are perceived as "natural" must be questioned, such as the expectation that Hawaiians have "aloha" or must perform only in Hawaiian forms, such as hula. It almost seems silly that I have to say these things. Cocoa Chandelier actively queers Hawaiian performance by not performing anything "Hawaiian" against a hypervisible backdrop of Hawaiian performance and notably in a tourist environment that rewards such Hawaiian performances. Further, she performs her aloha in drag.

"Drag" as a concept has become so pervasive in mainstream American popular culture that there is a common definition of what it is. RuPaul, perhaps the most famous drag queen in the world, recently won an Emmy for her reality drag competition show. Many scholars have labored to describe the transgressive possibilities, the normative dangers, and the overall social meanings imbued within drag performances in their various contexts. The celebration of drag also represents a liberalist attempt at so-called tolerance and acceptance of nonnormative gender presentations, performances, and ways of being on stage and in everyday life, while also profiting off of an emergent gay capitalist market niche that requires a heteronormative spectacularization of queerness.[26] Early scholarship on drag documented that the most simplistic act of drag is that of one gender performing another gender.[27] Drag performance—in terms of gender—unifies the category of "woman" or "man" through reiteration, in other words, through the constant performance of traits attributed to "women" or "men." Drag exposes the "normal" constitution of gender presentation that is constituted by a set of "disavowed attachments or identifications."[28] Drag reveals the ways that gender norms are naturalized, but as Judith Butler stresses, drag is also contingent, open to interpretation and resignification.[29]

Within LGBTQ communities, "drag" often refers to the way we all perform identities. Within queer communities, drag performers offer comedic relief, a space of performative fantasy (notably in the lip-syncing of pop hits), and at times political commentary that lay bare the precarity of queer lives. Drag has unifying power, even in what it unifies to disavow. Drag performance often parodies the very notion of an original, revealing that the supposed "original" is fabrication to begin with. Drag performance, then, is contingent on its audience having some kind of shared understanding that allows them to recognize the construction of whatever is being performed. When drag is performed before an LGBTQ audience, there is a shared commonality that allows the normative performance of gender to be exposed as a construction. By employing drag as a method, Cocoa Chandelier bucks expectations of Hawaiian performance and allows us to, as Sarita See explains in *The Decolonized Eye* (2009), "think about identity as a politics of evading rather than securing visibility and legibility."[30] This move, as See explains, enables thinking about American empire or imperialism itself as abstracted and hidden through particular kinds of performances. At other times, resistance is performed through seemingly apolitical performance genres.[31] In the Hawaiian context this is personified in stereotypical perceptions of hula that the untrained eye would mark as apolitical because they appear to embody "aloha."

I hold in productive tension "queer" as an identity formation alongside "queer" as a way to disrupt the norms of Hawaiian scholarship. This is not a study of how this artist identifies as queer or how this artist is queer. Cocoa Chandelier's body of work queers how we think about Hawaiian performance. Bringing the subjectless critique of queer studies to Hawaiian performance moves us away from making "the Native" the primary object of Native studies to challenge how studies of Hawaiian performance frequently position performers or performances as containers or transmitters of essential Hawaiian truths.[32] I am not going to tell Cocoa Chandelier's life story or examine her cultural performance as a means to comment on the natural essences of Kanaka Maoli indigeneity or even to connect her performances to a precolonial Kanaka Maoli way of being. Cocoa Chandelier's power comes through her resistance to this kind of ethnographic entrapment, because her performances disrupt the practices of ethnography that attempt to contain her narrative.[33] Even as I write about her, Cocoa

Chandelier does not confess, and I will not make her. Instead I offer a critical reading of her body of work as a way of meditating on the state of Hawaiian performance.

Serving Ka'ahumanu Realness

Figure 3, submitted for Cocoa Chandelier's participation in the Diva of Polynesia drag queen competition, is an image that conjures pride, erasure, and resilience for Kanaka Maoli viewers, LGBTQ ones especially. Reposted by Cocoa Chandelier on March 28, 2013, it began recirculating on her Facebook entertainer page as part of her effort to become a contestant on the reality drag competition television show *RuPaul's Drag Race*.[34] The first comment on this image was "Serving Ka'ahumanu Realness!!!" The comment and the image is everything. Representing those unexpected moments of Indigenous recognition and rearticulation, the comment names and calls out a public of viewers, of fans, and of community who know who Ka'ahumanu is and why such an image is necessary. Conjuring the memory of a pivotal figure in Hawaiian history, a revered queen, inferred in the image and the comment is the ongoing relationship between Hawaiian history and performance, making evident the interlocking threads of Hawaiian self-determination, gender expression, and contemporary politics. The image and the comment represent what I term Indigenous realness, a performance of indigeneity that builds upon popular cultural perception, yet at the same time prioritizes Indigenous knowledge and belonging rather than the obliterating force of colonialism that seeks to erase the diverse expressions of indigeneity that both challenge and authorize indigeneity itself.

"Realness" is a term invoked in drag culture. Realness can be connected to any number of identities, from businesswoman, to clown, to president. It might be an expression of humor; it can also be a matter of life and death. When realness is named, it is a way to recognize the labor that the performer has gone through to make a look or performance appear "real" in contrast to that which lies beneath the surface. As Marion Bailey describes, realness is a performance that adheres to particular racial and gender performances in an attempt to capture authenticity.[35] Realness functions as a guide, a communal form of recognition, and is a way to understand quotidian forms of performance as they contribute to subjectivity.[36] The image performs Indigenous realness because it references a shared set of imagery associated with an Indigenous people—Hawaiians in this case—and it is acknowledged by the audience as such. In this invocation of Indigenous realness,

FIGURE 3 Cocoa Chandelier entry, Diva of Polynesia Pageant, 2006. Photo by Charles Monoiki Ah Nee-Bahn. Hair and makeup by Wade Ah Nee-Bahn.

the viewer knows that the image is not a rendering of reality, but is representative of the performers intent is to stage and honor Hawaiian aliʻi (royalty), as clearly recognized by the user's comment, reminding viewers (at the posted moment and now), especially Hawaiian ones, of our regal past. Also, as a drag queen, Chandelier signals the presence of nonheteronormative gender expressions as also part of the Hawaiian past, present, and future.

Indigenous realness demands an awareness of ongoing Indigenous presence. It means acknowledging that Indigenous people have not been erased and that colonialism did not kill all of us, even if it is still with us. It generates its power from this fact. A performance of Indigenous realness might pull from a shared material way of knowing based on what it means to be Indigenous in a specific space. It also is a performance that draws from stereotypical imaginings of what indigeneity appears to be on the surface. And in this putting on and taking off of indigeneity, it both disrupts and maintains such imagery. Realness is a purposeful performance that is crafted to be seen in a particular way, and it is authenticated within a specific performance space. It is a performance that works only if there is an agreement on what that performance ought to "serve" or give. What a performance conveys to the audience through visual markers and cues "works" only if the people present—the audience of judges, so to speak—identify and acknowledge the performer's intent. Otherwise, it doesn't perform. It is necessary to reference a shared set of signs even as those signs are disrupted or discarded altogether. This interplay is what underpins racial and gender performativity and holds the potential of its force.

Foregrounding this idea of "realness" in the same way that realness is typically invoked in drag culture can transform the way we think about indigeneity. Indigeneity is something that is both real and performed, and it comes with associated imagery and expectations that people internalize and accept as natural. In the same way that gender differences were constructed by heteronormative colonial binaries rooted in Western religion and so-called science, what we code as "Indigenous" was created under the violences of the colonial encounter that created "the Native." These performances reference the expectations of Nativeness to challenge the forces that continue to frame Natives as an unchanging antimodern subject position. Indigeneity thus represents both the latter and a contemporary lived reality that is part of our experiences, our knowledges, and how we enact our identities every day. This can be both a burden and a blessing that individuals are constrained by as well as uplifted by through performance. Of course, it is not my intention to completely negate the necessary material performances that are required of indigeneity to be seen as "real," specifically when the state or tribal sovereignty is involved. But we must constantly remind ourselves that it was the colonial gaze that blurred the lines between staged performances and performances in everyday life.[37] Centering a theory of Indigenous realness reminds us of the hurdles, hoops, and bureaucratic nonsense that Indigenous peoples endure to prove how "real" they are. Indigenous peoples must perform this realness in order to be tribal citizens, to be recognized by their own kin, and to survive.

The prerequisites for Indigenous realness also illustrates its limits. As Bailey explains, realness is a necessary, strategic, and creative response to the dangers of gender and racial subjectivity.[38] Expanding this theorization to indigeneity, Indigenous realness also contains the material and psychological stakes of Indigenous performativity, which includes ongoing erasure as well as the danger of appropriation. Appropriation by outsiders is a practice far too familiar to Indigenous peoples, but it is more dangerous to constrain Indigenous performance and identity to a set of prescribed actions or norms than it is to worry about the loss of authenticity and cultural theft. There is certainly a risk in opening up the floodgates of indigeneity when I argue that indigeneity is performative and has no true essence or core. By this logic, then, aren't the kids at Burning Man performing Indigenous realness in their headdresses? These are troubling analogies. This is why Indigenous realness and aloha in drag are valuable strategies, because they show how we live, how we create knowledge, and how this is only possible through community connections. If we spend all our time focusing on demarcating what is real and authentic as a means to protect what keeps getting stolen or appropriated, we lose sight of our own innovation and connections. The benefit of Indigenous realness is that it exposes perceptions and fallacies at the same time that it might support them.

What makes these performances of indigeneity different? Realness requires shared definitions that are negotiated by an audience of peers who share an understanding about something. It also retains a constant challenge to the boundaries of realness. Akin to the archive of knowledge that is linked to debates about Indigenous membership, community recognition in these performance spaces is predicated on a deeper archive of knowledge that draws from being in community and centers genealogy and relatedness. As Audra Simpson describes, this archive of social and genealogic knowledge can function as a way that identification refuses the logics of the state.[39] In other words, the play that Indigenous realness allows supports a kind of community recognition of indigeneity, understanding that realness is about both authenticity and illusion.[40] Within performance space realness is adjudicated, albeit tentatively, by an audience, and this temporality is also what generates its defiance and contributes to Indigenous survival (a point I return to in my analysis of aloha in drag in the next section).

Other comments on the image of Cocoa Chandelier also make the connection to Hawaiian royalty, for example, "Very real I love serve the aliʻi."[41] This response is another example of the power of this kind of representation for viewers who connect with Hawaiian history and Hawaiian monarchs in particular because they serve as reminders of Hawaiian independence. Cocoa Chandelier brings to life Kanaka Maoli genealogies and connection to our royalty in an LGBTQ environment that mainstream or some of the more conservative elements of Hawaiian political life would seek to marginalize. The image in figure 3 does more than enter Cocoa Chandelier into the Diva of Polynesia pageant. When later shown and circulated, it is an image that speaks to the marginalized LGBTQ community in Hawaiʻi. Despite Hawaiʻi's so-called status as the Aloha State, where diversity and love abound, residues of colonization and Christianization remain, and LGBTQ folk are often shamed or ignored in modern Hawai'i. But many within the LGBTQ community know that Hawaiian culture was very expressive sexually and that nonheteronormative gender and sexual arrangements were rather common in Hawaiian society. This image of Cocoa Chandelier challenges the so-called annihilating force of colonization, situating her (and the community she represents) as part of a proud Hawaiian genealogy that remains and did not exist in the shadows.

What kinds of knowledges about Hawaiian indigeneity are then necessary for this image of Cocoa Chandelier to generate a response such as "Serving Ka'ahumanu Realness" or even for it to be celebrated by the many comments and likes that it received? While the specificities of Ka'ahumanu's prominence and rule might be lost on many people, her significance in Hawaiian history is widely known. Ka'ahumanu, like Kamehameha and Lili'uokalani, is heralded as an example of Hawaiian greatness; the three are memorialized with holidays, street names, schools, shopping centers, and hula festivals named after them. This is something that most Kānaka Maoli and people educated in the Hawaiian public and private school systems would have notably learned, as would anyone familiar with the history of the Hawaiian Kingdom. Curriculums in Hawai'i's schools openly celebrate Hawaiian ali'i as a strategy to avert a real conversation about Hawaiian politics, kingdomhood, or sovereignty in the present. The emphasis on the past functions to keep the present realities always out of focus and Hawaiian independence as an impossibility because Hawaiians are considered incapable of self-government.

Queen Ka'ahumanu herself was a high-ranking ali'i nui (highest royal rank), often described as the "favorite wife" of King Kamehameha I, the Hawaiian ali'i who organized the Hawaiian Kingdom under his rule. Beyond being a "favorite wife" of King Kamehameha, Ka'ahumanu was a kuhina nui (regent) and ruled alongside Kamehameha, not as his kept woman. Ka'ahumanu, who lived from 1768 to 1832, was the queen consort of Hawai'i (1795–1819), and kuhina nui of the Hawaiian Islands (1819–1832) and served as prime minister during the reigns of Kamehameha II (Liholiho) and III (Kauikeaouli). She participated in the 'aikapu, the transformation of spiritual order through eating practices, ending the kapu system, an intricate system of rules pertaining to lifestyle, gender roles, politics, and religion. She usurped her own hānai (adopted) son Liholiho's power over the islands by marrying the king of Kaua'i, Kaumuali'i (his loyalty to Kamehameha was in jeopardy), as well as later marrying his son Keali'iahonui to affirm her power—keeping Kaua'i under the kingdom—but she did so for her own power, not her son's.[42] She is recognized among Hawaiian historians as one of the most powerful figures in Hawaiian history, having encouraged conversion to Christianity, ended the kapu system, and brought in marriage laws. These details may not be particularly prominent or even important to a nonspecialist audience, but Ka'ahumanu's legacy is crucial in Hawaiian culture.

The online user naming of this royal lineage and history is a source of pride for Kānaka Maoli and local people who feel connected, in whatever form, to the Hawaiian monarchy. During the mid- to late nineteenth century, the Hawaiian Kingdom rapidly modernized and was internationally recognized by Great Britain, France, Japan, and Germany, to name a few. And as in those countries, Hawaiian royalty and other people of high status often had their pictures taken or posed for paintings. Kānaka Maoli today know what these personages looked like and look to these images as evidence of how civilized Hawaiians were and that we were and are fit for self-government in the present (even if settlers do not see it this way).

One of the things that marks images of Kanaka Maoli royalty is the presence of kāhili feathers. When one looks closely at the image of Cocoa Chandelier, the black Victorian-style dress (or what is termed a holokū in Hawaiian) is reminiscent of the dresses worn by women of the Ka'ahumanu Society—a mostly Christian Congregationalist Hawaiian organization known throughout the islands. The kāhili feathers she holds were used as markers of royalty. Cocoa Chandelier uses these items, which are revered markers of Kanaka Maoli royalty, to place herself in the genealogy of Hawaiian indigeneity. It is telling that, as perhaps Hawai'i's most well-known drag queen, she chooses to display herself as part of Hawaiian history in this way. Here, the drag queen is staging an actual queen, our queen, in an effort to reclaim the past and to put it in direct relationship with the present. Cocoa Chandelier engages in the melancholia that is common within contemporary Hawaiian culture as we attempt to reconstruct our identities, honor our dead, and fight ongoing colonial violences.[43]

The image invokes the spirit and legacy of the ali'i. As a māhū, Chandelier connects herself to this genealogy that people in Hawai'i would be hard pressed to deny. Now, one might argue that it is disrespectful to impersonate an ali'i. But I want to make clear that Chandelier herself did not name the connection to specific ali'i; it is only implied in the performance. It is the viewers, the commenters, who make this connection. This relays that the viewers, the community, seek this kind of recognition and that it is emblematic of such needs in a Hawaiian cultural environment that problematically accepts "traditional" Western gender expressions that are buttressed by heteropatriarchy and its Christian undertones. The image ultimately opens up a space for a reimagining of how the realities of colonization can be seen as temporary, articulating that the moment captured in this image does not exist only through performative reenactment. Indeed, many Kānaka Maoli have begun to argue very seriously for a reconsideration of the legal status of Hawai'i's annexation because we now know that our kingdom was never ceded and that it is still intact, albeit occupied. This image simultaneously gestures at the realities of the Hawaiian Kingdom still existing in the minds of many Kānaka Maoli in a melancholic mode of nostalgia, loss, and defiance. As Muñoz explains, mourning and melancholia can be used to map the ambivalences of identification and the conditions of (im)possibility that shape minority identity, which can function as "a necessary militancy and indispensable mourning."[44] Chandelier thus travels through time, allowing us to see that we are all connected to this genealogy. This is defiant indigeneity personified. It also puts out a call of aloha. She honors the history of Kanaka Maoli royalty by staging a scene wherein she, as a Kanaka Maoli drag queen, can honor them 120 years after the kingdom was overthrown.

While this image is an overt display of Cocoa Chandelier's indigeneity, it is curious and strategic that many of her other performances disguise or refuse to conjure indigeneity. A reading of the various demands of Hawaiianness can be observed in one of her performances at the Diva of Polynesia pageant. In 2006 Cocoa Chandelier resisted expectations of the pageant, wherein contestants are expected to represent their respective Polynesia heritages, by refusing to perform her Hawaiianness for the crowd. She performed instead a commentary on the various demands of "ethnic" performance. A video posted on YouTube on May 15, 2014, shows her performing at the pageant; this video was reposted through Cocoa Chandelier's Facebook page on "#TBT" (throwback Thursday).[45] The scene is of the talent competition during the pageant. Cocoa Chandelier enters the stage and announces herself as "contestant number one." A prerecorded voice-over (conceivably a judge) asks, "You ready?" and she says, "Yes, I am. I just have to warm up." Then the theme from *Flashdance* comes on and she takes off her trench coat to reveal herself wearing a black leotard as she begins to stretch. The crowd laughs, recognizing the iconic song "What a Feeling" from the movie, conjuring an image of Jennifer Beals in a leotard (very pre-*LWord*). The shared reference becomes obvious through the sound of laughter. The voice returns, saying, "This is a Polynesian dance audition. Can you do something more Hawaiian?" Then a calypso song begins to play, and she returns to the stage wearing a long skirt and with a lei around her neck, dancing calypso. The voice returns, this time saying with an irritated tone, "Polynesian dancing. Can you do that?" Cocoa Chandelier responds, "Oh, you mean like Samoan?" in a Valley girl–inflected voice. Then she sits and starts doing a Samoan slap dance. Someone screams, "Work, Cocoa!" The song playing is reminiscent of 1950s James Bond girl music as she continues the Samoan siva dance. The voice-over finally returns, saying, "This is Diva of Polynesia. If you got anything Polynesian this is your time." The music changes to a Brazilian samba tune, and she comes out with an African headpiece and starts doing a stereotypically Brazilian dance. The crowd is in stitches. The beat begins to pick up speed, and she starts doing cartwheels. The voice-over returns to end the scene, saying, "Next."

The annual pageant is a fund-raiser for Kulia Na Mamo, a Honolulu-based nonprofit focused on supporting māhūwahine (women-identified māhūs) and other transgendered individuals. At Diva of Polynesia, contestants usually perform a Polynesian dance. This is an example of how Cocoa Chandelier differentiates herself from other performers by refusing to follow the norms of the pageant. As a commentary on the expectations of ethnic performance, at each opportunity to perform something "Hawaiian" she refused, until she finally did a Samoan dance when urged. She utilizes humor in such a way that everyone can identify that she is supposed to be "Hawaiian," but instead she performs the dance traditions of other groups. These are groups that have been similarly hypercommodified in the global imagination, so much so that the audience can identify this and find it humorous. If you are not attuned to it, you will not get it.

Evasive performances like this one participate in the abstracting practices that Sarita See references.[46] They show how indigeneity can be represented in the abstract by performers like Cocoa Chandelier as a way to comment on the imperative to perform one's ethnicity or, in this case, indigeneity. This scene of abstraction ultimately questions how Kānaka Maoli are supposed to perform and disrupts the very meaning of "Hawaiianness," centering an awareness of how ethnic subjection is manifested in the ongoing conflation and exoticization of "the other" and their cultures. This is just one example of the demands of indigeneity and Chandelier's refusal to perform it, which she does through referencing other ethnic groups that are held to the same performative expectations. The performance produces commentary of these similarities and provides opportunities to queer the study of Hawaiian performance. The next section takes this a step further by explaining my concept "aloha in drag" as yet another strategy that can be used to disrupt the norms of Hawaiian performance.

Aloha in Drag

Aloha in drag takes many forms. It is simultaneously an experience and a performance. It is the performance of Hawaiian indigeneity by means other than through direct references to supposed Hawaiianness. Aloha in drag is also an over-the-top performance of Hawaiian signs done in such a way that other Kānaka Maoli can connect and identify the aloha in the performance (such as in a tourist environment). Aloha in drag can be understood as a process through which Kānaka Maoli perform hidden messages or transcripts to strategically conceal facets of Hawaiian indigeneity while highlighting others. This could also be a performance of aloha that is not recognizable to most audiences, but can be recognized by other Kānaka Maoli and locals. Cocoa Chandelier does not perform in ways that physically and culturally mark a performer as Kanaka Maoli to an outsider. By performing aloha in drag she performs aloha in such a way that aloha cannot be identified—you cannot see the resistance, nor can you *see* the aloha. In these spaces, aloha takes on its meaning as a word that brings Kānaka Maoli together, as a feeling that we know and experience because we have grown up experiencing it. It is an understanding of aloha as a practice and affect that brings people together and binds people to community. Paired with temporal processes of drag performances that are predicated on contextual understandings of a specific event or scene, this allows aloha in drag to emerge.

To support my claims, I look at how a shared understanding of what "aloha" is can be performed in drag, to expose how aloha became a critical concept tied to Hawaiianness and how it is performed in drag in particular spaces to unify and disrupt understandings of aloha and Hawaiianness. Aloha in drag lays bare the constructedness of aloha itself, in the ways that other drag performances make plain the constructedness of gender. In effect, aloha in drag produces a kind of uneasiness around Hawaiian indigeneity and aloha because it refuses to perform what Hawaiianness is supposed to represent. At the same time, it creates aloha in specific performance spaces because of the connections and communal work that go into maintaining these spaces. This can be achieved only in spaces where Hawaiian indigeneity is known (that is, experienced) among the audience. The audience members must have an understanding of Hawaiian culture as a whole and also, to an extent, of local culture in Hawaiʻi. This does not exclude Hawaiians in the diaspora either, as frequent trips back and forth can certainly contribute to this collective understanding and knowledge. While this has the ring of blanket inclusivity, let me be clear: there are those who are "one of us" and those who are not. "One of us" can be a tricky status. It is one that is earned by understanding what it is to live like and among us. It means living, experiencing, and doing. To be in on the joke, you have to belong with us; you have to do aloha with us. And to belong with us you have to live and perform differently.

Drag performances can certainly be transgressive, and they work predominantly because they expose the precarity of social norms; but they have to be recognizable by the community in order to be effective. Like Indigenous realness, aloha in drag is an extremely contextual practice and experience. It requires a basic shared cultural understanding—it is profoundly tied to lived experiences that are gathered because of the world one lives in. Aloha in drag emerges in Hawaiian spaces that center a communal understanding of aloha, pointing to the pressures that Kānaka Maoli face to perform aloha and acceptable forms of Hawaiianness. In the section that follows, I analyze how the purposeful ambivalences and complexities of Cocoa Chandelier's performance at the Universal ShowQueen (USQ) Pageant offer a space to imagine and engage the agonizing realities of Kanaka Maoli indigeneity. As a disidentifying subject, Cocoa Chandelier holds onto the loss of Hawaiian life, but also reinvests in it.[47]

At the 2008 USQ Pageant, held annually in Honolulu since in 1984 "for the enlightenment of the transsexual experience as a contestant, fashion model, and spokesperson," Cocoa Chandelier transformed the neocolonial juggernaut known as the Hawaiʻi Convention Center into a Bollywood "Harem of the Underworld." Situated at the mouth of Waikīkī and adjacent to Ala Moana Center, the Hawaiʻi Convention Center, which opened in 1998, is known for its purported "Hawaiian sense of place." The convention center was built as part of a large-scale revitalization and rejuvenation of Waikīkī, designed and inspired by Hawaiian concepts. The space is adorned with Hawaiian plants and features rooms with names like Kamehameha I. The convention center promotes nā mea hoʻokipa (translated as Hawaiian hospitality)[48] and also houses the Hawaiʻi Visitors and Convention Bureau. The design and decoration of the convention center are perfect examples of the ways in which Kanaka Maoli indigeneity is actively incorporated into public space throughout Hawaiʻi in the service of the tourist industry.[49] But, draped in Hindu accoutrements, Cocoa Chandelier transformed the space and herself as she played the role of a bride-to-be who was kidnapped and forced to live in the Harem of the Underworld. Dancing to the tune of a world music montage and a remixed Jay-Z Bhangra hit, she performed a mishmash of scenes from a Bengali epic. The performance ended with her hanging upside down by her feet from the convention center ceiling, giving herself up to the specter of Orientalism. Cocoa Chandelier's performance of aloha in drag in this fabricated space of "aloha" is thus all the more provocative. Refusing to be a Hawaiian subject in this convention center that intends to produce a "Hawaiian sense of place," she figuratively sacrifices herself. In her performance, she refuses to give up her brown body by not answering the call. This returns us to my earlier question: Can we turn away from the call? What happens when the call is not answered? When called, Cocoa Chandelier does not answer.

"Hung Up" at the Feet of Orientalism

In this performance, Cocoa Chandelier plays the role of the muse, a bride-to-be who is forced to live in the so-called Harem of the Underworld. Throughout the six-minute spectacle, Orientalist signifiers run amok, performed in drag by an abstracted Kanaka Maoli body. The performance begins with a prerecorded video and narration in which Cocoa Chandelier is adorned with bindis and surrounded by other Hindu accoutrements and motifs. Along with the audio narration, Cocoa Chandelier is shown in front of a backdrop of turquoise and orange silks. She herself is dressed in turquoise silk, with gold pearls wrapped around her wrists. She wears a scarf on her head, giant gold earrings, and a necklace in a similar style (see Figure 4). She introduces herself:

> The legend was foretold that a muse was taken on the day of her wedding to the bowels of the underworld, deep beneath the desert sands, where she would remain with her haunting voice that which [sic] would lure a man's soul to his death to be devoured by this creature of the underground, placing these men under a trance with her intoxicating dance and her beckoning harem of lost brides-to-be. But this would not remain true, for the gods had forsaken such acts placed upon unwilling mortals. And so the sun-god, Syria, sent forth a ray of light to penetrate the darkness that from which [sic] she had climbed out into the light, but at the last moment, she heard the call of the cihade and fell from the light, back under her unbefitting spell of bewitching darkness.

FIGURE 4 Cocoa Chandelier as "the muse" from the talent portion of the Universal ShowQueen Pageant DVD, 2008.

This visual imagery is lit through high-contrast black-lighting. Her head is facing downward as the camera pans the perimeter of her body, stopping at her eyes. While her voice-over explains an attempt to "penetrate the darkness," Cocoa Chandelier is shown holding and pulling on a rope, trying unsuccessfully to escape from the underworld. She is pulled back.

This prerecorded video sets the stage for the live performance that takes the audience into the underworld, where the brides-to-be perform their songs. The song that begins the piece, "Harem," was originally recorded by the British world music star Sarah Brightman. At first, Cocoa Chandelier dances alone, but soon she is joined by a young man to whom she sings the lyrics "I hold your Eastern promise close to my heart, welcoming you to my harem," immediately after which she kills him. At this point the music switches, and a group of women and men begin to dance a scene from the 2002 Bollywood film *Devdas*, which is based on a 1917 Hindi novella by Sharat Chandra Chattopadhyay.[50] (The novella is a classic and has been adapted to film dozens of times.) Next, three other men approach and lift Cocoa Chandelier above their heads, carrying her away in a cross formation. The song changes to Kavita Krishnamurthy's "Dola Re Dola," with the choreography matching much of the dancing in *Devdas*.[51] Soon, Cocoa Chandelier begins disrobing. The dancers lift her up and spin her around as the song changes to Jay-Z's 2003 release "Beware of the Boys," which features a popular Bhangra music sample, "Munddian to Bach Ke," by Punjabi MC.[52] The dancers exit the stage, and Cocoa Chandelier begins dancing with another man in a mash-up of hip-hop and Bhangra. After this brief dance, the group of dancers returns and the song switches back to "Dola Re Dola" as Cocoa Chandelier scales a long piece of red fabric that is hanging from the ceiling. Presumably this is the "ray of light" that was sent to save the bride-to-be. As she begins to scale the fabric, the crowd is screaming in disbelief. When she gets to the top, she spins upside down, and slides down slowly. The dancers all continue dancing below her. The music is blasting in Hindi, and as it crescendos, Cocoa Chandelier wraps her feet around the red fabric and again begins to ascend, only to suddenly flip upside down in an apparent unsuccessful bid to climb out of the dark "harem." Hanging by her feet, she sacrifices herself at what might now be understood as an altar of Orientalism. Hanging thus from the Hawai'i Convention Center ceiling, she receives a rousing standing ovation. In an interview, she has described this story as one in which the woman who attempts to flee her fate, even with the help of a godlike figure, is doomed to remain a prisoner forever. This performance encapsulates modern Kanaka Maoli indigeneity and subjection. While Cocoa Chandelier renders her own Kanaka Maoli heritage completely invisible by not performing anything that can be identified as "Hawaiian," she offers the possibilities of a radical alterity, one that is achieved by appropriating the subjection of a feminized Oriental. My read attempts to straddle these problematics.

The bride-to-be portrayed by Cocoa Chandelier is evocative of the Sirens from Greek mythology. Because of her ability to lure men to their death with her song, she must stay in the harem, for she is dangerous. Cocoa Chandelier crafts a performance that references the fears of women's sexuality and the emotive power of the Sirens' songs. When the bride-to-be is given a chance to escape, she cannot; she is continually pulled back into the Harem of the Underworld, to perform her song among the other lost brides-to-be, where no one can see them (even though everyone knows they're there). The bride is being punished for her intoxicating dance and song. She is being punished for what makes her different, her culture. A godlike figure in the story, which I interpret as the liberal multicultural subject, unsuccessfully tries to save her. In spite of her song or culture, the godlike figure offers her a chance at freedom, but as she attempts to climb out she is hailed and interpellated back to the underworld, unable to escape. Her performance is ultimately insufficient, and she is therefore not able to climb out. In the underworld she is fated to live out her subjection forever as a racialized subject. Her race pulls her back down; she cannot overcome it through the performance of her culture.

This story relays a message that efforts to overcome subjection through recognizable forms of cultural performance are ultimately futile because the very discourse through which such performances must occur is fundamentally colonial. Put another way, cultural performance might change the perspective of the onlooker, but not the act of gazing. This exemplifies that the very need to recognize cultural difference is proof that "the other"—or the bride in this story—is inherently unassimilable and cannot be saved. Denise da Silva contends that (1) it is "culture" and not "race" that now (doubly) disempowers us, and (2) this results in a double binding through discourses of culture rather than through discourses of race[53]—reminiscent of debates in postcolonial theory around "Can the Subaltern Speak?" or the deeper question, Can the screams of the subaltern subject even be heard in an ontohistorical formation that has already mapped out its existence as one that is marked for death?

Further, what does it really mean to be "hung up" at the feet of Orientalism? Such forms of being hung conjure a visualization of a brown body hung upside down by the feet, signaling the global subjection of abject brown bodies. This is an example of what da Silva has described: the "other" is always racially encoded, always a prisoner of her or his own cultural difference, and never self-determining.[54] This is why the bride cannot climb out of the harem. Under liberal multiculturalism, racial overdetermination can be combated only through the recognition of cultural difference, but in this story the call of the state cannot save you.

Answering the call means performing a recognizable mode of cultural difference. The performance of "cultural difference" as a necessity, as a survival strategy, cannot so easily be dismissed when talking about Native or Indigenous peoples whose claims to sovereignty are based on their difference as Indigenous peoples; such claims differ considerably from the claims that U.S. racial minorities might advance. Native peoples cannot stop performing their culture—they need to perform it in order to be recognized, in order to remain Native to begin with. But these performances have risks, as I have explained, such as making certain aspects appear natural (like aloha) or perpetuating violent forms of colonialism handed down by the state and the Native governments it "authorizes." Instead, Glen Coulthard advocates working toward mutual self-recognition in Native communities that does not rely on statist forms.[55] I am somewhat torn when I advance an argument that advocates for disguising Kanaka Maoli identity because the need for Kanaka Maoli–only resources has a material reality.[56]

We know that Indigenous peoples need visibility and must perform in recognizable ways to be deemed worthy of resources from the very state that dispossessed them of their way of life to begin with. As Elizabeth Povinelli explains, aboriginal groups are forced to perform in certain ways to show themselves as worthy in the eyes of the state. The continual performance of particular types of aboriginal cultural practice, then, is sanctioned by the state through a multicultural imaginary that defuses struggles for liberation and ensures the functioning of the modern liberal state.[57] In sum, Native aspirations for decolonization and self-determination are predicated on their cultural difference, and must be "recognized" by people in power in order for such claims (for example, land claims or entitlement programs) to be acknowledged. The spectator dominates and controls the exchange because, more often than not, underrepresented groups are scripted to "sell" or "confess" to someone (a theatrical "audience" or government official) who is in a position to buy or forgive the performer.[58] Ergo, state forms of recognition are undoubtedly important, but they should be understood as temporary rather than being the end goal of decolonization. Furthermore, the idea that cultural performance can educate audiences about cultural others is not a means to an end. As argued in the introduction, being forced to perform a particular type of cultural difference—sanctioned by the very government that is requiring you display that difference—to legitimate your claim to sovereignty is an inherently colonial practice.

Aware of the problematics of performance and recognition, at the performance's end, Cocoa Chandelier or the bride sacrifices herself at the feet of Orientalism. This act of self-sacrifice is instructive for rethinking Kanaka Maoli indigeneity. Remember, Cocoa Chandelier's performance of the bride's death is a commentary on the bride's inability to overcome her racial subjection because the performance of her culture was insufficient. So, rather than continue trying to climb out of the harem or being imprisoned there, she sacrifices herself. The interpellation fails. Within the context of Hawaiian cultural performativity, Cocoa Chandelier's performance exposes how Hawaiian performance and bodies are deeply inscribed as racialized (and culturalized) objects within a representational system and yet provides resistance to that very system.

This racialization (and culturalization) occurs in tandem with the perception that Kānaka Maoli are performing our interior selves all the time, and this is where the idea of the "aloha spirit" comes from. In short, Cocoa

Chandelier refuses the aloha-filled expression of aloha as a marker of Hawaiian culture. Historically, the aloha spirit has been fabricated as a Hawaiian essence that is shared and transferrable to non-Hawaiians. But aloha's market value only counts when people believe that Kānaka Maoli naturally emanate aloha. If aloha is identified as a performance, its worth depreciates. Cocoa Chandelier, like Krystilez, shows us how aloha and "Hawaiianness" itself are performances because neither of them performs aloha in recognizable ways. Cocoa Chandelier especially performs on multiple levels of drag and invokes the trope of the harem to confuse the Western gaze that sees Kānaka Maoli only when they perform aloha. Cocoa Chandelier hides in plain sight. On the verge of this perhaps liberatory performance, Cocoa Chandelier's performance simultaneously exhibits Kanaka Maoli complicity in the racial overdetermination of another subjected group through her appropriation of another "other."

Native Appropriations

In June 2008, at the time of this performance, the United States was engaged in its so-called War on Terror with the ongoing military occupation of Iraq and Afghanistan as well as a military buildup in the Pacific (Guam and Hawai'i especially) unseen since World War II. Additionally, the American media had renewed fears of terrorism because of the 2008 Mumbai bombing attacks in India.[59] Cocoa Chandelier's performance of South Asian Orientalism is evidence of the manner in which the War on Terror revived American interest in Middle Eastern, Arab, Muslim, and South Asian cultures that is both an embrace and a distancing from the brute realities of U.S. war making. Celebrating "others" and their culture has always been a tactic of colonialism and nationalism, whereby the inclusion of certain "others" requires the exclusion of undesirable "others," such as "terrorists" or "bad Indians," for example.[60] Therefore, there is space to critique Cocoa Chandelier for indulging a vague Orientalist notion of a generalized Eastern world. Her usage of the Jay-Z song is a classic example of Arab and South Asian rhythms being incorporated, whether through dialogues or sheer appropriation.[61] This repackaging of culture—via the remix—enters the public sphere and marketplace as a commodity to be enjoyed through a multicultural imaginary that celebrates difference without critiquing the political economy upon which it relies. Throughout the performance, Arab and South Asian cultures are abstracted, which is common in the post-9/11 era, when Arabs, South Asians, and Muslims, as well as anyone else perceived to be from a nation with a large Muslim population, are wrongly clumped together.[62] For example, "harems" of the abstracted Arab world are also conflated with Indigenous culture when remixed into the *Devdas* Bollywood spectacle that is based on a Bengali novel. Cocoa Chandelier's appropriation of *Devdas* choreography and the story she tells about the harem exhibits this conflation. Historically, harems were imagined as an alluring and tantalizingly forbidden world because the Western male gaze could not penetrate them.[63] By embodying this performative realm—the so-called harem—Cocoa Chandelier may well be replicating Orientalism, but she may also be understood to be availing herself strategically of a space that cannot be penetrated by the Western gaze, a space that can be liberating for Natives, especially for Kānaka Maoli, who continue to be hypervisible subjects. This kind of "liberation" for one group, however, comes at the expense of another. It makes the appropriation of culture appear both individual and universal, which is at the core of American notions of liberal democratic freedom, where multiculturalism means appropriating and commodifying ethnic difference to hide ongoing subjection.[64]

Subjection is something Kānaka Maoli know all too well, as it has been through the embrace and celebration of Hawaiian culture and performance that the material realities of Kanaka Maoli dispossession have been concealed. But Kānaka Maoli internalize these processes in complicated ways. By appropriating Orientalist signifiers, Cocoa Chandelier temporarily destabilizes the grounds upon which Hawaiianness is built because she refuses to perform in prescribed ways. Her "truth" is revealed and hidden at the same time. This is what made this performance so spectacular. Cocoa Chandelier's performances do not present a desire to be represented or "recognized" in an easy way; the actual references she uses are difficult to track. However, the Orientalist tropes are also easily conjured. And yet, by not performing anything that can be named "Hawaiian," Cocoa Chandelier refuses to be a confessing subject fated to live out her subjection forever as a Kanaka Maoli. In this performance of Orientalist drag, she obstructs the disciplinary gaze that seeks to further normalize, contain, and commodify Hawaiian culture. Throughout her performance repertoire and discursive strategies, she is rarely seen or heard explicitly talking about herself. Her work, therefore, confounds disciplining technologies that seek to understand "Hawaiian" identity expression and performance. Cocoa Chandelier's performances help us think about how we understand and constitute Hawaiianness. Her performance, ultimately, pushes Hawaiian performance to interrogate the ever-mutating and disciplining technologies of colonialism. Linking back to how Cocoa Chandelier queers Hawaiian performance, her performance of aloha in drag circumvents the wide optics of neoliberalism.

I am aware that I might perhaps be letting Cocoa Chandelier off the hook for her appropriative moves, but I would contend that her numerous performances exemplify what Sarita See has called "abstraction as a practice."[65] I view Cocoa Chandelier's usage of the abstract as a tactic, one that See explains is an aesthetic practice, alongside other strategies of indirection, trickery, and mimicry.[66] Cocoa Chandelier is not associated with a specific kind of Orientalism; her performances vary widely, and as she told me in an interview, she is trained in numerous types of dance and draws inspiration from many different cultures.[67] This approach to performance is not necessarily novel, but what is apparent is the ways that in actual public performances, as I have mentioned, she chooses not to perform in "Hawaiian" forms. In her disguising of the Kanaka Maoli subject, she resists the ghosts of stereotypical Hawaiian iconography. Cocoa Chandelier's impersonation and performance of Orientalist tropes thus operate as a strategy to resist a commodifying gaze that, in seeking out the "Hawaiian," always seeks a new cultural product.

Another example of this abstracted performance is found in the "showgirl" portion of the competition. Many of the contestants dress in elaborate headpieces, and are covered in brightly colored feathers and sometimes even mechanical moving parts of the headpieces or capes themselves. Frequently, the costuming involves large capes underneath which the contestants wear very little clothing, showcasing their bodies, particularly their breasts and hips. Cocoa Chandelier enters the stage, along with her entourage, on stilts and dressed as a court jester. She wears a skin-tight black-and-white-checkered bodysuit and holds a long scepter. Reminiscent of the jester tricksters of carnivale and Mardi Gras, Cocoa Chandelier invokes these notorious scenes of performance play to further set herself apart from the other contestants. In this, she performs what Simpson describes as a mode of triple, even quadruple, consciousness that engages in constant play, at times mocking those who seek to make sense of it. Looking further at Cocoa Chandelier's performance from Simpson's perspective, the play the latter engages in, as Simpson explains, reveals itself only through refusal.[68] Cocoa Chandelier refuses the hypercommodification of Hawaiian identity and produces a momentary performance event for a specific audience that, as Peggy Phelan has noted, finds its greatest strength by "eluding the economy of reproduction" because it "clogs the smooth machinery" of capitalism, as the performance is not easily re-created or marketable to a mass audience.[69]

Performances of this nature tap into public fantasies, leaving a trace that produces and alters cultural repertoires, making visible not just the live event but also "the powerful army of the always already living," as Diana Taylor explains.[70] These performances thus speak to the presence of a community that can be uplifted by Cocoa Chandelier's performance and the possibilities of a collective sense of defiant indigeneity. In this case, as Taylor suggests, the army or community of Kānaka Maoli already living— whether or not they are recognizable—is always already there. This can be seen in the Kanaka Maoli presence in the convention center space, throughout Hawai'i, and represented through Cocoa Chandelier's very body. In the contained performance event a sense of pride and strength emerges for this particular community, be it of māhū, Kānaka Maoli, as well as all the muffies and the butchies, or the wider LGBTQ community in Hawai'i. Cocoa Chandelier performs Orientalist discourse as the audience acknowledges her brilliance as a performer, with her "true" identity abstracted because the audience is already familiar with her. Aloha in drag makes this possible.

To perform aloha in drag is to narrate a version of contemporary Kanaka Maoli life that contends with images of Hawaiian culture that have been bastardized through the "spirit of aloha." In the prerecorded video (explained earlier) Cocoa Chandelier as the muse or the bride-to-be who possessed difference through her song (that is, culture) knows that she will be a prisoner forever. Kānaka Maoli occupy this space amid the realization of the constructed ideal they are measured against. Aware of this bastardization, activist iterations of Kanaka Maoli sovereignty have been particularly invested in narrating a version of Kanaka Maoli indigeneity that is situated in a dynamic and confrontational imagining of Kanaka Maoli identity. As explained in chapter 2, Kanaka Maoli performers often embody the antithetical perception of "aloha" by refusing aloha as a way to produce counterhegemonic imagery against the trope of a happy Kanaka Maoli filled with aloha. Yet, as many Kānaka Maoli will tell you, aloha is still something we deeply believe in, even as we pretend to disavow it or publicly critique its commodified nature. We struggle with finding ways to balance this contradiction. Aloha in drag allows that contradiction to be held in productive tension when performed or expressed in the appropriate spaces. Cocoa Chandelier's performance at the USQ competition is one such space, where it appears that Kanaka Maoli indigeneity is not limited or overdetermined by the specter of aloha and all that it carries. Even in the Hawai'i Convention Center space, marred as it is in Hawaiian appropriation at every turn—with rooms named after Hawaiian royalty and Hawaiian imagery adorning its insides—Cocoa Chandelier manages to hide her "Hawaiianness" while also asserting her Kanaka Maoli indigeneity. In this space, the call of aloha is ignored when she does not perform Hawaiianness; it is instead disguised and answered only because the audience recognizes her, knows her, knows her work, has aloha for her—shares in her performance and in its success.

Phelan explains that performance must be experienced live—honoring the idea that a limited number of people in a certain place and time can experience something that leaves no visible trace after the performance.[71] Disrupting the representation necessary for capitalism, Phelan explains that once the performance is documented and put into a reproduced form, in this case a DVD, it is no longer a "performance"—it is an archival video document consisting of a multitude of images of a performance that took place.[72] Now, my reveal: I was not at the USQ Pageant that I have just spent half of this chapter examining. I bought the DVD online. I did not experience its liveness the way the audience there did. Indeed, I only saw the performance on DVD and had heard about it through word of mouth, during my annual return to Hawai'i over the summer of 2008. I had been back about a week before a friend showed me the DVD, which she had purchased a week earlier.

I watched Cocoa Chandelier's performance at the USQ Pageant on DVD, blown away, transfixed. The fact that I "had to see this," as my friend put it, spoke to the way that word of mouth operates in a small LGBTQ community. The spectacular nature of Cocoa Chandelier's performance was spreading through what people in Hawai'i call the "coconut wireless," that is, the rumor mill. I was told that I had to see it to believe it. It was true. As the audience members left the Hawai'i Convention Center after the performance, word surely spread. *OMG Cocoa did this Bollywood thing. OMG girl she did that aerial ribbon-dancing thing. OMG she hung herself upside down*, and so on. These were actual things people had been saying. The performance produced this immense feeling of pride; everyone was talking about it. The community felt uplifted in it; they felt connected and affirmed in the fact that this small community was part of this spectacular performer who represented the best of the community, something *we* could be proud of. The performance in general overshadowed the figurative death that is staged at the end. In watching the DVD, I was witness to a reenactment of a woman's sacrifice. Her powerful act, in the face of her unbearable existence, could be dealt with only through death, by hanging herself. The song ends. The crowd is heard screaming on the DVD. Cocoa Chandelier chooses to ignore the call of aloha, but through her performance she sends out her own call of aloha.

In this call of aloha, the audience witnesses Cocoa Chandelier's performance of self-sacrifice, forcing it to experience her—the bride's—figurative death. The death is not just that of Cocoa Chandelier. It is of the subjected Kanaka Maoli body and, to that end, it is a staging of the death of aloha. Phelan describes this kind of performance as "hardship art" or "ordeal art," a process by which the audience views pain through one performer as a way to engage their own pain. The performance calls witnesses or the audience to the individual's death. The audience is pushed to see the significance of an individual's death and is asked to "do the impossible," to share the death by rehearsing for it. Like the ritual that takes place in the Catholic mass, it is a ritualized performative promise to remember and to rehearse for "the other's" death (that is, the way the mass reenacts the death and resurrection of Christ through "transsubstantiation"—the turning of bread and wine into body and blood that is further ritualized in communion). The performance evokes a promise to learn and remember what is lost, to recall not only the meaning but also the value of what cannot be reproduced or seen (again).[73]

While Phelan and other scholars have focused on the ephemerality of live performance, I believe, like Muñoz, that the "burden of liveness" functions to deny minoritarian subjects of history and futurity, existing only in the moment.[74] As the stories of the performance traveled, it had an afterlife that contributes to our Kanaka Maoli future. Remember, aloha is "the call" of Kānaka Maoli because aloha became the essence of Hawaiianness through a ritualized performance of aloha that is attached to colonial commodification. In the performance, the audience witnesses the bride attempting to climb out of the underworld (because aloha is calling her), but the bride transforms into Cocoa Chandelier, as a member of the community. And the community, I would argue, because it is small and because of Cocoa Chandelier's prominence, knows that she is Kanaka Maoli. Attempting to break out of the underworld, she chooses death. The audience witnesses Cocoa Chandelier's sacrifice, the performance of her death. In this death scene, the screen flashes and the music comes to an abrupt halt. Cocoa Chandelier's body hangs by her feet, her arms spread in a cross formation, an upside-down crucifixion without the cross, without Jesus (without aloha).

As the death occurs, we are forced to ponder what is lost in this enactment of death. As a viewer you see the bride sacrifice herself because she knows that she will never break out of the Harem of the Underworld. She chooses to opt out of subjectification. After unsuccessful attempts to climb out, she chooses death because she knows that outside of the harem she is dead anyway. Put another way, the specter of Kanaka Maoli indigeneity is sacrificed; the call of aloha is turned away from and thus rendered irrelevant, moot, dead. As this death of aloha occurs, a new formation of aloha becomes possible.

Hawai'i's Queen

One of the contestant slots on *RuPaul's Drag Race* is reserved for a "fan favorite" who gets voted onto the show by online votes. During Cocoa Chandelier's campaign to get on the show in the spring and summer of 2014, she and her supporters posted on their Facebook, Twitter, Instagram, and other spaces their calls to support "Hawai'i's Queen." It was a heart-warming showing of the kind of love, the kind of aloha, that people have for Cocoa Chandelier within Honolulu's LGBTQ community. Cocoa Chandelier posted daily, asking people to vote for her. Many of her fans (including myself) and other queens retweeted her statuses. By the end of the first week, she was in the number one spot, which she held for close to two months. It was unclear how long this voting challenge was going to go on, but people voted every day. It was clear that she had the support, the aloha, of the community behind her. In post after post, people expressed the need for a Hawai'i queen to get on the show, to represent *us*.

The rallying around Cocoa Chandelier suggested that a huge community of supporters, local and nonlocal, stood behind her and believed she should be the one to represent Hawai'i on the show. There are many talented and popular performers within the community, but her ongoing work and innovation set her apart from everyone else. It is her ability to take chances—to defy the conventions of her indigeneity, her gender, her body, her performances, to strive always for more—that makes her remarkable. She is seen as a representative of the best that we all could be. In many ways, that's what the ali'i were supposed to be. So when she serves Ka'ahumanu realness, it is not to say that she actually becomes an ali'i or even questions how we come to understand the role of ali'i in a Hawaiian cultural worldview. Rather, what this image does is assert her leadership role, showing how she operates as a symbol, as a "queen" who reigns because the community recognizes her value.

After it had become clear that Cocoa Chandelier had not been selected to compete on the seventh season of *RuPaul's Drag Race*, she asserted that she was very humbled by and grateful for the outpouring of support from everyone. She also reaffirmed that she was now going to focus on performing and gaining new knowledge. Like Krystilez's, Cocoa Chandelier's aspirations for stardom were an organizing force for the communities she (and he) represented. Rather than focusing all their energy on attaining mainstream fame, these performers expanded their influence and importance through their community roles. They serve as inspiration for other Kanaka Maoli and non–Kanaka Maoli performers who are able to see that Kānaka Maoli can perform all types of ways. They show us that performers always grow and change, even if at times it seems as though the community or your indigeneity holds you down or back, or literally pulls you down, but that when you know, share, and understand the significance of aloha and being Kanaka Maoli, the community stands with you and holds you up.

CHAPTER FOUR

The Afterlife of Princess Kaʻiulani

You've looked into those eyes, what did you see reflected? Beauty?
Youth? Joy? Sorrow? Hidden promise? Is she a mirror for your
mind? A looking glass of all your romantic feelings and fantasies
about these islands in a time gone by? Well, she was real, and she
was more than that to me. My grandmother remembers her
funeral. She remembers the long, slow process. She remembers the
hundreds of faces. She remembers the horses' hooves that pulled
her casket all wrapped up so that they made no sound. She
remembers the silence, the silence of the dying hope. I see my
people in her death. Cut off by things that came across the sea.
In 42 years, half of our race was gone. Someone wrote in 1822 in a
journal, "there is hardly a day goes by we do not hear the wails of
death from the village of Honolulu." Death from introduced
disease, death from ships, death from sailors, death from white
men. Now we are a minority in our own homeland. There is talk
today of reparations to the Hawaiian people. Reparations for our
stolen land, our stolen kingdom. But you can't ever really repay us.
Imagine all those people dying, hear the wails of death every day
for thousands of my people. Stamp it in your mind like it's
stamped in mine. And every time you see her picture, remember it.
They may give us money, they may give us land, they may give us
"educational opportunities," but they will never be able to replace
what was killed: our people, our race, our Kaʻiulani.

—Excerpt from the play *Kaʻiulani* (1987) by DENNIS CARROLL,
      VICTORIA KNEUBUHL, ROBERT NELSON, RYAN PAGE

Princess Victoria Kawēkiu Kaʻiulani Kalaninuiahilapalapa Cleghorn died
on March 6, 1899, of an apparent case of pneumonia brought on by her previous condition of inflammatory rheumatism. Her death was a result of
horseback riding in the rain in Waimea on the Big Island of Hawaiʻi, or
perhaps she died of a broken heart, as the *San Francisco Call* reported.
Kaʻiulani perished less than two years after she had returned home to
Hawaiʻi, a year into her engagement to Prince David Laʻamea Kawananakoa,
nine months after Hawaiʻi was annexed by the United States through the

Newlands Resolution, six years after the U.S. military backed an illegal overthrow of the Hawaiian Kingdom, and eight years after she had been declared heir to the throne. More than a century later, Princess Kaʻiulani continues to be memorialized in hula, mele, film, narrative, and live productions. Audiences are fascinated with Princess Kaʻiulani for multiple reasons, as this chapter details, but for Hawaiians in particular, she allows the lāhui to live through her memory.

The monologue quoted above from the script of the play *Kaʻiulani* lays bare the juridical, political, historical, and affective stakes of Hawaiian cultural memory and performance. Articulating the various ways that Hawaiʻi and, by extension, all things Hawaiian continue to be viewed through a gendered colonial frame, this monologue comes in the third act of the play, as the narrator addresses head-on the competing narratives that memorialize and feminize Hawaiʻi as a site of white masculinist fantasy as well as the locus of Hawaiian cultural power and profound sadness. The narrator, named Maile, a young Hawaiian girl, explains that Kaʻiulani is real to her, in contrast to the fantasy of Kaʻiulani, to the fantasy of Hawaiʻi. The emphasis on the realness of Kaʻiulani is experienced through the narrator's grandmother, who remembers Kaʻiulani's funeral. Identifying herself through genealogy exhibits how Kānaka Maoli link what is maoli, what is "real," through genealogies and cultural memories. For Kānaka Maoli, the kingdom is so close that we have family who remember it. Maile notably refuses reparations for Hawaiians, affirming some *other* form of restitution and renewal that might take place today, a reinterpretation of Kaʻiulani's legacy, a Hawaiian reenvisioning of our future, not the one supposedly foretold in Kaʻiulani's death (and broken heart). In Maile's defiant turn away from the state, we ponder Kaʻiulani's life, our loss as a people, and what could have been. Recall that in ancient times Kānaka Maoli had processes and practices in place that allowed for public mourning. Sometimes referred to as a kanikau or a dirge, the mourning chant was a common form of public wailing. The sound "uwē" expressed deep lament over the loss of a loved one. But we don't have these rituals today. The texts and performances I analyze in this chapter function as modern-day forms of mourning that force Kānaka Maoli to reimagine the life of one of their most famous aliʻi and to rethink the future of the lāhui.

The representations analyzed in this chapter leave Kaʻiulani's legacy open for interpretation by audiences, particularly Kanaka Maoli audiences. So let me be clear: I am not interested in declaring a definitive truth about what or who Kaʻiulani is or what really happened in the events leading up to her death or the time following it. In what follows, I consider the afterlife of Princess Kaʻiulani—on a ghost tour, in film, and on stage—and why her narrative has become so important to Kānaka Maoli today. I discuss my experience on a ghost tour of Waikīkī that included a walk through the Sheraton Princess Kaʻiulani Hotel. I analyze the 2009 film *Princess Kaiulani*, and I examine the restaging of the play *Kaʻiulani*, which was revived at Kumu Kahua Theatre in Honolulu in March 2015. Since Kaʻiulani's death in 1899, she has continued to be memorialized in countless mele and in a number of historical biographies, including children's books.[1] Today there is an elementary school named after her in Nuʻuanu, Honolulu. She is honored with an annual keiki (children's) hula festival in October, usually around the time of her birthday. The event, hosted by the Sheraton Princess Kaʻiulani Hotel, includes a reenactment of the royal court of the Hawaiian Kingdom. The Sheraton Princess Kaʻiulani Hotel supposedly honors her legacy. It sits on the site of Kaʻiulani's former lands at ʻĀinahau and is yet another example of the insidious tactics of settler colonialism. In 1999 a statue of her was erected at the quadrangle of Kuhio Avenue (which later intersects with Kaʻiulani Ave) and Kanekapolei Street in Waikīkī. The statue was commissioned by Outrigger Enterprises (Outrigger Hotels) to demonstrate their commitment to Hawaiʻi's past. A small park sits adjacent to the statue. A play titled *Kaʻiulani the Island Rose* was written by Jennifer Fahrni and Carol Harvie-Yamaguchi and has been performed throughout the islands and in Scotland as well. There is also a short documentary about her, *A Cry of Peacocks* by Kristin Zambucka. The play *Kaʻiulani*, which is analyzed throughout this chapter, was penned by Dennis Carroll, Victoria Nalani Kneubuhl, Robert Nelson, and Ryan Page and first staged in Honolulu in 1987, followed by performances in Los Angeles and Washington, D.C., and in Scotland at the Fringe Festival. The play was revived in 2015, when I had the pleasure of viewing it.

This chapter curates an unexpected archive of materials about Kaʻiulani to ponder what happens when we allow ourselves to fully experience a performance, to arrest belief, and to ignore historical inaccuracies. My analysis bleeds through the multiple texts, engaging them as multidirectional and fluid with intentions of unsettling the way we think about Princess Kaʻiulani. I move back and forth between my reading of these performances and texts to highlight the ways that audiences interact with multiple texts simultaneously, drawing from their own memories of history and other events, mixing them with the current situation. Popular Hollywood representations of Hawaiʻi and the Pacific produce a monorhetoric, an archive of performances that identify the islands with an irreversible linear history associated solely with dominant representations. Monorhetoric maintains the islands in the European imagination, outside of Indigenous culture, history, knowledge, and practices.[2] But Indigenous viewers and their interpretations of texts offer something else. The cultural productions discussed in this chapter not only intervene in Kanaka Maoli absence and erasure but also challenge injustice and engage cultural memory through performance. Cultural memories function as sites of knowledge that get activated in performance space. These spaces include everyday life and staged performances, such as the streets of Waikīkī, online commenting spaces, and of course theater space. In this sense, space can also become a multidimensional entity as history becomes a character in the performance itself.[3] These stages are haunted by what came before, carried in the space and among the audience, shaping how a performance is received.[4]

The focus on how Princess Ka'iulani's memory is performed builds on my theorization of Cocoa Chandelier's honoring of ali'i in drag. Whereas the previous chapters looked at the marginal subcultural spaces on the fringe of Hawaiian performance, here I turn to mainstream cultural productions that celebrate Hawaiian royalty as part of Hawai'i's rich history, because these representations are also indicative of how particular forms of respectability work to conceal everyday pressures to be Kānaka Maoli. These performances uphold forms of Kanaka Maoli respectability that Kānaka Maoli and settlers can rally around and easily celebrate, but they also represent a deep desire to reconcile the legacies of the overthrow and can often produce new forms of resistance. Many performances that honor our culture are often overlooked, as I have explained in the previous chapters. There is an official state-sanctioned tourist version of Hawaiian culture, and then there are divergent Kanaka versions that overlap and interweave with one another. Consider, for example, Cocoa Chandelier's image of herself in drag adorned with a kāhili, a noted marker of royalty (see figure 3). An image like this would never grace the front page of the local newspaper or the cover of the Office of Hawaiian Affairs annual report, and yet it circulated widely on social media and prompted the reactions I explained in chapter 3. In the video for the song "Karma," Krystilez points at an image of Queen Lili'uokalani and rips up an image of Sanford P. Dole, one of the conspirators of the overthrow, referring to him as a "greedy bastard."[5] These performances enable Kānaka Maoli to express their reverence for nā ali'i (the chiefs or the royals) in settings that are not always in the desired forms associated with the commemoration of ali'i and Kanaka Maoli respectability.

These performances push us to negotiate mainstream performances and re-think what could be possible when the state narrative is reappropriated in a countercultural space to advance a political critique or to contribute a reinterpretation of the political significance and reach of the ali'i. Subcultural spaces thus interweave with mainstream spaces of performance and commemoration, sometimes unexpectedly, allowing alternative expressions of memory and mourning that facilitate communication with our kupuna and Hawaiian history in a way that neither erases a vibrant Hawaiian indigeneity nor fully prescribes anything in the realm of governmental politics, but is indelibly linked to both.

These performances of the Hawaiian Kingdom challenge settler-colonial efforts to politically domesticate the Kanaka Maoli people, allowing Hawaiian performers and audiences to question and make these cultural productions and performance spaces vibrant with reinterpretation and openness for the future of Hawaiian indigeneity. The constant return to Ka'iulani affirms that Kānaka Maoli had a kingdom, one that was internationally recognized, and it represents Kanaka Maoli connections to our past. It also points to the failure of Indigenous autonomy and femininity. The focus on Ka'iulani by Kānaka Maoli and non–Kānaka Maoli alike is indicative of investments people have in particular kinds of narratives about Indigenous women, U.S. colonialism, Hawai'i, and Hawaiian sovereignty. In spite of the so-called inevitability of the overthrow of the Hawaiian Kingdom, it is through the power of cultural memory and the performance of those memories that Kānaka Maoli continue to make sense of our histories and restage them in imaginative and unexpected ways to oppose the ongoing occupation of our country.

The Hawaiian Kingdom is memorialized ad nauseam in state-sponsored parades, Hawaiian civic club ceremonies, and different forms of Hawaiian cultural performance (such as the Merrie Monarch Festival, the Aloha Week festivities, the various hula festivals held to honor ali'i, and so on). The state and even the federal government honor the integrity and political status of the Hawaiian Kingdom with state holidays such as Kamehameha Day and Kuhio Day. For many, honoring the kingdom happens primarily in memory and performances, sometimes for spiritual purposes, sometimes for entertainment, and oftentimes both. The way we choose to memorialize and honor nā ali'i is indicative of a kind of nostalgia that can function as a form of managed celebration authorized by the settler state. As explained in chapter 1, the state sponsors performances that are depoliticized forms of "hybrid" local culture that serves tourists and a multicultural imaginary.

The state lets us remember only momentarily and evacuates our desires for the future. As Jodi Byrd explains, Indigenous people (Indians) are lamentable but not grievable; they belong in the past. The difference, as Byrd describes, is that the act of grieving "calls people to acknowledge, to see, and to grapple with lived lives and the commensurable suffering" as a means to apprehend the policies creating "unlivable, ungrievable conditions within state-sponsored economies of slow death."[6] In other words, celebrating indigeneity for its cultural difference and its contributions to humanity does not challenge settler colonialism or white supremacy directly while the power structure remains unquestioned. The political claims of the Hawaiian Kingdom or an independent Hawaiian nation are, in effect, neutered through various performances, seemingly reduced to cultural parades, historical reenactments, and ceremonial meaning without political possibilities.

Honoring our aliʻi and performing Hawaiian culture is also a way that Kānaka Maoli learn about who we were, who we are, and who we could be again. Nostalgia for the kingdom plays a crucial role in decolonization because it allows us to bring our aliʻi back to life, to bring Kanaka Maoli independence back to life. This is also an act of mourning. Rather than focusing on our prior life or on our political afterlife manifested in "culture," as the settler state constantly encourages us to do, we honor our aliʻi as part of our shared sense of self; it is how we know who we are, and it is built into every understanding of what it means to be Kānaka Maoli. While the outside world tells us (Hawaiʻi and Hawaiians in the discursive imagination) we are just their playground, a sexy culture, a Disney film, a football player, a military landing and staging site, honoring our aliʻi reminds Kānaka Maoli that we were royal, civilized, respectable people—not incarcerated, druggedout, homeless, or noble savages who live in the past.

Cultural memories are embodied in and through performances that are social processes of memory and forgetting. Performances invoke and conjure, bringing into being what often does not need to be said or get to be said. These performances are transferred in sacred ceremonies, in parades, onstage, and in everyday life.[7] Hula performance, for example, is a way that the immense depth of Hawaiian knowledge and culture is communicated, and aliʻi especially are honored through mele (song). From a young age, Kānaka Maoli in Hawaiʻi are taught about who our aliʻi were and what they did. We learn this from our families and through public and private school education, field trips to ʻIolani Palace and the Bishop Museum, participation in May Day parades, hula practice, and so on. On a community level, hula hālau, Hawaiian charter schools, Hawaiian civic clubs, and other organizations all work to honor the legacy of the nā aliʻi and do important advocacy on behalf of Kānaka Maoli. During hula festivals, parades, and other cultural events, these groups represent the link to our aliʻi and serve a vital cultural function through their ongoing visibility. These educational opportunities are also uneven; not all Kānaka Maoli have access to them (even in Hawaiʻi, where they are part of the school curriculum), and not all families transfer cultural memories, especially those who have suffered the consequences of decades of colonization, which taught Kānaka Maoli to be ashamed of our culture and history. Keep in mind, too, that not all Kānaka Maoli dance hula and that many Kānaka Maoli living outside of Hawaiʻi do not learn about their aliʻi in formal institutional settings such as schools, but may learn about them through more mainstream Americanized sources such as children's books or Hollywood films. All these acts of connecting to and of desiring to see ourselves in representations are acts of mourning and become crucial spaces in which we can account for the past, present, and future.

Haunted Hawaiʻi

The filming of *Princess Kaiulani* in 2008 produced quite a bit of intrigue. There were rumors that the filming was cursed. During filming at ʻIolani Palace, some of the production assistants had felt, heard, and seen spirits or said that strange apparitions appeared on film. This fueled the controversy surrounding the film, as Kanaka Maoli activists were already protesting its production, questioning its historical accuracy. In an ominous turn of events, one of the production managers working on the film perished in a tragic accident at the Sheraton Princess Kaʻiulani Hotel during preproduction.[8] Many stories circulated. *Someone fell from a hotel balcony. A hotel room caught on fire from a cigarette. The "accident" happened because the production was hewa (wrong).* I heard that the film was not honoring cultural protocols. The rumored haunting of the hotel and the intrigue surrounding this production exemplify the long-standing tensions that exist in Hawaiʻi over contested histories and claims to political power that include the sprits of those no longer living.

An industry around ghost tours has popped up in Hawaiʻi. A version of this story of a producer dying while working on the *Princess Kaiulani* film was told to me on a tour of ʻIolani Palace in 2008. Kaʻiulani's memory was also invoked on a ghost tour I took in July 2013. Indigenous hauntings trouble settler colonialism by reminding us all that something is unfinished.[9] Maintaining Indigenous presence, hauntings and ghost stories denote the power of cultural memories that can belong to individuals and also reflect group histories. Being haunted in a particular location is a product of the social and cultural histories of that space. Both real and imagined, Hawaiian indigeneity informs not only political rhetoric or cultural investments but also a profound commitment to place that is felt by Kānaka Maoli, settlers, and tourists alike. Hawaiian history, culture, and governmental politics literally haunt the public sphere in Hawai'i. As Avery Gordon noted, hauntings are a way people are notified that what has been concealed is alive and present, interfering precisely with those incomplete forms of containment and repression.[10] The ghost in a sense symbolizes what Eve Tuck and C. Ree describe as the "relentless remembering and reminding that will not be appeased by settler society's assurances of innocence and reconciliation."[11] Hawaiian ghosts question how Hawai'i came to be part of the United States and how it became a tourist destination. The ghost tour experience compels audience members to confront their own complicity with the erasure of Hawaiian indigeneity in Waikīkī. It reminds us all that something has not been said, that someone or something is lingering because of an injustice, and that we are all complicit if we refuse to listen. The ghosts' intention is to get you to think and to act differently.

Social relations produce space and thus are never empty; they are full of histories of what came before and what is to come. Space in the abstract and as a commodity is a mechanism used to control and dominate everyday life.[12] The rewriting of Hawai'i's geography served a critical role in the colonization process by disappearing Kanaka Maoli understandings of land and replacing them with settler formations predicated on unchecked capitalist development, at first in the form of plantations and later in the form of a tourist economy. This process has been ongoing, an illustration of what Gerald Vizenor has described as a simulation of "the Native" or "the real" that is always a signal of its absence.[13] Nowhere is this more evident than in Waikīkī, a place synonymous with Hawaiian tourism in the global imagination. The fabrication of "Hawaiianness" throughout Waikīkī in Hawaiiana motifs, streets named after prominent ali'i, and so-called Hawaiian culture at every turn caters to tourists' fantasized image while simultaneously denying counternarratives that may contradict or threaten this fantasized image.[14] Waikīkī is a case in point of the way in which Hawaiian culture can be celebrated, representing our Hawaiian cultural capital at the same time that Kānaka Maoli themselves remain on the bottom of society.[15] Recent efforts to curb the homeless "problem" in Hawai'i, where many are Kānaka Maoli, often focus in Waikīkī because the presence of houseless people bothers tourists, making obvious the kind of Native purging and removal that is necessary to maintain "paradise." No one wants to confront abject poverty and the legacies of colonial dispossession when they are trying to get their mai tai on. This is yet another example of the ways in which settler colonialism appropriates Native culture at the expense of actual Native people.

From receding shorelines to increased street policing, the so-called naturalness of Waikīkī as a playground denies the violence necessary to make and maintain it. In 2011, during the Asia-Pacific Economic Cooperation meeting, a young Kanaka Maoli man, Kollin Elderts, was tragically shot to death by an off-duty federal agent, Christopher Deedy, at a McDonald's near the Princess Ka'iulani Hotel. The agent was later acquitted of all charges. The defense argued that racial tensions between haoles and locals played a role in the encounter that resulted in Elderts's death, depicting Elderts as an intoxicated and aggressive Native who provoked the off-duty Deedy. As in the cases of the murder of other people of color by police officers in the continental United States, protesters and legal appeals by Elderts's family made these connections, but Deedy's first trial and his appeal to the Hawai'i Supreme Court resulted in an eventual acquittal. This is representative of the ways in which Waikīkī (and Hawai'i in general) is a site of ongoing violence and tension despite state and corporate interests that seek to sanitize these histories.

The intentions of the settler state and the tourism industry are to always establish the "natural" presence of Hawaiian culture and history in Waikīkī by emphasizing it as a space of recreation for ali'i (and now tourists) while erasing Waikīkī as a social, spiritual, and political place for Kānaka Maoli.[16] Hawaiian history and culture are then used to construct a "unique" sense of place that attracts tourists in order to compete in the tropical resort market, offering Hawai'i's distinct sense of indigeneity, which is welcoming (because of aloha) and civilized (to an extent because of our royal history). The Sheraton Princess Ka'iulani Hotel can honor and memorialize the former glory and power of the Hawaiian Kingdom throughout its interior, through its dining room performances, and even through educational cultural activities intended to craft a more nuanced tale of Hawaiian history; but such celebrations are handled in a manner that denies the possibilities of contemporary Kanaka Maoli governance. Waikīkī disappears Kanaka Maoli people through the appropriation of numerous Hawaiian aliʻi for street names and Hawaiian concepts such as "aloha" to serve the larger purposes of settler colonialism and capitalism. Through a process of renaming and settlement, settler colonialism transforms an Indigenous space into colonial space. It makes modern, breathing, vocal Natives (and the presence of cultures that do not threaten settler colonialism) antithetical to "progress" or Hawaiʻi's multicultural future. Setter colonialism and the complexities of spatial practices at play in Hawaiʻi naturalize a settler narrative, replacing them as normative, while erasing any Indigenous relationship to space.[17] As Jacques Derrida explained, hegemony is haunted by ghosts—by memory, history, fears, and desires that the present structure seeks to repress.[18] Settler colonialism as a structure is thus required to maintain social relations that contribute to the production of historical amnesia and denies the ongoing presence of Native peoples. In a settler-colonial Hawaiʻi, Kānaka Maoli haunt settler hegemony.

Prior to the 1970s in Hawaiʻi, many people were dismissive of Kanaka Maoli aspirations for sovereignty, but since the 1990s the question of Hawaiian sovereignty is definitely on people's minds. Even when not discussed directly, the specter of Hawaiian indigeneity is felt. This presence takes place at governmental levels and also pervades the subconscious of all of Hawaiʻi's people, especially for Kānaka Maoli themselves. It is no coincidence that ghost stories and ghost tours emerged as an industry in Hawaiʻi in the early 1990s. Glen Grant, a haole storyteller and cultural historian, became well known in the local media. He was a scholar and an educator who wrote about Hawaiʻi's ethnic diversity as told through ghost stories and changing historical conditions. He argued that the rise in Asian ghost tales occurred as Asian immigration increased and the Native Hawaiian population declined. His popularity, however, had less to do with this emergent critique of Hawaiian erasure and the ascension of Asian settler colonialism (although he would never call Asians "settlers") than with the content of the chicken-skin-inducing scary ghost stories themselves. Grant conducted extensive research on these topics, and during the late 1980s he was known for a *Honolulu Star-Bulletin* column, "Murder, He Wrote," which documented various occult and ghost stories of Hawaiʻi. He published local literary hits such as *Obake Files* and *Chick'n Skin* and went so far as to copyright "Chicken Skin."[19] He parlayed his writings into walking ghost tours of Waikīkī and downtown Honolulu and Chinatown and was featured on local television shows.[20] Stories of the "choking ghost" and the "faceless ghost" became familiar in Hawaiʻi. Many of these tales came from the experiences of Asians in plantation-era Hawaiʻi and areas in urban Honolulu where many Asians settled after leaving the plantations. The only mentions of Hawaiian ghosts were of "the Nightmarchers" (ghosts of Hawaiian warriors) who in these stories appear at random, holding torches and beating drums on their way to a battle. While Grant described Kānaka Maoli as the "spiritual bedrock of modern occult occurrences," he noted that they were tolerant and happy to make space for the later immigrants and their supernatural traditions.[21] Grant's interpretations of ghost stories played into settler ideologies that portray Hawaiian culture as simultaneously lost in the past and as the embodiment of "aloha" because he claimed that Hawaiian ghosts were inclusive. Prior to Grant's telling of these stories, they circulated in folk networks via Hawaiian oral histories and plantation rumor mills; their circulation was also aided by a robust print culture in Hawai'i dating back to the mid-nineteenth century in multiple languages (Hawaiian, Chinese, Japanese, and so on).

The popularity of these stories in the late twentieth century coincided with the growing prominence of the Hawaiian sovereignty movement. The ghost stories cannot be read separately from these political realities, which were quite literally unsettling the narratives of Hawai'i as an inevitable U.S. holding. As a venue for entertainment, the stories reflected a deep anxiety about Hawai'i's past, present, and future. Ghost stories represented settler anxieties of the contemporary Hawaiian present, functioning to relegate Hawaiian culture to the past in a manner that pretends to "remember" the greatness of Hawaiians while also producing nervousness about the precarity of Asian settlers in Hawai'i. As explained by the editors of *Asian Settler Colonialism* (2008), Asian Americans in Hawai'i need to address how their presence functions as a multicultural alibi for settlement.[22] The ongoing fear of ghosts points to the significance of these stories and to the anxieties over the Hawaiian past and our shared island future. Ghost stories embody the political claims of Kānaka Maoli and what refuses to stay in the past despite over a century of U.S. military occupation.

Kanaka Maoli ghosts embody haole and Asian settler guilt and question who the rightful inheritors of the land in Hawai'i are. When Kānaka Maoli are written off as ghosts, they are written off and removed from their lands and are placed in a local/settler imaginary where Kānaka Maoli signify the past and always haunt the future. This is why Hawaiian culture can be invoked at every turn—in every hotel lobby, on the beaches, in every song, in every advertisement. It gestures toward a spectral Hawaiian presence without political consequences, and it supports a neoliberal sense of multicultural belonging that is assumed to be supported by Hawaiian culture's welcoming and inviting essence (that is, aloha) and proven through the brown bodies that welcome tourists—eschewing the economic realities that require such performances. Simultaneously, the consistent returning to Kānaka Maoli as the "host culture" references the actual presence of Kānaka Maoli and an acute sense of guilt experienced subconsciously by settlers in Hawaiʻi. These forms of guilt and the invocation of Kānaka Maoli exemplify the unsettled nature of Hawaiʻi and reveal that American hegemony in Hawaiʻi is an ongoing colonial project that is already quite precarious. Tales of a "haunted Hawaiʻi" teach us that Hawaiian indigeneity and the way it is represented and remembered exist at a nexus of competing desires and memories with multiple constituencies, including those that exceed the dead. Kanaka Maoli ghost stories remind Asian settlers that they can be disappeared in Hawaiʻi too, replaced by white settlers. Hawaiian ghosts remind Asian settlers of the possibility of that loss, which is why Asian ghost stories that take place in Hawaiʻi are so critical for Asian settler colonialism. They permit Asian settlers to stake a place in Hawaiʻi's future by invoking its past.

In the summer of 2014, while doing fieldwork in my homeland, I had plans to attend a ghost tour, similar to the one I had been on a few years prior, of Downtown and the ʻIolani Palace grounds, where I learned about the ghostly encounters experienced by the *Princess Kaiulani* film crew. At the time, I had no intention of focusing my research on Princess Kaʻiulani or cultural memory at all. In fact, in the previous ghost tour I had been on, with the exception of learning about the rumors of the film's haunting at ʻIolani Palace, the focus was almost explicitly on Japanese or Chinese ghosts, which led me to my initial theory that even through these ghost stories, Asian settler presence was working to erase Hawaiian indigeneity. My thoughts were based on the popularity of Glen Grant's Obake Files series, which was very popular during my youth (and in my own home). I was planning to go on as many different ghost tours as possible. I was excited to see a "Groupon" for a ghost tour by the Mysteries of Hawaiʻi Ghost Tour company led by Lopaka Kapanui, a kumu hula and Hawaiian cultural practitioner and also the protégé of Glen Grant. On a steamy August evening in Waikīkī, I expected to be on a terrible tour with a bunch of tourists; instead it was with a local couple and their teenage sons. I anticipated being surrounded by tourists looking for an experience with an authentic Hawaiian ghost, but I was sharing this experience with a local family looking to spend time with one another. As locals who share an experience of what it means to grow up in Hawaiʻi and value it, there was a shared sense of place, discomfort, and interest in Hawai'i's ghostly presences. As we traversed Waikīkī's busy tourist-infested streets, it became clear that while our tax dollars may have invested in this place, we had a distinct sense that it was no longer our place, and we expressed how irritated we were by the experience of having to weave in and out of Waikīkī's nightlife (which includes countless tourists, street performers, homeless folks, and various other solicitors). Whereas tourists might seek out these tours in search of the Hawaiian occult with tinges of that ever-present exoticism that pervades Hawaiian touristic fantasy, our tour did not deliver that. There were no over-the-top explanations of Hawaiian culture. Kapanui seemed to hold it back. He warned us that we must honor the spirits we encounter and that he would respond if necessary because he had the spiritual and cultural tools to do so. In these moments, we kept quiet.

Our first stop was across the street from the Hyatt Regency Hotel. As Kapanui told his first story, we stared upward at the towering glass building at the corner of Kalākaua Avenue and Uluniu Avenue a block from Ka'iulani Avenue. I recalled my sister's wedding there in 1998. Kapanui told his story and quickly moved us to the next location because security guards—who had warned him not to go near the hotel—were watching us. We proceeded to the Sheraton Princess Ka'iulani Hotel, which sits at the entrance to Ka'iulani's estate, known since the 1880s as 'Āinahau. The estate was gifted to her by her aunt, Ruth Ke'elikolani. During Ka'iulani's youth and adulthood, the estate hosted many high-society functions. After Ka'iulani's death, 'Āinahau passed into her father's care. When Ka'iulani's father, Archibald Scott Cleghorn, died in 1910, he willed the land on the Territory of Hawai'i to create Ka'iulani Park, but they refused it, so the land was divided up and sold. The old Victorian mansion was converted into a small hotel, which operated from 1913 to 1917 and later burned down, in 1921.[23] The nearby Moana Hotel, which had been in operation since 1901, expanded, building bungalows on the 'Āinahau lands; they were demolished in 1953. The Matson Line constructed the Princess Ka'iulani Hotel in June 1955, and in 1959 it was sold to Sheraton Hotels. A second wing was built in 1960 and third in 1970. The Japanese company Kyo-Ya purchased it in 1963 and continues to own it along with a slew of other Waikīkī hotels—Moana Surfrider, Royal Hawaiian, Westin, and Sheraton Maui. Consisting of two towers, the hotel boasts a thousand rooms. It is also the site of a new stage show, *Te Moana Nui*, which premiered in August 2015.

Walking through the hotel, looking at images of our ali'i on the walls, seeing Filipino maids push carts through the halls, being almost blinded by the white marble floors, hearing the faint sound of Hawaiian music as Japanese and haole tourists in surf shorts and towels covering bikinis and bad tans scampered by, I was confronted with the violence that was necessary for this scene to take place in front of me. As a Kanaka Maoli who grew up in Hawai'i, I had maybe been to one of these hotels once or twice, perhaps outside of a prom that I did not go to, or at a hotel party in high school, but unless you work directly in this industry, the Hawaiian hotel experience (as a guest) is not one that most locals and Kānaka Maoli are familiar with. We know that Waikīkī is not for us to enjoy.

We began this part of the tour in front of a picture of King David Kalākaua. Kapanui explained Ka'iulani's lineage and why it was significant that this hotel was named after her. In this area, a few blocks from the Royal Hawaiian Hotel and five blocks from the Queen Kapi'olani Hotel, it's common for Waikīkī to boast of its connection to our royal past. Hotels feature large portraits of ali'i, paintings done in their honor, and rooms named after them. These kinds of decorations perhaps relay to tourists the importance and power of Hawaiian culture. The ghost tour presumably also shares a taste of this, but everyone on this particular tour was local, and Kapanui explained that the majority of his tours are for local people, unlike those conducted by some of the more flashy tour companies in the islands. By giving a tour of Waikīkī he hopes to remind us all that Waikīkī can still be a Hawaiian place, despite the artifice of its Hawaiianness. The ghost tour experience produces a rupture in the tourist narrative of Waikīkī, encouraging us to think about its history of transformation, violence, and Native erasure. The tour reminded us that it is very possible that ali'i still roam these beaches, streets, and hotels and that the stories told about them are not what they seem. Throughout the tour, Kapanui took us to sites where Hawaiian spirits are known to dwell, where particular trees are the loci of 'eha (pain).

As we walked through the Princess Ka'iulani Hotel, he spoke quietly, showing us pictures of Ka'iulani on his iPad. The hotel lobby has a life-size portrait of Ka'iulani and a collage of images of her as the backdrop of the concierge area. These images of the Kingdom of Hawai'i served as stark reminders of Hawaiian modernity. The tourists who pass these large portraits daily are presented with imagery of the Hawaiian Kingdom as a thing of the past whose majesty and royal magnitude are not lost culturally, but certainly politically, thus reifying the settler-colonial formation of Hawai'i and its illegal occupation by the United States. There were moments when we stood at the periphery of the hotel space, careful not to draw attention to ourselves. Hotel staff did not like that Kapanui brought attention to the possible haunting of the hotel. The smell of fish, plumeria, and maile mixed with the sound of Hawaiian music and dinner service in the background as we walked quietly through the hotel lobby, where Kapanui told us the story of Kawēkiu.

Kapanui recounted the experience of a hotel security guard and her encounter with Kaʻiulani's ghost.[24] Meaning "the highest rank or station," "Kawēkiu" is part of Kaʻiulani's name. The guard's personal story weaves through a history of drug abuse and incarceration; her job at the hotel is a second chance for her. Highlighting the problems of drug abuse and incarceration that occur in Hawaiian communities, Kapanui connects the story to a reality that many Kānaka Maoli are familiar with. The encounter with Kawēkiu is no coincidence. The security guard's ʻaumakua caused the encounter with Kawēkiu. In Hawaiian culture, an ʻaumakua is a personal family god or protector who can communicate across spirit worlds. The guard has a connection to Kawēkiu because of their shared indigeneity too. Kawēkiu reminds the guard that she still roams her lands, despite the towering concrete and the desecration of the land on which it is built. Indeed, the interaction between the guard and Kawēkiu transcends Western time and logic. Kawēkiu comes to life and provides meaning for the guard, making her job more than a second chance; the security guard is no longer just a laborer in this space. This encounter represents the way that Hawaiian indigeneity haunts Hawaiʻi, particularly in settler spaces. Kawēkiu tells the guard that she will always be there. In this declaration, her ongoing presence can never be totally erased in this space, on what are still her lands, haunting a hotel named after her. Her presence cannot be denied even if only materially commodified throughout the hotel interior.

Dying of a Broken Heart

In 1875 Princess Kaʻiulani's birth was celebrated widely as the highest-ranking royal birth of the Kalākaua dynasty.[25] She was heir to the throne of the Kingdom of Hawaiʻi and was named crown princess by her aunt, Queen Lydia Liliʻuokalani, on March 9, 1891.[26] Educated in England, the princess traveled across Europe and the United States in her early twenties, spreading awareness about the overthrow. On March 2, 1893, the San Francisco *Morning Call* described her as a "beautiful young woman of sweet face and slender figure," remarking on her dark skin and soft eyes, which were common among the Hawaiians.[27] This was a typical characterization of her, among other descriptions that attribute her pleasant countenance to her British education and her father's Scottish bloodline.[28] Rather than reducing Ka'iulani to her appearance, Hawaiian-language newspapers wrote about her with the utmost respect, expressing deep aloha toward her. Hawaiian-language newspapers would publish the mele that were written about her. Ka'iulani is honored in name songs. "He inoa no Kalaninuiahila-palapa" by Miss Kekoaohiwaikalani and "He inoa no Ka'iulani," written by Queen Lili'uokalani, compare her to the most sacred vines, describing her as one whose voice and presence bring joy to Hawai'i. She is celebrated as being a budding flower of proud ancestry representing the flag of Hawai'i.[29]

In a newspaper article dated April 9, 1899, roughly a month after her death, Colonel Macfarlane told the *San Francisco Call* that Ka'iulani said to him, "I think my heart is broken," in reference to the current state of the kingdom. Because of this statement, Colonel Macfarlane commented that Princess Ka'iulani died of a broken heart, the result of an ongoing illness that was exacerbated by the political situation in Hawai'i. Ka'iulani was reported to have a heart condition that began when she first heard news of the overthrow and worsened as the annexationists took power. This alleged comment by Ka'iulani (which I cannot find elsewhere in other media of the time), quoted by Macfarlane and recirculated in the media, then and now, carries a narrative power that was seemingly built for catchphrases and one-liners about her that came later as illustrated in the film *Princess Kaiulani*. The final scene in the film culminates with a slow-motion close-up of Ka'iulani horseback riding; before the scene fades to black, words appear on the screen explaining that many believe that Ka'iulani died of a broken heart. The constant focus on the heart, on the affective, emotive valences of "dying of a broken heart" juxtaposed with the focus on Ka'iulani, indicates a kind of mourning for what could have been. It romanticizes Ka'iulani's life and the past, obscuring the violence of the time, which marked Kānaka Maoli as too weak for modernity because attempts to reestablish the kingdom ultimately failed.

When we focus on her broken heart, we lock her in time, erasing her resistance and the resistance of all those who came after her. This in turn justifies ongoing U.S. occupation, positioning Hawai'i as always in the space of the feminine, servicing colonialist viewpoints that figure Ka'iulani (and Hawai'i and all "small" island nations) as helpless in the face of colonialism and naturalizing the taking of the Hawaiian Kingdom by a global superpower, the marriage between Hawai'i and its white suitor, the United States.

FIGURE 5 *Princess Kaiulani* film poster.

This inevitability is clearly reflected in the film, which provides a fictional depiction of the events leading up to and surrounding the illegal annexation of the Kingdom of Hawai'i by the United States—the so-called day our nation died, as spoken by Q'orianka Kilcher, the actress portraying Ka'iulani in the film (Figure 5). Portrayed as a predestined moment of Indigenous independence ceding to Western power, the illegal overthrow of the Hawaiian Kingdom is merely a backdrop to a love story between the princess and her suitor, Clive Davies, the son of Theophilus Harris Davies, who owned one of the "Big Five" sugar corporations in Hawai'i and acted as Ka'iulani's guardian in England. As explained by Noelani Goodyear-Ka'ōpua in "Domesticating Hawaiians," tropes of marriage and romantic love between royals and haoles accomplished political and cultural work to naturalize the union between a Hawaiian heiress and a son of a Scottish businessman who had financial stakes in Hawai'i (and whose family still does).[30] This is the modus operandi for Hawai'i in the Western imagination—an inevitable possession, an object that against perhaps its better judgment has no choice but to submit to the seduction of Westernization (of the white man) and our own desire to become its subject. In the film, Ka'iulani resists American annexation and never marries a white man, but the viewer still walks away with a sense that her protest (and by extension her people's protest), while noble and beautiful, did not matter. The film portrays that the people's and the monarchy's resistance to the overthrow was unimportant and ultimately ineffective because the overthrow was an inevitable occurrence that even Ka'iulani acceded to under duress (through her very death).

These representations place the kingdom in the past and in many ways lay the blame on women for inadequately defending their nation. From a Western viewpoint, the ocean, the island, the nation, the people themselves are all feminized and unable to rule. Scholars have discussed at length the ways in which colonization is a gendered process, and the representation of Ka'iulani's aunt, Queen Lili'uokalani, in particular is indicative of the way that "world powers" viewed her as inept because of her gender and indigeneity. Images in the 1890s reflected deep-seated biases toward people of color and other Indigenous peoples that were rooted in views of slavery, Reconstruction, and European imperialism, which represented Hawai'i, Cuba, Puerto Rico, and the Philippines with similar traits.[31] The blackening of Lili'uokalani naturalized the legitimacy of white or haole American businessmen (that is, the annexationists who made themselves the "Provisional Government") as more capable statesmen in contradistinction to the Kingdom of Hawai'i and to the queen in general. References to "Dusky Queen Lil" symbolized the racism that was common in political cartoons that portrayed Lili'uokalani—and by extension, Hawai'i—as black, savage, and female, a tactic used to denigrate all Hawaiians.[32] Lili'uokalani was drawn as loose, disheveled, and unintelligent. Ka'iulani, in contrast, was described as lighter-skinned than her aunt and treated with an air of respect because of her appearance (even though she was frequently referred to as a princess from a savage, primitive, and backward place). Fast-forward a century, and the story of Ka'iulani is retold, couched in a universal feminist narrative of a young, intelligent, beautiful princess torn between her nation and her heart. The film recounts a story that young women, Anglophiles, Kānaka Maoli, and other viewers can latch onto.

Ka'iulani, who was known for her attractive appearance and sophistication, concurrently operates as a modernized Indigenous femininity that

Kānaka Maoli can celebrate for her resistance, but also for non-Kanaka audiences who might celebrate subconsciously her failed resistance. Kaʻiulani in all her respectability works as the foil to the "dusky maiden." As Lisa Taouma explains, "The 'dusky maiden' functions as a metaphor for the colonization of the Pacific in that she, like our social, economic and religious structures, was shaped to fit a colonial agenda."[33] As a stand-in for the land and the tumultuous and mysterious Pacific Ocean, the "dusky maiden" is an inspiration of its fertile depths, which fascinated so many European colonists. Early European journals and travelogues noted that Pacific women were sexually available, existing in a kind of Garden of Eden with no mores or rationality. Pacific women running wild in turn reflected the lack of power Pacific men had because they could not control women and society, thereby warranting the conquest of the Pacific itself and its women. Unlike her dusky Pacific sisters, Kaʻiulani was a proper "half-breed," and her so-called civility was always attributed to her Scottish ancestry. She was held up as exceptional, not emblematic of her people. Native women are often blamed for colonization as a way to question their loyalty to their people. La Malinche, Pocahontas, and Sacajawea in particular have been framed as Native women who collaborated with colonists. This, however, does not happen in the film. Kaʻiulani is instead shown as a woman with agency who lobbies in New York City and with President Cleveland in Washington, D.C., and is depicted as a fighter for her kingdom. The film even credits Kaʻiulani with proposing voting rights for all people in Hawaiʻi, which in actuality she did not do.

In this way, the film does not squarely blame "woman" for Hawaiʻi's colonization; it in fact credits the princess with advocating for "equality" in the form of voting rights for all, which becomes possible only because of the liberal sentimentality of Sanford Dole. The viewer is left with the sense that Dole would then lead the new Hawaiian government into an American democratic future where all men are created equal. The film completely fails to acknowledge the resistance of Native women and the role they played in fighting to save the kingdom. Kaʻiulani's contemporaries in Hawaiʻi were responsible for the anti-annexation petitions that are today known as the Kūʻē Petitions. These wahine koa (women warriors) traveled from island to island and village to village collecting signatures from Kānaka Maoli (and non-Kanaka subjects of the Hawaiian Kingdom) opposed to annexation. Women like Emma Nawahī and Abigail Kuaihelani Campbell of Aloha ʻĀina o Nā Wahine (Hawaiian Women's Patriotic League) rejected Western social conventions that relegated women to the domestic sphere and

were key figures in Hawaiian women's resistance.[34] The film fails to document the resistance of Kānaka Maoli who organized 38,000 signatures opposing annexation and that women were responsible for much of this
resistance. Overlooking this huge part of history, which was certainly within
the time frame of the film, displays the limits of cinematic representation,
even in a situation where the filmmakers (I am giving them a lot of credit
here) are attempting to supposedly "get it right." Intentional inaccuracies
like these represent very clearly the ways in which the emphasis on Kaʻiulani
marks ongoing non-Hawaiian fascination with images of Hawaiian women
and love stories about Hawaiʻi but is not interested in Hawaiʻi's complex political history (and present) when it challenges ongoing American military
occupation and settler colonialism.

Overall, the film sacrifices a political memoir for a universal love story.
The long scenes set in Scotland with Kaʻiulani making out with Clive Davies feel like Victorian-era Downton Abbeyesque soft porn rather than an
understanding of the agency that Native women may express in situations
where they are believed to have none. In a modern feminist twist, Kaʻiulani
will not give up her kingdom for Davies because she quite plainly outranks
him. She refuses to marry him, asking, "Do you think I love you more than
my country?" This is a powerful affirmation, to be sure, but a later scene
shows her making out with Davies passionately again, ostensibly in public in
Hawaiʻi, lending support to the colonial idea that her desire for this white man
cannot be controlled. While tourists view Hawaiʻi (and the rest of the Pacific) as their sexually free wonderland, since colonization Natives have
become quite demure and would never partake in such displays of public
affection! This occurs in the film in total disregard of the princess's engagement to Prince Kawananakoa, portrayed as "Koa" in the film. Her engagement
is certainly within the time line the film crafts, yet it is never mentioned.
Kaʻiulani and Koa became engaged in February 1898. On screen, Koa
and Kaʻiulani rarely interact, and when they do he is depicted as grumpy
and punitive toward servants and appears overprotective and foreboding.
It is never explained that he is a high-ranking prince and that the couple
were friends from a young age and grew up together. Nor does the film ever
hint at their future union. Rather than explore the relationship between
Kaʻiulani and Koa, the story line focuses on the trope of the young Indigenous woman protagonist who would of course fall madly in love with her
white suitor. In countless Hollywood films, Hawaiʻi is generally represented
through the image of a hula girl and her inevitable suitor, the American

businessman or soldier, thus making Kānaka Maoli American masculinity's possession. In the retelling of Kaʻiulani's story, we are forced to confront the scenario of conquest, which Diana Taylor describes as acts of possession that restage battles for power throughout the Americas; but these scenarios can also be subverted from within.[35] Unlike many aliʻi wahine (chiefly women) who married white men (including Kaʻiulani's mother), Princess Kaʻiulani does not get married off to a white man, nor does she consent to marry a Japanese prince, Higashifushimi Yorihito, as her uncle, King David Kalākaua, might have intended. She remains "single" in the global imagination, and her would-be fans or commemorators need not see her as a woman who was defined by who her husband was. The film does not end in marriage or betrayal, but instead in death.

It is imperative to present a different reading of this film, which has been criticized as apolitical or historically inaccurate by Hawaiian academic and activist communities. We must read the broader implications of these so-called flawed objects because they reach a wide audience of Kānaka Maoli, many of whom cannot touch Hawaiʻi or who have limited historical and cultural knowledge. These images function as a liminal space for many Kānaka Maoli to connect to the Hawaiian past and to mediate their relationship to an emergent independent Hawaiian future. This is why these images are so disruptive, because they represent competing forces that seek to decolonize our past and articulate "accurate" visions of the past as a means to usher in a liberated Hawaiian future based in historical truths. The desire to produce the "truth" is necessary to rewrite and challenge Hollywood and incarnations of Hawaiian history that left out the Indigenous perspective, but it also has the damaging power to occlude multiple interpretations that might be generative for new forms of resistance. We have to account for why images of "the Native" that affirm stereotypes can also be so empowering for Native people. As Michelle Raheja explains, "The realism of film resides in its ability to function as a placeholder: as a representational practice it does not mirror reality but can enact important cultural work as an artform with ties to the world of everyday practices and the imaginative sphere of the possible."[36] We must take these images seriously because they allow us to reckon with our affective connection to our kupuna and the lāhui, shoring up emotions that reveal themselves through sadness, anger, and, yes, even aloha, as seen in response to the film. Today, it is often difficult to grasp what the kingdom might have even looked like because so much has changed in Hawaiʻi. Settler colonialism in Hawaiʻi has become so pervasive and damaging that an Indigenous understanding of place often feels out of reach. If we are lucky, we learn these stories from our kupuna or in school, but there is a visual limit to our imagination. Visual media like television and film have become the predominant form of knowledge transfer. Historical documents and archives reveal a story most people are unable to access themselves (or are uninterested in doing so). It is through visual and audio media that the majority of people come to experience their own memories and histories, particularly among Kānaka Maoli. Films serve as sites of pedagogy and knowledge production for spectators.[37] Further, Indigenous spectators critically examine in television and film the residual elements of imagined cultural knowledge that comes from films, which harken to a long political narrative and historical context that may be lacking visually.[38] The visualization of the kingdom in the film therefore enables Kānaka Maoli to connect with our kingdom in a way that is arguably more powerful than the lived experience that can come through taking a tour of ʻIolani Palace, dancing hula, or reading a book. The film, despite its flaws, is generative for modern resistance because of the way it performs cultural memory work and lets Kānaka Maoli visualize the Hawaiian Kingdom.

There is no shortage of films about Hawaiʻi, but there has yet to be a film that documents what the Hawaiian Kingdom might have looked like when it was rapidly modernizing. The film *Princess Kaiulani* visualizes what the kingdom looked like, complete with arch-annexationist advisers, lavish displays of wealth and power, and hula dancers preparing for a special event that brought electricity to ʻIolani Palace in 1886 before the White House had it. We get to see Kalākaua in full regalia and Hawaiian servants speaking ʻōlelo Hawaiʻi (Hawaiian language). For Kānaka Maoli this is important because it counteracts the mass-produced imagery of Hawaiʻi (as explained throughout this book), and it shows us in full high definition as close as we can get to the kingdom in our memories, one that leaps out of history books and materializes what is learned in mele. Live, vibrant, and maoli, the film allows Kānaka Maoli viewers to reimagine our aliʻi. The implications of this film for Kanaka Maoli audiences are illustrated in its celebrated reviews and related events in Hawaiʻi. A community "talk story" took place at ʻIolani Palace, giving an opportunity for the directors, actors, and cultural advisers to comment on some of the criticisms. The takeaway point of the event and other reactions shared online is that the film brought to light a history that has been widely hidden and that many Kānaka Maoli were leaving the theater in tears, experiencing both sadness and joy. The film's Facebook page is flooded with comments from Kānaka Maoli discussing the film, particularly those in the diaspora, who repeatedly ask if it is going to be shown in their town or how they can get the DVD.[39] The film provides an opportunity for Kānaka Maoli to access these images, which are especially important for Kānaka Maoli in the diaspora. The film allows a visual presence in everyday life and in a representational field defined by absence.[40] When we consider how Kānaka Maoli interpret this film, we acknowledge ourselves as contemporary consumers of mass culture with agency to make these images our own.[41] This is a form of resistance and survival, for Kānaka Maoli often have to encounter a painful "unreality," which, as Simon Ortiz explains, is the process of having to contend with mass-produced stereotypical images of the self that misrepresent your language, culture, history, place, and everything else—creating a distance from "our lives as they really were."[42]

Thus, the performances in the film work to protect, honor, and preserve Hawaiian culture and political claims even if on the surface they appear to be benign expressions of cultural heritage or can easily be dismissed as nostalgia or as historically inaccurate. These images function to create cultural memories and remain critical locations for dream-work, where the staging and restaging of Hawaiian history allow Kānaka Maoli to mourn and engage their own pain. Engaging it as a form of spectatorship-as-resistance, we are able to make meaning and interpret the film in ways that constitute a form of ownership that reorganizes the original relations of media production.[43] The representational spaces where we are seen and legitimated, especially when we do not even have to contend with touristic fantasy, become ever more crucial spaces of attachment and radical reimagining of our histories and our place in the future. Representational critique notwithstanding, visualization generates a space of agency otherwise not available to Kanaka Maoli viewers. It is better to be represented, even if problematically, than to remain invisible and not be seen in the national imaginary at all.[44] Kānaka Maoli can be critical of this film while also feeling profoundly moved and inspired by it. While much has been said about the power of mele and oli and Hawaiian-language newspapers to recontextualize our relationship to the kingdom, this visualization has extreme power to tap into Hawaiian sentimentality, which aches for historical representations of the time before we became dashboard ornaments. This film, despite its tepid reception in the media, is actually beautifully staged, well acted, and full of powerful portrayals of Kanaka Maoli greatness that are much needed for Kanaka Maoli audiences.

Alas, these images are not without fault; furthermore, I would be remiss if I did not critique the misrepresentations in the film. In rather public displays of protest in person and on YouTube, a number of prominent Hawaiian actors, musicians, and cultural practitioners took issue with the film's authenticity and historical accuracy.[45] At the same time, several Hawaiian cultural historians and language specialists worked as advisors on the film. The larger question emerges: Does the power of this film's visuals and representational possibilities override the dangers it presents because it misinterprets history? For example, as the Hawaiian musician and actor Palani Vaughan explains in a YouTube video, the portrayal of Sanford Dole as a benevolent and reluctant annexationist is inaccurate, as many sources have noted the pivotal role Dole played in annexation and through his late service as territorial governor from 1900 to 1903.[46] Additionally, there are a number of web pages and even a Facebook page dedicated to presenting "the facts" and telling "the truth" about Ka'iulani's life. I appreciate the work involved in these endeavors, and my intention is not to dismiss the validity of these efforts or even the futility of documenting historical accuracy; but in some cases the film starts a conversation that may not have ever happened before.

Princess Kaiulani has the power to influence non-Hawaiian and Hawaiian viewers in ways that may not clearly align with a particular Hawaiian nationalist or political configuration. Scholars and critics, then, have the duty to make sense of what these visuals mean for Hawaiian indigeneity broadly and what Kānaka Maoli take away from this film. Native activists and scholars have labored extensively to combat the misrepresentation of Native people and histories in film, television, and popular culture in general. A critical contribution of this labor has been the emphasis on a more complex rendering of historical events that takes into account the Native point of view or, at the very least, represents the Native as an actor with political agency in moments when such agency was being increasingly curtailed. When we give these images too much power, we neglect to make space for the agency of audiences to reinterpret and remake these cultural productions in different ways. The visualization of the kingdom enables us to see not only the magnificence of our lāhui but also their profound resistance to annexation. We must think of our understanding of Ka'iulani and the history she represents as always active, as both Avery Gordon and Walter Benjamin urge us, so that we can fight for our oppressed pasts through engaging the traces in the present.[47] In the stage production, subversion becomes possible by giving voice to Ka'iulani, who is critical of her suitors and white society, and ultimately rejects both.

The Two Victorias

The play Ka'iulani is in the style of a Greek chorus, allowing multiple characters to convey divergent and perhaps painful interpretations of Ka'iulani's psyche. Interspersed with narration by a young woman character who is tasked with the assignment of writing about Ka'iulani for a university Hawaiian history course, the play oscillates through time. The play is set in the present, and the young woman struggles to make sense of the life of Princess Ka'iulani, who in the face of U.S. military power was powerless. The student's discomfort ultimately comes from having to make sense of a glimpse of history that offers only a partial portrayal of a person, a historical time, or a memory. The play first ran in 1987, the product of a collaboration among Dennis Caroll, Victoria Nalani Kneubuhl, Robert Nelson, and Ryan Page. Kneubuhl, who was a graduate student at the time of its writing, later became a renowned playwright. The play is billed as a "cantata for the theatre." When it premiered during the 1986–87 Kumu Kahua Theatre season, it created a buzz that got the wider Kanaka Maoli community interested. The production traveled to Hana, Maui, where the performance was lit by storm lanterns. It toured across Hawai'i in the summer of 1988, traveling to Kaua'i, Big Island, Maui, and additional venues across O'ahu in Kaneohe, Waianae, Leeward Community College and at Kamehameha Schools, proving its reach into the Hawaiian community. It also traveled to the Edinburgh Fringe Festival in Scotland as well to Georgetown University in Washington, D.C., and Los Angeles, thus showing the reach of the interest in the content. This was the first time since Hawai'i had become a state that a production "co-authored by people of Hawaiian ancestry [was] given outside Hawai'i," as the playbill explains. When it was restaged in 2015, the woman who played Ka'iulani in the original was recast as Ka'iulani's mother, Dowager Likelike. As reviews have noted, it is compelling to consider the difference in the audience's knowledge of Hawaiian historical events related to the overthrow in 1987 versus 2015.[48] In 1987 people could have still lived in a space of denial in regard to the illegal overthrow, but after decades of protest and cultural revitalization, Hawai'i has changed. Less than a year after the Department of the Interior held public meetings across the islands, the question of Hawaiian sovereignty was certainly part of public consciousness. For this reason, the play does not need to go in depth to set up the plot or backstory of Kaʻiulani because the audience already knows the time, place, and characters portrayed.

Throughout the play the women characters all take center stage. Four different actresses portray Kaʻiulani (Victoria) at three different points in her life. In the script, two different actresses portray her when she is living in England. Victoria is portrayed by the actress pictured kneeling in the foreground in figure 6, and the actress in the back plays Kaʻiulani. Another actress, not pictured, portrays Kaʻiulani as an adult when she returns home to Hawaiʻi after the overthrow. Over the course of the play, the girls and women all wear the same costume and create circles with their hands, singing and dancing together through different scenes. The feminine spirit is felt within the space, which is apt, since the story is about the princess of a kingdom, of a place, that has been so thoroughly feminized in the global imagination. These actresses look like everyday people, reflecting the diversity of Hawaiʻi and the Hawaiian community; this allows the audience to imagine Kaʻiulani as more than a royal from the past—she becomes a present-day figure who is representative of a universal sense of womanhood.

Men are secondary and superfluous to the story line. The only men portrayed by name are Kalākaua, her father, and Robert Louis Stevenson, a close friend of both, who was a well-known writer who traveled extensively in the Pacific. Stevenson's obsession with Kaʻiulani is inferred and documented in the play. As he sings a song to her, he is quickly ushered offstage by another character, who dismisses him. This garnered a chuckle from audience members who were well aware of the awkward relationship between Stevenson and Kaʻiulani. Stevenson was known for naming her "the Island Rose" in a poem he wrote for her, published in his book *Songs of Travel* (1896). He is also known to have shared many stories with her during her youth and to have written her letters while she was attending school in England.[49] It seems strange for a man who was twenty-five years older than her to be obsessed with a young girl. The chuckle from the audience signaled public knowledge of this rather inappropriate relationship. Other portrayals have been celebratory of this relationship, possibly because of Stevenson's stature in Hawaiʻi and across the Pacific. It is telling that the playwrights explicitly depicted the relationship as somewhat inappropriate, even if portraying it in a humorous tone, thus displaying the interplay that occurs within theater space where community knowledge of events is accessed without it being obvious within the performance itself. The chuckle from the audience shows the level of historical and cultural knowledge

FIGURE 6 Three actresses portray Kaʻiulani at different stages of her life, from the play *Kaʻiulani* by Dennis Carroll, Victoria Nalani Kneubuhl, Robert Nelson, and Ryan Page. Produced by Kumu Kahua Theatre, 2015. Directed by Harry Wong III. Photo credit: Denise De Guzman.

within a specific space. Kaʻiulani treats other suitors with ambivalence in the play. She is centered as the one with the power. The conflict of the two Victorias—played by two separate actresses to represent parts of Kaʻiulani's psyche—emerges when she relocates to England for her proper elite Western education.

Kaʻiulani is portrayed as Everywoman, a princess, but one who shares similar experiences with all women. Kaʻiulani goes into monologues that contemplate the experiences of women who know their worth, despite the place and time period they are living in, and that being a woman comes with power. She is positioned to represent a universal womanhood without sacrificing Indigenous or even Kanaka specificity. By visualizing these real-life modern characters who look like us and do not conform to the representations of Kānaka Maoli in the global tourist imagination, the play is able to confront the audience with the fact that Kaʻiulani is symbolic of the experiences of all women, especially Indigenous women. Through this play, we are able to speculate what her voice might have sounded like, especially in the second and third acts, because of the way Kaʻiulani is resistant to forms of European respectability that are pressed upon her.

When Kaʻiulani is sent to England for her "proper" education, she must battle internally with pressures to perform Victorian respectability and represent Hawaiʻi and her Hawaiian royal background while balancing European expectations of both. Her experiences in England cause her to question herself. In the film *Princess Kaiulani*, upon hearing that the Davies family hid information about the overthrow from her, Kaʻiulani flees and shouts, "There is no Victoria, there never was!" This tension and ultimate disavowal of "Victoria," Kaʻiulani's so-called respectable self, are embodied in the stage production as well. When Kaʻiulani, who has just been sent to England, graces the stage, two Kaʻiulanis emerge, holding hands, embodied by two actresses who weave their lines together in a dance. This movement of the two actresses together as Kaʻiulani's double consciousness conjures the trope that Native people "walk in two worlds." It teaches the audience (who may already be aware of it) of the double bind of indigeneity that must always perform in certain ways, balancing outsider expectations, personal desire, kuleana or responsibility to your culture, and the ongoing awareness that your Indigenous culture is valuable, yet denigrated. On stage, one character speaks to the audience while the other whispers in her ear. One Kaʻiulani is shy and unsure, whereas the other is an assertive woman who encourages her counterpart to take risks, have fun, and speak out. The two Kaʻiulanis vie for control of Kaʻiulani's public actions and voice.

The feminist priorities of the play become obvious, as Kaʻiulani consistently critiques the pressures exerted on women, and Native women especially. What we might today refer to as "Native feminism" is evident in Kaʻiulani's analysis of the heteropatriarchal expectations of her and the taking of her kingdom. Kaʻiulani knows that she is representative of the kingdom itself and that the suitors who seek to win her affections want her as a trophy, to, as she phrases it, "push me down with your 'love' like a stone . . . you want to use me." Kaʻiulani is uninterested in her many suitors and does not trust them because she knows that they desire her as a prize. She briefly considers marriage with one of them and sighs, saying that she'd "die a little more each day." Correlating marriage with a civil and slow death, Kaʻiulani's character leverages a critique of heteropatriarchy not heard of at the time coming from women. The script allows this critique to come through for a modern audience to ponder the motivations and actions of Kaʻiulani. The reinterpretation of history through performance thus grants a revision of how we understand our aliʻi and what we speculate Kaʻiulani's so-called truth might have been. We simply do not know. She did not leave behind journals. She did not compose mele that might have hinted at her innermost thoughts. We are left with artistic interpretations of what might have been, and in this way we can use these speculations as springboards for contemporary resistance.

Knowing full well the level of exploitation involved in marriage, particularly marriage with foreign men, the play depicts the absolute opposite of the film *Princess Kaiulani*, which prefers a narrative that erases all Indigenous men as possible partners and favors white masculinity as the obvious choice. The story of Kaʻiulani, contained as it may be in a seemingly universal narrative of an Indigenous woman torn between worlds, is actually not realized in the play or the film. She is not linked romantically to any man in the play. Perhaps Kaʻiulani would have gone on to marry David Kawananakoa and had children with him. Or maybe she would have become a territorial legislator like her cousin, Prince Jonah Kūhiō Kalanianaʻole, and helped to draft the Hawaiian Homestead Act of 1921. Maybe she would have stood with Alice Kamokila Campbell and protested statehood. Maybe she could have helped to get our country back or have somehow stopped what happened. But she didn't. She died.

The Hope of Hawaiʻi

In the final moments of the play, the audience knows what is coming: the princess's death. The script implies that Kaʻiulani may have committed suicide. As this chapter has summarized, the official history is that after horseback riding she contracted pneumonia and died prior to her marriage to Prince David Kawananakoa (although the latter is conveniently left out of many accounts). This is the official story of her death. Colonel Macfarlane told the *San Francisco Call* that her illness was exacerbated by the loss of the kingdom. Kapanui tells a different story about her death, inferring that she died in a different way and that perhaps the Kalākaua dynasty did not end with her.

I am careful about how I portray this *other* cause of Kaʻiulani's death that Kapanui shares. He insinuates that the kingdom lied about the cause of her death and covered up the real reason to protect future heirs. We must remember that Kaʻiulani was an aliʻi, and her family had the power to craft stories and disseminate certain kinds of information. Kaʻiulani was often called "the hope of Hawaiʻi." It was noted in the newspaper account that it seemed fitting that Kaʻiulani died, because as the highest-ranking heir of the Kalākaua dynasty, it made sense that she would die because the kingdom did. The narrative that her death symbolized the death of a kingdom served the arguments of annexationists who in 1899 were celebrating their successful overthrow of the government. In the play script, Kaʻiulani explains, "In those last days of mine . . . as an ex-princess I wasn't much use to my people and perhaps I knew that in my death I could be more use to them. I was young. I died at home among them. They had seen me." Then the stage goes dark, the entire space is without light, and all you can hear is the sound of funerary wailing. The sound of "uwē, uwē" can be heard for a few minutes as oli and hula envelop the perimeter of the circular stage set of Kumu Kahua Theatre. Inhabiting this space and witnessing the play cannot be fully captured in my readings here or in my quotation of the script. The space we share in the theater connects us to the creative process of all those involved in the production. As witness to this creativity, our presence challenges our contemporary absence.[50] The play, like all performances, takes on a life for those who were present in the space. When one is able to experience the performance, the affective power of the history it invokes can be felt. At the performance I saw, the audience was mostly local, and while few may have had extensive knowledge of the kingdom, everyone there had an investment in Princess Kaʻiulani and what they imagine she represents. The play moves through multiple layers of kaona, as its descriptions of plant life, bodies, hula, and movement interweave to craft a narrative of an important woman who has come to be a metaphor of the kingdom's failure.

Returning to the scenes of her death in the film and in the play, my thoughts mix these sites and bring together a nonsequential understanding of history that does not process from or in an autonomous past; it is organized by violence that has repressed and processed it into a past.[51] These voices are alive because we are open to hearing them. Kānaka Maoli are always open to hearing from our kupuna, like the security guard in the story about Kawēkiu; this has been an ongoing process that may not make itself evident in prescribed political forms but that is slowly contributing to a contemporary resurgence. The ghost tour makes you realize that history is alive and that we have an obligation to protect the dead from the dangers of the present.[52] Indigenous hauntings are powerful and maybe even magical. As Gordon notes, hauntings are about "reliving events in all their vividness, originality, and violence so as to overcome their pulsating and angering effects. Haunting is an encounter in which you touch the ghost or the ghostly matter of things. The ambiguities, the complexities of power and personhood, the violence and the hope, the looming and receding actualities, the shadows of ourselves and our society. When you touch the ghost or the ghostly matter (or when it touches you), a force that combines the injurious and the utopian, you get something different than what you expected."[53] My experience on the ghost tour led me to this research. It would have been easier to focus on circuits of Asian—particularly Japanese— immigration to Hawai'i and how the folktales of Japan and China worked to erase Hawaiian presence, as I had originally planned. I did not intend to write about Ka'iulani. In fact, prior to this research, I was somewhat dismissive of her story (although I was moved by the film, which made me bawl like a baby every time I watched it) and felt that people focused on her only because she was normatively beautiful. I was not open to thinking deeper about her life and its modern significance. I thought the honoring of ali'i, while surely an important activity, was too mainstream, an acceptable form of Kanaka Maoli respectability that was reserved for May Day parades, Hawaiian civic clubs, the Royal Order of Kamehameha, and graduates of Kamehameha Schools, and not resistant enough. I thought, *How does honoring nā ali'i challenge how we think about Hawaiian indigeneity?* But when I heard Kapanui reinterpret the cause of her death, I knew why I was there. Perhaps my kupuna and 'aumakua had something to do with it. I realized I was approaching my research in response to what people say about us and the narrow versions of Hawaiian indigeneity that have been damaging for us. I was not centering all the different performances we enact to mourn, to remember our histories, to cultivate our knowledges, and to build lāhui. The ghost tour experience is different than when you watch a play or a film. It compelled me to consider my kupuna as part of this active process, feeling myself move through colonized space, a space of violence and erasure—a familiar feeling, having grown up in Hawai'i and now living in Oregon as a settler myself, on Kalapuya land. The monotony of everyday settler colonialism requires us to push down our anger so that we can survive and perhaps live happily; it teaches us not to mourn or grieve. When moving through these cultural productions, I had to ignore knee-jerk skepticism and my own fear to focus on what becomes possible when we let the spirits move us, when we tune in to the layered histories and unspoken narratives, when we let the ghost touch us.

The play, film, and ghost tour together form spaces of survivance that prioritize and affirm undeniable Kanaka Maoli defiance.[54] The performances relayed the ways that we connect to our kupuna, to each other, and to our ali'i through memory, witnessing, and physical movement. Through performances in these multiple spaces, our claims to political primacy are evident, and the hegemony of settler colonialism is arrested. These forms of resistance may appear to be minor ones, but they actually function as subtle waves of disruption that redirect the perceived natural path of capitalist "progress" and ongoing settler colonialism. When we tell these stories, we honor Ka'iulani by thinking about her life critically, reclaiming the spaces that seek to erase or exploit us, producing defiant possibilities through our own interpretations. In these acts, we affirm the resistance of our kupuna, of Ka'iulani herself, and we empower our memories and the future of the lāhui to proliferate.[55]

CHAPTER FIVE

Bound in Place

Queer Indigenous Mobilities and "The Old Paniolo Way"

According to the 2010 U.S. Census, 45 percent of self-identified Native Hawaiians live outside of Hawai'i, a proportion that has nearly doubled since 1990.[1] One-third of off-island Kānaka Maoli live in California and nearby states. Economic realities such as the high cost of living in Hawai'i and increased job opportunities that exist beyond the islands have led to what many have referred to as the "brain drain" and what others have gone as far as to describe as an example of ethnic cleansing.[2] It is seldom discussed that Kānaka Maoli leave for noneconomic reasons. I say this not to undermine the economic justifications but to highlight that colonialism, curiosity, and even a rigid articulation of cultural nationalism can cause someone to move, signaling that the motivations behind diaspora go deeper than the high cost of living or lack of employment options. The experiences of those living in the Hawaiian diaspora, where Kanaka Maoli populations continue to call Hawai'i "home," are often an afterthought within Hawaiian studies despite this growing population. As J. Kēhaulani Kauanui astutely observed, there is little understanding that Hawaiians who may have never lived in Hawai'i also "cultivate vital links to Hawai'i as 'home.'"[3] Thinking more broadly about diaspora is required if we are going to account for what its exponential growth means for the future of the lāhui. The benefit of this conversation would be a more expansive practice of belonging, one that is grounded in genealogy and kuleana (responsibility), not in statist forms that have worked to colonize, remove, and divide us.

What kind of Natives would choose to leave their land? In what ways does making a choice to leave mark a Native as somehow *queer?* My intention is to disrupt the perception that Natives who do not live on their ancestral lands are somehow inauthentic, suffer from cultural loss, and do not have a place in the lāhui. To combat this perception, it is necessary to change our discussion of indigeneity as something always bounded by and to the land. Our genealogies and responsibilities to the land should be prioritized, but we should not lose sight of the diversity of experiences that exist within Native communities. We need to have a more robust conversation about how ideas of "the Native" are constrained by discourses that privilege presence on the land in contrast to living in the diaspora, and the impact these discourses have on belonging within our nations, communities, and ʻohanas. Ranging from economic dislocation, to land struggles, to the forms of exclusion that we internalize among ourselves, place-based forms of indigeneity tend to take precedence over the Indigenous histories of movement and travel.[4] This chapter aims to recenter our histories of movement and travel through a close reading of the short story "The Old Paniolo Way" by Kristiana Kahakauwila, in her book, *This Is Paradise*. The story offers an ambivalent response to the problem or crisis of the Hawaiian diaspora, rejecting an eventual homecoming as the only path to belonging.

Indigeneity has many routes. In the Indigenous Pacific in particular, our kupuna took many routes, traversing two-thirds of the globe's southern oceanic hemisphere. This is a 4,000-year-old history of Native globalizations, reliant solely on Indigenous technology and knowledges, with a navigational reach that populated regions from modern-day Thailand to the coasts of South and North America. These transoceanic routes have been passed on to us through our moʻolelo and "proven" by Western science, but the contemporary circuits through which we route our claims to place and belonging remain centers of precarity. For Indigenous peoples who have been displaced by the machinations of settler colonialism, the desire to come "home" is a wish that many are unable to attain. Our diaspora is in fact required, especially when we are in Hawaiʻi. As the educator, scholar, and activist Kaleikoa Kaʻeo asserted in the film *Noho Hewa* (2009), Kānaka Maoli are always at risk of being removed, even when we're in the ground.[5] Given this terrain of epistemic and physical violence, Kānaka Maoli who live in Hawaiʻi struggle daily with multiple levels of settler violence and U.S. military occupation in our own homelands. Being Kanaka Maoli can make you feel consistently out of place and, indeed, literally push you out of your place. This is the paradox and price of "paradise." Kānaka Maoli are celebrated in earnest yet saccharine representations of "Hawaiian culture," while actual Kanaka Maoli people struggle to live a good life in the islands as we are dispossessed of our inherent right to sovereignty daily. This ongoing struggle thus makes it appear that Kanaka who chose to leave Hawaiʻi are somehow giving up on their indigeneity. Setting up a binary wherein on-island Kānaka and off-island Kānaka are seen as opposites, Kānaka Maoli living away from Hawaiʻi are perceived to have abandoned their indigeneity, choosing to assimilate into American society, and those who remain on the land have not.

Our Indigenous Pacific epistemologies offer a more vibrant way of thinking about this. Tevita Kaʻili's theorization of the Tongan concept of the tauhi vā outlines how Pacific Islanders have always been in movement, noting that their long-distance travels made islanders some of the most widely dispersed peoples in the world and that this allowed them to link distant island communities and to establish far-reaching exchange and social networks.[6] "Vā" in Tongan is also "wā" in Hawaiian. The "vā" is defined as the space in between—not empty space that separates, but space that relates, bringing separate entities together.[7] Contrary to the politics of size that understands our islands as disconnected dots on a map, our world is expansive—Oceania is a sea of islands, not a bunch of islands in a distant sea. The scholar and novelist Epeli Hauʻofa's game-changing concept of the "sea of islands" reframed the supposedly "empty" and isolated oceanic island expanses that characterized the Pacific as a full and connected Oceania where the sea was the source of life and the way Pacific peoples were all genealogically connected to each other. Acknowledging our oceanic mobilities as well as our landedness is exceedingly necessary in the contemporary moment, when our "smallness" continues to be used as a justification of our colonization and occupation—both in terms of policy and in our minds. This works to further distance us from the Indigenous dreaming that motivated our travel to begin with. Rather than allow a belittling determinist view of the Moana Nui (Oceania) to define who we are, Pacific Islanders have taken up the conceptualization of the "sea of islands" to reorient how we view ourselves and the natural and spiritual worlds—including especially the surrounding ocean, the underworld, and the heavens.

Like the sea of islands concept, Kaʻili's theorization emphasizes connection across the diaspora—not division—through a discussion of space and transnational practices.[8] Transnational migrants reconfigure space as they live in two or more nation-states because of the ways that they are sociospatially connected through genealogy.[9] As David Gegeo explains, indigeneity is formed through sociospatial ties. The Kwaraʻae people of the Solomon Islands, for example, carry their homelands with them wherever they travel.[10] Kwaraʻae people do not stop being Indigenous when they migrate; rather, they carry their place and indigeneity with them to new spaces. My point is not to overly romanticize diasporic indigeneity, but to challenge the pernicious notion that Indigenous people who do not live in their homeland become less Native the longer they are away from "home."[11] Drawing on Renya Ramirez's concept of "native hubs," we must include diasporic

Natives in nationhood but not in a way that prioritizes either landedness or being in diaspora. Rather than affirming the so-called authenticity of "the Native" on the land or viewing "the Native" in diaspora as superior or "hybrid," all Kānaka are seen as valuable parts of the lāhui, which breeds the possibility of alliances and connections. This strengthens our indigeneity wherever we are.[12] As Vicente Diaz and Kēhaulani Kauanui remind us, we can acknowledge Natives who are defined by landedness while also centering the sea and recognizing these distinctions, but not to place them in hierarchal relation with one another. Keeping this flexibility is a tactical formation for Indigenous political and cultural struggles.[13]

Returning to the ʻōlelo noʻeau invoked in the preface, "I ulu nō ka lālā i ke kumu" (translated as "The branches grow because of the trunk") describes what it means to be rooted in the land, but at the same time it also reminds us to think about the Kānaka Maoli who are routed to the ends of the branches and leaves, those who are most at risk of falling off. This tree is crucial to the histories of mobility in Pacific, as Hauʻofa explained:

> The people of the island of Tanna in Vanuatu conceive of their universe in terms of the tree and the canoe. The tree symbolises rootedness in culture, while the canoe stands for movements along sea routes that connect people of different island locations. The canoe is history—the working out of relationships established through travel and movement of materials from one island to another. One may extend this metaphor to include present-day connections between Oceania and the surrounding continental landmasses and cultures. One may even say that since it is made of wood, the canoe is part of the tree, and its potentials are to a large extent determined by the qualities of the tree from which it was made.[14]

The tree as canoe is a useful metaphor—even if we travel in jumbo jets now—because it is a central system through which our genealogies are rooted, routed, connected, and held. This is the core of our Indigenous circuitry. ʻŌlelo noʻeau came from the way our kupuna viewed the world. The tree represents our roots and routes, making possible our ongoing movement and accountability toward one another and the performances of aloha that are necessary to remember and maintain these connections. We must recall the multiple purposes of the tree in order to focus on what sustains our ʻohana and lāhui. The tree and the canoe constitute both the rooted and routed realities of Pacific diaspora where connection should be more important than distance and division in Oceania.[15] "The Old Paniolo Way" describes a form of indigeneity that is old and rooted; but when it becomes routed, it facilitates a certain kind of mobility that queers both understandings of diaspora and indigeneity itself.

Bringing together Native Pacific cultural studies, Native feminist analysis, and queer of color critique, I examine how aloha is performed when it comes home from the diaspora. I build upon Elizabeth Deloughrey's application of Kamau Brathwaite's theory of "tidalectics" to the Indigenous Pacific. As a methodological tool, tidalectics provides an approach to explore the interconnected realities between the land and sea, diaspora and indigeneity, and routes and roots.[16] Based on a cyclical model of movement, tidalectics "foregrounds alter/native epistemologies to western colonialism and its linear and materialist biases."[17] In addition, I draw from works on queer diaspora to contest and rethink the pervading rhetoric that "situates the terms 'queer' and 'diaspora' as dependent on the originality of 'heterosexuality' and 'nation.'"[18] I invoke queer diasporic critique not to erase the specificity of indigeneity to lands or oceans, nor to turn Indigenous peoples in the diaspora into settlers who deny the indigeneity or nationhood of peoples on whose lands they reside, but to contemplate the ways in which national belonging is stripped from Indigenous peoples in the diaspora, which denies our Indigenous self-determination. Centered in this chapter is the subject of the diasporic indigene. As Hokulani Aikau has described them, diasporic indigenes are Natives who are no longer living in their homeland yet carry their history of dispossession with them while settling in the diaspora, troubling binaries of native/settler and colonized/colonizer.[19] In defiance of binaries, the diasporic indigene is also queered because it questions the underlying logic that binds "the Native" to the land and the perceived normalcy of heteropatriarchal nationalisms. My analysis reminds us that "the Native" is in movement and that indigeneity can also be understood in terms of mobility and transformation without compromising its genealogical links to the land, ocean, and other Indigenous peoples. "The Old Paniolo Way" makes multiple allusions to the ways that indigeneity and Hawaiian belonging require certain performances that are bound by old ways of being, but when in movement produce new forms of indigeneity that are always connected to the past. Together, this framework can address the complexities of Hawaiian diaspora, emphasizing Indigenous epistemologies that do not rely on narratives of linear progress, landedness, and material evidence, thus opening up a space to reimagine and put into practice a more dynamic performance of diasporic connectivity and Indigenous mobility. In what follows, I perform a close reading of "The Old Paniolo

Way" to highlight the various ways that Kānaka Maoli maintain relations within our community and within our ʻohana. The story ultimately requires us to be accountable to one another and to teach ourselves that this kind of belonging in or out of the diaspora takes work.

Despite living most of their lives on "the continent," those in the diaspora maintain a connection to home and solidarity with Hawaiian political struggles, as evidenced in the outpouring of support for the protectors of Mauna Kea who are opposing the construction of a thirty-meter telescope on this sacred mountain, which for Kānaka Maoli is not only a site we revere for its sacredness but also our kupuna, our ancestor. It is where our islands began. In the spring of 2015, Hawaiian social media networks erupted over images of the Kanaka Maoli celebrity Jason Momoa posting "We are Mauna Kea" on his Instagram account. Bringing worldwide attention to this struggle, Momoa inspired Kānaka Maoli all over the world to post images of themselves in the same way that he did, with the words "We are Mauna Kea" etched on signs and frequently on their bodies. He made visible the Hawaiian diaspora to the world and, most importantly, to Kānaka Maoli in the islands. Himself a product of the Hawaiian diaspora, growing up in Iowa with his mother, and estranged from his Hawaiian father, Momoa has spent much of his adult life reconnecting to his Hawaiian ancestry and portraying characters who marshal their indigeneity as the source of their strength. In a very public forum, his celebrity status compelled these images to be shared and reposted. Momoa's diasporic body harnessed others in the diaspora to stand up for Mauna Kea, showing that the Indigenous Hawaiians of the diaspora were not lost, assimilated, depoliticized, or disappeared. As his original post faded into the background, the ongoing flurry of images of Kānaka Maoli all over the world displayed the presence of a thriving and dispersed sense of lāhui, one with deep routes and roots affirming an expression of Hawaiian indigeneity that had not been compromised, despite its presence across Turtle Island and in other places, some as far away as Japan, Denmark, and Brazil.[20]

This online moment initially felt like a blip, but it turned into a flash point for the Kanaka Maoli people. It brought visibility to the diaspora in a way that expressed explicitly our solidarity with the protectors of Mauna Kea and our unwavering indigeneity. As the Hawaiian diaspora continues to grow and as the fight for Hawaiian federal recognition or independence continues to produce heated debates about the future of the Kanaka Maoli people, efforts must be made to include the diaspora. Recognizing Kānaka Maoli outside of Hawaiʻi can help to strengthen sovereignty rights based on indigeneity, by acknowledging that even those not in residence have national claims.[21] Additionally, accounting for the way that belonging is achieved "at home" and in the diaspora can teach us a great deal about how we can uplift and sustain the diversity of our lāhui. Thus, one of the primary goals of this chapter is to challenge how we think about diaspora as solely a product of colonialism or settler colonialism, to create space for the range of Kanaka Maoli indigeneity, and to disrupt the perceived heterosexuality of an emergent Hawaiian nation. To answer the question, What kind of Natives would choose to leave their land?, I highlight the intimate, affective lives of Kānaka Maoli who left, those who are difficult to track because hard data about their lives does not exist or is assumed to be insignificant, because these voices and sentiments are on the edges of how we think about Hawaiian indigeneity. To change this, we must reconceive the future of our lāhui and what it might look like for Kānaka Maoli who now live in the diaspora. We need a renewed understanding of the ways in which we maintain relations and connections (not how we lose them) in the diaspora within our community and families through practices of aloha.

I have lived ten years on the continent. I continue to meet so many Kānaka Maoli and their ʻohana who have lived away from Hawaiʻi for multiple generations, and they tell a familiar story. Their mom married a guy in the military, so they moved to San Diego. Their dad was disgruntled with statehood, so he fled. Their grandfather was a laborer who eventually stayed in Washington. They went away for college and decided to stay. They wanted to move back but didn't know where they would fit or how they could sustain themselves. It seemed okay out here. There are more opportunities here. Hawaiʻi was no longer the place they left. "I believe in sovereignty, but I'm not sure how it applies to us out here" is a common sentiment. Admittedly, before I left Hawaiʻi I never pondered what life was like for Kānaka Maoli who lived away, even those in my own family. I just counted on seeing them during their regular summer trips or at funerals, weddings, or baby lūʻaus every few years. The longer I lived in the diaspora and the more I learned from Kānaka Maoli there, the more I realized that as a lāhui we have largely ignored the concerns of those living in the diaspora, neglecting to consider the ways we could help the diaspora feel more connected to movements in the islands; nor have we examined how the emphasis on living on the ʻāina as a determinant of our indigeneity can isolate Kānaka Maoli who do not share that experience. This is not to negate that we come from the ʻāina and have primordial and contemporary claims to it; of course we must assert this in the face of settler colonialism. Across the Indigenous

Pacific there are place-based indigeneities tied to the land, and there are others that understand their indigeneity as inextricably linked with the Moana. Kānaka Maoli have reached a moment when the latter must be expressed alongside our indigeneity on the land. Rather than focus solely on what is lost, we should cultivate strategies to produce new forms of belonging and possibilities for Indigenous connection and mobility. We need more stories about Kānaka Maoli who live in the diaspora, and we need more stories about queer Kānaka Maoli in the diaspora. This is more than a call to talk about queer Natives, although that is necessary too. We need to queer the way we currently talk about a lived relationship to the land as the only way to be Indigenous or belong in the Hawaiian community.

"The Old Paniolo Way" provides a detailed glimpse of the diasporic Kanaka Maoli experience that we rarely hear, representing how quotidian Hawaiian spaces serve as crucial sites of making and remaking home and the attendant struggle to maintain connections in the diaspora. Within the quotidian, life is performed. We see the enactment of relationships that cannot be archived, those that cannot be fully captured by outsiders. In her short stories, Kahakauwila offers an opportunity to animate the actual complexities of coming home from the diaspora, exhibiting varying senses of Indigenous belonging and Indigenous understandings of place, history, and time. Kahakauwila's characters exhibit new ways of thinking about Hawaiian diaspora because they prioritize oceanic movement as well as land-based indigeneity. While the characters certainly aspire to be home and belong, they also express those feelings with some ambiguity about the need to "come home" permanently in order to feel welcomed, and they revise the notion that Kānaka Maoli in the diaspora do not have a place in the Hawaiian future.

Queer Indigenous Diasporas

It is a common trope in Hawai'i that when you are gay you move to the mainland, usually San Francisco (back when it was affordable). I cannot even count the number of friends I had who ran off to San Francisco as quickly as they could. Within the Hawaiian gay community there is a sense that there has got to be more somewhere else. I recall many young gay Hawaiians (including myself and Asian settlers) aspiring to move to San Francisco, New York City, Seattle, or Los Angeles because they imagined these continental cities as spaces of queer urbanity that promised the possibilities of fabulousness. Most of the ones who were able to actually move were men.

Some got into school on the mainland and went to college. Others hustled their way working retail and waiting tables, eventually moving together as a group, or one person went and then everyone slowly followed. It was something we all aspired to. Some people moved away to come out, but never came out at home. Others came out and then came home as a kind of strategy to show themselves that they could make it on their own "on the mainland." Their motivations were not unlike the fantasies of rural people about moving to urban centers, or the desires of islanders to relocate to continents—anywhere but the smallness, the seemingly antiquated space, of home. Reminiscent of the longings of postcolonial subjects who yearn to live in the metropole, relocating to the mainland is promoted as a modern experience that separates those who can travel from those who must stay in place, static and unchanging. Often, leaving Hawai'i is seen as a mark of success, being able to make it in a non-Hawaiian space, as though you have transcended your meager Indigenous beginnings. This desire for movement is not inherently negative, but there are certainly risks of erasure—around indigeneity and, in this case, sexuality too.

"The Old Paniolo Way" tells the experience of Pili, who comes home to the Big Island of Hawai'i from San Francisco to take care of his ailing father. Pili comes from a family of paniolos, which in the Hawaiian context is shorthand for cowboys. In the early nineteenth century, Mexican vaqueros were contracted to work on the Parker Ranch in Waimea on the Big Island. Vaqueros trained Hawaiians to herd cattle and ride horses, creating a paniolo culture across the islands that remains to this day. Pili left his family's ranch to live in San Francisco, where he works in advertising. Not being out to his family—his sister, Maile, and his father, Harrison—Pili struggles with what it means to come out in the diaspora but not at home. Harrison is on his deathbed and is nursed by Albert, with whom Pili begins a relationship. As Pili contemplates coming out to his father, Maile and Albert urge him to consider who he would be coming out for. Pili manages to do so in his own way before his father passes away. The story ends with no resolution for Pili and Albert in terms of their relationship, and Maile is left wondering whether Pili will stay or go back to the mainland for good (as is the reader), as the story ends with Pili saying that he will be back "as soon as I can."

The story begins with an interaction between Pili and his father, Harrison, as the latter is telling him to grab something—"Dat thing!," spoken in pidgin English. Harrison motions for Pili to grab a wool turquoise saddle blanket decorated with a pattern of dark blue waves, which Harrison gave to his deceased wife (Pili and Maile's mother) when they got married. Setting up the relationship within a family, which is one of shared understanding of things that do not explicitly get said, the blanket is a recurrent object throughout the story, functioning as a vehicle for dreaming, warmth, and belonging. Pili recalls how as a child he would use the blanket as a magic carpet to transport him to faraway places and at other times use it to jump off the hayloft in the barn, slowly floating into big heaps of hay. Memories of childhood pepper the story as Pili rethinks his life choices and his desire to leave behind the smallness of the ranch.

Albert has never left home. Unlike Pili, he does not feel out of place because of his sexuality. He has found a place, even though he is in the closet. Albert's behavior is indicative of what Deceno Carlos Ulises describes as a necessary shift in how people think about self-definition and coming out. Queer people of color (and I would add Indigenous people too) often refuse the "reductionism gayness engenders in the public sphere" because sexuality is not the only factor in their identities.[22] Albert is content to stay on the Big Island, where he is known as a good person, especially because he cared for his grandmother, and has not left his family or the community behind. While Albert admits that he sometimes longs for other places, he is less conflicted in his life than Pili, who lives on the mainland, "out of the closet" and supposedly more "free" in San Francisco. Through his relationship with Albert, Pili slowly begins to understand how his time away has inhibited his relationship with his family. As Pili takes care of his father, he struggles with explaining to everyone—his father, his sister, and the surrounding community—why he isn't married, why he doesn't have children, and why he has stayed away for so long. He learns through this process the sacrifices that he has made (and those his sister has made) in order to live his life openly away from Hawai'i. The story questions, at first blush, the need to come out in queer Indigenous contexts.

Diaspora has a long history within LGBTQ communities. Since the late nineteenth and early twentieth centuries, same-sex-desiring men who had the means began traveling the globe.[23] The rise of gay identity coincided with the proliferation of industrialization, which transformed the ways that people sought intimacy and pleasure. This allowed sexuality to be separated from procreation, making possible the formation of urban communities of LGBTQ populations and a politics based on sexual identity.[24] Movement from small towns to urban locations has been a common tale for the creation of LGBTQ social networks that at one time were termed "queer." By moving, subjects could come out, but only when "home" is left behind. To fully free oneself from the binding that comes with home and cultures of heteropatriarchy and their attendant domesticity, leaving was necessary. As an act of agency, these movements were made as a choice to secure physical and psychological well-being, and in this choice, relocation to more sexually open cities and towns was imagined to free queer subjects of the shackles of their respective homes.

White gay liberal subjects especially benefited from the creation of gay communities and the rights-based campaigns that characterized the late twentieth century. In the process, they have normalized a version of the LGBTQ community that does not challenge the status quo of the settler state. The collusion of the respectable LGBTQ subject with the U.S. nation-state operates in a different way for people of color and queer Natives, who may at different moments be purposefully excluded or included in state narratives of "tolerance" and inclusion. Natives especially bear the brunt of ongoing settler colonialism because, as Scott Morgensen asserts, when non-Natives (including people of color) form shared identities and movements to claim sexual citizenship, they do so through settler-colonial formations that naturalize settlement, thus creating settler homonational-ism that is predicated on Native disappearance.[25] As Qwo-li Driskill has written, while queer people of color resist empire and heteronormative nationalism through a critique of diaspora, such a critique also requires an interrogation of what diaspora means for Indigenous peoples in the United States and Canada, who are often excluded from the queer of color critiques of diaspora.[26] Driskill describes a "two-spirit critique" that diverges from other queer critiques because it roots itself in Native histories, politics, and decolonial struggles to challenge both white-dominated queer theory and queer of color critique's near-erasure of Native people and nations. Driskill and others foreground tribally specific traditions that contest heteronormativity and the ongoing impact of colonialism on the expression of Indigenous sexualities and sovereignties.[27]

For queer Natives, leaving home might provide freedom from the colonial imposition of heteronormativity in their communities, where it has taken on the semblance of being natural, rather than a missionary introduction, such as in the case of Hawai'i. This is similar to what Manolo Guzman refers to as a "sexile," defined as the "migration of queer folk globally, a neologism that refers to the exile of those who have had to leave their nations of origins on account of their sexual orientation."[28] The movements of Kanaka Maoli queers to places like San Francisco and Los Angeles are an example of a Hawaiian "sexile," which we see in the example of Pili in the story, although this motivation is seldom discussed within Hawaiian communities. While sometimes liberating, these movements contain huge risks and consequences, such as cultural isolation and the discrimination Natives face from LGBTQ communities who sometimes have little or no knowledge of (or interest in) the history of Indigenous genocide in the Americas or colonialism in the Pacific. Further, because of the limited space for queer Native organizing on the continent and within LGBTQ communities, queer Hawaiians run the risk of further distancing themselves from indigeneity when they also fail to make connections with the Indigenous peoples of the lands they live upon.

Much of the dominant discourse within LGBTQ communities is that coming out is a necessary personal act for nonheterosexual folks that ushers them into the public sphere as a "queer" or as a nonnormative heterosexual person. Queer people of color have since rejected coming out and leaving your community as being a "white" and homonormative requirement that isolates queer people of color from the social networks that they need to survive as persons of color in a white supremacist system and world. White queerness can certainly be colonizing, prioritizing homonormative political agendas such as marriage quality. Hawai'i was notably the first U.S. state to hear legal arguments for same-sex marriage when three gay and lesbian couples filed for marriage licenses in 1991. Media coverage of same-sex marriage in local, national, and international media was extensive. In public testimony, newspaper articles, and editorials, supporters of same-sex marriage invoked the "spirit of aloha" as the reason same-sex marriage should be legalized in Hawai'i. The enduring residues of nineteenth-century colonial discourse, which painted the Pacific as a place where people were freed from moral constraints, causing them to "give in to their senses" and transgress sexual taboos, only exacerbated the perception that same-sex relations were "normal" in Hawai'i.[29]

Indeed, it is the knowledge of nonheteronormative relationships that continues to cast Hawai'i and the Pacific as spaces of the erotic and exotic, as cited repeatedly in the press. During the early years of the struggle for same-sex marriage in Hawai'i, the debate spoke to deep anxieties about Hawai'i's global image and its economic reliance on tourism. With Hawai'i's ailing economy based almost entirely on tourism, same-sex marriage and its impact on Hawai'i's reputation were certainly contentious issues. Hawai'i eventually became the first state to legally ban same-sex marriage (in 1998). Present-day representations of Hawai'i as a land of sand, sun, and fun, as a place where you can be free and "feel the aloha spirit," ironically hinge on the very processes by which Kanaka Maoli land and sexuality were colonized to fit within a Western capitalist model. Throughout the late nineteenth century, Kanaka Maoli sexuality was domesticated to serve Christian morality, to ready us both for salvation and for capitalist development.[30] These political transformations are rarely referenced in mainstream media coverage, particularly in the LGBTQ press, which typically favors a story about Hawaiian history that focuses on how Christianity transformed sexuality, while ignoring the role of the United States in the overthrow of the Hawaiian Kingdom or the way capitalist enterprise dispossessed Kānaka Maoli of our lands. Pili's narrative exists against this backdrop, representing the histories of colonialism that constrain Native lives, notably self-definition and gender and sexual expression. The tensions between mainstream American visions of LGBTQ life are referenced as antithetical to the Indigenous-based forms of gender and sexuality that get squeezed into Western categories but also continue to exist outside of them. While on a mainstream stage, coming out has lost its radical thrust and is now a "normal" part of becoming a gay subject, on an everyday level many people still struggle with discrimination within their families and communities. For many people of color and Indigenous peoples, coming out comes with a huge price.[31]

Pili never really comes out to his father in the conventional way that has been termed by some as a "confession" which rests itself on juridical forms of guilt and requests for forgiveness, as though the queer coming out were committing a sin (as explored in chapter 3). Albert is quick to warn Pili that he would be coming out at this point, as his father lays dying, only to make himself feel better. Albert rejects the dominant LGBTQ notion that one must assert one's independence to become one's true self or become free. Instead, Albert and Maile remind Pili what it is like to exist together as an 'ohana. Albert favors his own silence in order to remain connected with his family. As a form of coming out, Pili simply states to his father, while the latter is on his deathbed, that he has learned to appreciate men. Pili explains to his father how important Albert, his nurse, is to their family. Pili asks his father if he can give Albert the turquoise saddle blanket that belonged to their mother. This gifting maintains the reciprocal modes of aloha wherein "aloha is better understood in an 'ohana setting where all people contribute for mutual benefit."[32] In this gifting, Pili acknowledges the crucial role Albert has played for his father, his sister, and his family and wants to extend that aloha to him for the care he has provided (even if he is a paid nurse). Though Harrison lies in a coma, it is clear to everyone in the scene what is happening: it is a welcoming of Albert in relation to the entire family, not just in relation to Pili. Indeed, Albert was already part of the family even before Pili came home; this is illustrated in the relationship Albert has with Harrison and with Maile, who claims Albert as her only friend. The relationship of Pili and Albert is sidelined in favor of expressing the kinship that now exists for everyone in the family. Rather than name this as Pili's coming out moment, it is turned into an opportunity to acknowledge Albert, whose relationship to the other characters and ongoing presence exhibit how community belonging takes places through mutual reciprocity, respect, and care. The story culminates with this scene and Harrison's eventual passing. At the postfuneral gathering, the extended family of aunties and uncles thank Albert for the care he provided and welcome him to the family, not knowing the extent of his relationship with Pili specifically. Maile jokes that if Albert and Pili get married, Albert would be a hit. Despite the presence of this utopic moment near the story's end, my goal here is not to celebrate a story of LGBTQ inclusion, because it would be a lie. It would also be untrue to say that Pili and all the actual people he represents, including myself, have not gone through the multilayered experience of belonging and not-belonging in our communities because we are LGBTQ-identified. By explaining to his father the importance of Albert to the entire family, Pili refuses coming out in the way most people imagine it. The story reminds us that the feeling of belonging and welcome at the end of the story becomes possible only through the practice of aloha where family and kin networks, genealogies, and working together are prioritized over the self.

Bound in Place

The peopling of the vast area known as Oceania, what we call the Moana Nui, occurred through multiple migrations.[33] In other words, Pacific diaspora is not new; one might even argue that it is traditional. This is supported by oral and written archives and scientific and archaeological evidence—both Western and Indigenous. Our ancestors navigated the vast Moana that Magellan incorrectly named "the Pacific" and developed formidable cultures that honored the lands and seas. It does not mean that Kānaka Maoli in the diaspora do not ache for "home" at the same time they live happy lives elsewhere. The accoutrements of diaspora—displacement, dispossession, breaking up of the family, forced migration, colonization—are frighteningly common, and it is imperative to contextualize the specificities of these movements rather than subsume them solely under the negative. Holding onto only the negative valences of diaspora keeps indigeneity fixed. We must remember that it was colonialism and, later, anthropology that endeavored to keep Indigenous peoples locked in place. European men as travelers, missionaries, and colonial administrators imposed heteropatriarchy on the peoples they encountered and colonized. In the process, they undermined the Indigenous knowledges and epistemologies that viewed the land and sea as mutually constituting homelands.

The problem with representing "the Native" or Pacific peoples as "simply" rooted, as Margaret Jolly challenges, is that when you continue to "ground" people in the land, as a kind of static place and time, you represent Europeans or Asians as mobile explorers. This perpetuates a temporal language that portrays Islanders as stuck in the past, stagnant in tradition, making foreigners (mostly men) agents of change and transformation.[34] Jolly cautions that creating identities based solely on roots or routes (without the other) can create harmful dichotomies that deny the lives of those who have followed routes beyond the ocean yet still celebrate their roots back home. She describes what Pacific scholars have noted, that is, Pacific Islanders "deploy metaphors of both groundedness and mobility, settlement and detachment to articulate their being in the world."[35] During a fight with Maile, Pili feels "bound in place" (217). To be bound can have multiple meanings—tied in a bind; a legal or moral obligation; a destiny, or a path that is leading somewhere; a leaping movement upward or forward. Being "bound in place" for Pili represents familial pressures, but also those of indigeneity that might immobilize "the Native" on the land. Being bound connects to the other thematic of the story, which focuses on an "old paniolo way of life" and its tensions in the present. "Way," like "bound," signifies being as well as a movement along a path, a course of travel that leads somewhere. The experience of Pili represents the movement of indigeneity as it reaches and traverses its own territorial limits and the limiting values imbued in the performance of indigeneity itself. Bringing these ideas together illustrates how necessary it is, then, to push and leap toward a different course of indigeneity, one that is not absolutely bound to the land, yet recognizes that a connection to the land while living in the diaspora is another way in which indigeneity can be performed.

Returning to Teresia Teaiwa's theorizations of Pacific subjectivity, Pili defies colonial constructions that keep Native subjectivity as singular and unmoving, exemplifying an articulation of "the Native," that is both fluid and complex, not absolutely bounded. Pili is both bound in place and to it, as "the Native" is grounded in land and identifies itself through kinship networks that can provide mobility and fluidity that confounds and disrupts colonial, nationalist and even postcolonial representations.[36] The emphasis on mobility and fluidity connects to these histories that Pacific Islanders share and must prioritize when we think about Indigenous performance, identity, and diaspora. It doesn't have to be final and "Indigenous" and "diaspora" are two concepts that should not be thought of us opposite. As Pacific Island scholars have explained, Pacific indigeneity has always been about movement and that tradition was always a dialogic process, fusing different elements together throughout time, making new traditions.

"Diaspora" belongs to the Greek root *speirō*, meaning "to sow," with Greek derivations of this root used in scientific terminology, e.g. *sperma* meaning to "scatter seed," which infers that diaspora, that is, travel, can only be male, via the spreading of seed in the form of sperm.[37] This cannot stand. It is imperative to challenge the manner in which heteropatriarchy informs the discourse on diaspora and landedness; as Deloughrey writes, "The discourse of diaspora is constituted in relation to the stabilizing notions of femininity, nation, and indigeneity."[38] In Western history, specifically British maritime history, men had the agency to travel, explore, and be in movement. They did so in the name of women (and nation), leaving women and "home" behind in the domestic static space of the feminine. In the Indigenous Pacific, many stories detail the special role of women in navigation.[39] Because of colonization, this has of course changed. In Satawal, for example, which is part of the Caroline Islands in Micronesia, girls used to be trained as navigators, although now it is mostly a male activity. In the Hawaiian context, in the process of colonization, women were encouraged to adopt Christian forms of domesticity. Much of the early diaspora was gendered male too, often in the movement of sailors, fur workers, and Forty-Niners. In this sense, although there is a history of Pacific women who traveled, under colonialism Hawaiian women were relegated to domestic space. This is why high-ranking Hawaiian women—the queens and princesses of the Hawaiian Kingdom—troubled European and American men, because while on the surface they adopted the norms of Victorian womanhood, they still retained their chiefly rank and refused to be relegated to the private sphere (see chapter 4). These women and Hawai'i itself had to be domesticated and contained within the home under the physical and ideological control of an emergent U.S. empire. I bring this up to emphasize that the discourse on diaspora and landedness replicated colonial figurations of heteropatriarchy wherein men would travel and women would not. These ideas traveled across the Pacific. Thus, when we acknowledge the longer history of Pacific movement and the vital role of women both on the land and in the water, we honor the history of Pacific navigation and movement and recognize it as an ongoing process that should still be active today.

Despite the proud history of Pacific women in navigation and in movement—or what Disney's *Moana* hopes to sell you—in the contemporary Pacific it is often women who carry the burden of staying. Within "The Old Paniolo Way" there is a clear gender division within the home. Maile is surrounded by men—her brother, father, and Albert. Maile does everything for them. She takes care of their father, Harrison, and cooks for Pili, Harrison, and Albert nightly. Pili assumes that she does all this to impress Albert, but Pili soon begins to realize that Maile does all this in order to keep the family together and away from conflict. She sacrifices herself for the family. Living in the diaspora, Pili forgets what it is like to be home, but within the intimacies of domestic space the practices of aloha become clear to him. It is Maile who is most bound in place, which contributes to her subtle resentment of her brother, whom she covers for, telling her father that he hasn't yet found the right "wahine." Maile does not have children, which is also used as an example of her failed femininity despite her faithful performance of family duties, as her father worries how the ranch will go on, as Pili is given a subtle pass because he is living away from home. As the only woman in the household, she is the butt of frequent jokes among the men.

The confinement of Maile to the home is analogous to the binding of "the Native" to the land. Colonialism worked to contain Natives within certain spaces the same way that heteropatriarchy continues to curtail women's agency. These ideas are carried within the Hawaiian community in particular ways, as exhibited by Maile in the story. At the same time, we also know that in multiple examples, Native women actively refuse these forms of containment by prioritizing Indigenous culture and knowledge. Native peoples have always disrupted these notions of what they ought to be, contributing to an overall Native sense of flexibility and innovation. In the Pacific, Islanders similarly base their own common sense on a fluidity of being in the world.[40] In the interest of truly living this fluidity, the next section discusses how pursuing our liberation from settler colonialism requires foregrounding a critique of the heteropatriarchal undercurrents of nationalism. We must articulate a desire to take our lāhui somewhere else than where colonialism has taken us, or indeed, where colonialism attempts to leave us.

Desiring a Rudder

Returning to the earlier discussion of how diaspora is perceived as a masculine activity, Deloughrey writes that travel was possible only through the discourse of women as land and as sites of reproduction, in contrast to the masculine discourse of diaspora and globalization. As embodied in the word "diaspora" itself, these connections "arise from a complex metaphysical association between sperm, blood, and spatial dispersal (for trade and racial regeneration)."[41] When diaspora is privileged as a male activity, we further perpetuate it as a site of reproduction via sperm and blood, constituting a solely biological connection over the various forms of culture and belonging that question and reconstitute diasporic networks at home and abroad. Yet there are these moments when diasporic subjects are confronted with the loss of home, and they seek guidance by those who have knowledge of life on the land. Throughout the story, Pili is confused and inspired by Albert's ability to remain in the closet and appear seemingly content. Albert does not express regret, sadness, or anger over this choice. Pili describes Albert as the better part of his conscience (193). Enamored of Albert, Pili says that he desires a rudder in him, to guide and steer him.

As a crucial part of travel, a rudder is attached to the back of a boat or plane and used to steer and balance the craft. The desire for a rudder infers that Pili sometimes feels lost in the diaspora and that Albert, as a representation of Hawaiian culture and home, is the thing he desires to reconnect with. Certainly, living in the diaspora can make you feel rejected and lost. Kānaka Maoli take very seriously the idea that "to lose one's place, to not know where one's island is, or to no longer be possessed by that island, is to be perilously lost at sea." This issue is raised by Diaz and Kauanui, who ask, "What happens when the grounds of indigeneity (of Pacific Islanderness) get too fixed or move too far?"[42] The rudder is crucial to movement, but Pili's desire for a rudder is indicative of the gap between cultural expectations of what family duty and, in some sense, reproduction must look like and what, in practice, it means to belong to and care for your family. This is why the theories of queer diaspora are useful in the Hawaiian context.

Queer diaspora understood in a Hawaiian nationalist context declines the normative impulse to recuperate the lāhui in nation-state form, to celebrate heteronormative notions of social belonging and racial exclusion (based on blood quantum) that the nation-state would seek to naturalize and legitimate through the inherited logics of kinship, blood, and identity. Instead of valorizing a "traditional" Hawaiian or state-imposed theory of blood quantum, this method values Hawaiian forms of belonging and knowledge that uplift the actual meaning of helping each other, of having aloha for one another. The methodology of queer diasporas denaturalizes the racialized rhetorics that articulate lāhui with biological inheritance and frame queerness as antithetical to the lāhui and Hawaiian indigeneity itself. This idea connects to the ongoing margins of Hawaiian indigeneity that I have discussed throughout this book, and furthermore, to the disturbing notion that Kānaka Maoli cannot be part of the nation unless they are "reproducing it" in a heteronormative way. As Native feminists have discussed, Native women are penalized for their sexual and reproductive choices in ways that men are not. Haunani-Kay Trask wrote in the 1980s about her difficulties within the Hawaiian nationalist movement because she was viewed with distrust as an unmarried woman without children, thus putting her Hawaiianness in question; and worse, people feared she was a lesbian.[43] Similarly, as Kanaka Maoli feminists such as Kēhaulani Kauanui and Maile Arvin have both discussed, Hawaiian women face pressures to have children with Hawaiian men to "build the lāhui" or "save the race."[44] As Arvin describes, we should center critiques of blood quantum while also highlighting alternative modes of recognition and regeneration that keep Native communities together, not divide them.

Many Kānaka Maoli acknowledge the historical and contemporary diversity of gender expression and sexuality within Hawaiian communities. Certainly, ʻohanas were large, and hānai was a common practice. Some of the highest-ranking aliʻi were "hānai" (adopted) into other royal lineages. Queen Liliʻuokalani herself was hānai and had hānai children. When Christian missionaries and Europeans came to Hawaiʻi and inserted themselves (by invitation in many cases) in the government, rigid domestic family structures and restrictions on particular kinds of sexual practices were imposed and were institutionalized in the nineteenth-century legal codes. Many Kānaka Maoli actively adopted these practices as they converted to Christianity, but they also retained other "traditional" practices. There were indeed legal consequences for not adhering to gender and sexual behaviors based on biological sex and Christian morality. As a result, many Kānaka Maoli are very attached to performances of Hawaiian respectability as it is wrapped up in heteronormativity. At the same time, we can be very inclusive and welcoming of those within our ʻohana who stray from the norm, for example in the case of māhūs, because we know that they have a connection to precolonial Hawaiian culture. This dynamic interplay of belonging within our communities is again precarious, but also evidence of the profound aloha we have for one another, even when we appear to be in conflict on the surface. In order to challenge the heteronormativity within our communities or at the very least to make space for diverse gender and sexual expressions, we must foreground the violent processes of this history.

Pili purposefully distances himself from māhū in Hawaiian culture. He uses the deviance of māhū (under Western heteropatriarchal binaries) to assure himself of his own normalcy. Pili otherizes māhūs both to his father and to himself. Pili recalls a moment in his childhood when an effeminate boy was called a māhū and ridiculed for it, teaching Pili that māhū is a negative identity. He also reflects on an excursion to Waikīkī when he mistaked a māhū for a "real woman," and his father and aunt made fun of him. This is his first recollection of the division he feels with his father, because he knows that he does not fit into heteronormative desires, but also knows that he does not want to be māhū. Pili struggles with his "divided heart" (220)—between family and self, "mainland" and "island"—relying on hetero (or perhaps I should say homo)patriarchal strategies in order to increase his proximity to masculinity. This represents what Kalaniopua Young describes, that is, that māhūs are "brutalized and codified as disposable," even by other Hawaiians, because they "subvert the dominant narrative about the lāhui as a puritanical project."[45] Young brilliantly analyzes the ways in which the lāhui must commit itself to indigenizing and decolonizing forms of gender captivity; anything less would be yet another assault on our Indigenous self-determination. Pili's formulation of his gay identity as something compulsorily separate from a māhū identity represents an importation of American concepts of gender and sexuality in Hawaiian culture. Even though Pili learned to be proud of his sexuality in supposedly liberal San Francisco, it is evident that his views of māhū are dependent on Eurocentric constructions of sexual identity that divide homosexual and transgender, representing the deep divisions within the larger LGBTQ community as well as the Hawaiian community. Just as U.S. white gay politics are often predicated upon instrumentalizing, demeaning, and discarding trans women of color, Pili's insistence to himself that he is not māhū can also be read as analogous to Hawaiian and LGBTQ respectability politics that are based on a fear of subverting gender norms because of social exclusion. So, while māhūs are often held up by Hawaiians and others as a representation of the so-called inclusive culture of Hawai'i, we must be careful not to obscure the discrimination that still exists, the heterornormativity and homonorma-tivity that are also adopted within the LGBTQ community even among Natives, and the heteropatriarchy that is at the root of all of these divisions.

Fundamentally, then, we must use a rudder to direct ourselves away from the currents that shore up our deep complicity with Eurocentric ideolo-gies of gender, sexuality, colonialism, and heteropatriarchy. The process of decolonization for Kānaka Maoli must occur through a critique of gendered and sexualized forms of colonialism, which notably get performed in quo-tidian spaces. As Lisa Kahale'ole Hall describes, there are numerous ways that Kānaka Maoli feminists can "remap" the "sea of islands" to document our own histories, since we are so often literally outside of mainstream and even women of color feminist histories. By remapping the "sea of islands," Kānaka Maoli feminists are able to place themselves in a longer and larger history of Indigenous movement across the Pacific.[46] We view the sea as the site of our kupuna and as a place that generates life for Pacific Islanders wherever they are. Through a critique of the heteropatriarchal under-pinnings of travel that is always framed as male, we can challenge the idea of who gets to spread the seeds, who gets to be the subject of history, and who gets to be in movement in the Pacific. That is not to say that woman isn't a center of the home or that women don't reproduce the nation—indeed we do, and it is powerful—but we ought to acknowledge that this binary perpetuates colonialism and its attendant heteropatriarchy at the expense of Indigenous epistemologies that are more expansive in their conceptual-ization of 'ohana.

For example, Leanne Betasasmoke Simpson writes that sovereignty be-gins in the ways that we treat each other; it begins in the home and in our relations. As a lāhui, we must focus on the everyday acts that nurture and cultivate our relations rather than relying on state forms that police belong-ing. As Native feminists explain, our belonging as a people cannot be con-tained within a document, and our sovereignty and nationhood are about relationships with each other, the plant and animal worlds, and the land and water that surround us.[47] We also need to recall alternate Hawaiian forms of belonging and membership that extend beyond filial and blood relations, which include caring for the 'āina, plants, and animal relations in Hawaiian culture.[48] Throughout the story, Pili, Harrison, and Maile make reference to caring for their herd of cows. Their formation of ʻohana extends to Albert, the ʻāina, and the neighboring paniolos, as well as to the animals themselves ("the herd"), who are part of the family. Pili recalls past moments to connect with the land and the animals on the ranch as a way to reconnect himself to home.

Paired with Native feminist analysis and tidalectics, the land and sea become sites of movement and fluidity that refuse the phallocentric tendency to prioritize patriarchal configurations of sowing or scattering seeds and to articulate a more expansive understanding of how we all sow and scatter seeds. Rather than view diaspora as wholly masculine or negative, we should view Indigenous diaspora as an opportunity to spread and repropagate Indigenous cultures over settler culture. The seeds in this sense are not sperm or intended to displace Indigenous peoples from other lands, but instead will work to challenge settler force by asserting our ongoing Indigenous presence rather than absence and to forge connections with the Indigenous peoples of the places in which we too have become settlers. Diaspora can mean an uprooting and a reseeding somewhere else, but it does not need to be a denial or erasure of the indigeneity of the people who were there before us or are there with us.[49] Diaspora can re-create Indigenous life and share it, honoring a homeland and a new place, but not in a way that seeks to displace or to turn queer Indigenous peoples into hybrids who are used as the foil to land-based indigeneity. As the scholar and activist Fuifuilupe Niumeitolu explains, diasporic solidarity is both possible and necessary. She writes: "This new home we've created is a home that can shelter all of us, especially those of us that have been marginalized or cast aside. This is a new home built on our collective struggles, resistances, and inexorable love for our ancestors and each other."[50] It is in fact through feeling as though one still belongs within one's Indigenous community and homeland that one comes to understand the necessity of understanding and connecting with the Native people of a new place. This ultimately refuses distance as an inhibitor as well as the heteropatriarchal and colonial formations that keep us disconnected from our homes and each other. And by cultivating Indigenous connections, even when we are not in our homelands, we prioritize an understanding of the enduring relevance of Indigenous and alternative forms of recognition and belonging everywhere.

Pili's desire to find a rudder in Albert exhibits his desire to direct his boat back toward "home," but the ending of the story hints that this redirection might not be what Pili actually wants or what is required in order for him to feel like he belongs. This returns us to my earlier critique of the homecoming from the diaspora. When we prioritize the active movement of the Indigenous diaspora and alternate forms of belonging that take place away from the tourist gaze, we are able to recognize the ways in which Indigenous diaspora can work to challenge the heteronormativity of the family tree and kinship systems that structure "return narratives" and to think instead about the multiple roots and routes that foster identity through indigeneity and sexuality.

(Not) Coming Home

Pili is firm in his commitment to his family, but does not feel the need to come home permanently. The story ends with the death of Pili's father and a conversation between Pili and his sister. She asks him when he's coming back to visit, and he just replies, "As soon as I can." Rather than reduce diasporic Kanaka Maoli wellness to an eventual "homecoming," Pili illustrates a challenge to the telos of linear history that is common in Pacific cyclical models, and his ambiguity about coming home invokes the continual movement and rhythm of the ocean. Pili's ambiguous response is an indefinite expression of time. It could mean one month, two years, or five years. No matter the expanse of time or how vast the distance between island and continent appears to be, he knows that he can always return and maintain relations if he acts with aloha. Pili's response to Maile displays how he views the future as open and full of possibility after coming out to his father and family in his own way. This "way" required relating to his family by being there and helping to care for one another, which he learns to do through his relationship with Albert. In seeing how Albert navigates his own identity as gay and Kanaka Maoli in this small community, Pili learns what it means to be accountable and to belong within your 'ohana.

Kānaka Maoli need to remember that diaspora is a kind of tradition that is created not only out of necessity but also out of ingenuity and imagination. Diaspora is like performance in this way: adaptive, moving, imposed, full of power, and productive for re-creating culture and sustaining it. Since the diaspora keeps growing, we must center the flexibility and movement of Hawaiian indigeneity. We must locate our indigeneity as a kind of creativity that converges with the past and the future. We must view our travel between islands and continents as a part of our ongoing history that sustains us, and we must view *who we are* in terms of how the knowledge and belonging we perform are connected to our kupuna who came before us and those who will follow. Set in Waimea, the story provides multiple scenes with Mauna Kea against the backdrop of the night sky, which watches over this ʻohana. The looming presence of Mauna Kea in the background of many scenes reminds Kānaka Maoli of the ancestral significance of this sacred mountain, which is also an expression of Pili's late mother and a representation of how Kānaka Maoli relate to our place. As the origins of our piko (belly button), Mauna Kea is the site from which we emerge, so our collective and individual genealogies always root and route us back to it. The landscape itself in turn binds Pili to this place, not to confine him, but as a reminder that he will always be part of something larger than himself. The connection is revived through a knowledge that while things change, this connection is constant, as the land is.

Queer diasporic Kānaka Maoli can connect to Pili's experience in a manner that is about more than direct identification with the location being discussed. Indeed, most Kānaka Maoli are not from a ranch, and most certainly are not paniolos. However, many may share the experience of not being able to explain to your family why you have stayed away for so long or not being able to justify why you are "different" from everyone else. You also must grapple with the feeling that you may never have a place *in your place*, but you know that it is still your place because of your genealogy and your ʻohana there. "The Old Paniolo Way" exhibits a different way of thinking about the diaspora, teaching us that growing up or living in the diaspora did not compromise Pili's responsibility or connection to place. Pili worried about how people would react to his sexuality, but he never acts as though this would be in conflict with his indigeneity. Pili demonstrates what Deloughrey explains is a challenge to state-based forms of nationalism—that "Indigenous practices of national belonging are far more layered and inclusive than diaspora theorists would let us believe."[51] Therefore, we must articulate a more expansive understanding of belonging, community, and nationhood that is not reliant on landedness or statist, regional, and cultural differences that were fabricated by Westerners. It is time to put an end to the stigma attached to Indigenous diaspora, the kind of stigma that perpetuates the opinion that those who have left Hawaiʻi are unable to deal with the on-the-ground struggle that other Kānaka Maoli are engaged in. At the same time, those in the diaspora must also work to fight the opinion that Kānaka Maoli on the continent are somehow intellectually superior to those who have stayed.[52] This movement, then and now, is as much a result of Native agency and choice as of settler colonialism, but this movement and agency are uneven across the Indigenous Pacific, and our perceived relatedness with each other at home or in the diaspora is not a given. It requires labor to maintain the bonds of kinship and belonging.

In the end, Pili's behavior reminds us of the difficulties of coming home from the diaspora (albeit temporarily) and that belonging does not await us after a one-way ticket home. Maybe coming home is not always the only answer. The story teaches us that there are many ways or paths to be Indigenous, those that are "old" as well as new; sometimes on the 'āina, sometimes in the water, and even as a settler on the lands of other Indigenous peoples, you can still be Kanaka Maoli and conduct yourself with aloha. These realities need not necessarily be in conflict. We can retain our sense of indigeneity, our connection to our homelands, and our participation in our 'ohanas, communities, and lāhui by being accountable to one another and cultivating the many branches that stem from our genealogies.

Conclusion

Aloha as Social Connection

When I began this research in 2007, looking at how blood, identity, and claims to place were articulated in Krystilez's song "Bloodline," I presented many of the critiques that flow throughout this book, namely, that claims to place interweave with expressions of indigeneity that are administered through colonial logics, yet retain a defiant assertion of our abilities to exist prior to and without the state, in circuits that we cultivate and in ways that the state is unable to fully account for. Manifested in performances that take place in the courtroom, in the streets, in films, in songs, and in everyday realities, our Indigenous performativity is certainly a product of colonialism, but it is also a reminder that attempts to obliterate our indigeneity have been unsuccessful. This book has attempted to convey that the limiting boundaries around Hawaiian indigeneity need to be expanded to establish a greater sense of belonging within our communities. I have focused on examples of Hawaiian performance that exist beyond its radar yet are recognized as "Hawaiian" among the marginal sectors of the Indigenous community because of shared understandings of genealogy, cultural memory, and a commitment to one another. Ranging from online commenting spaces, gay bars, and hip-hop cyphers to small theater spaces, all of these performances of Hawaiian indigeneity are rooted in a desire to connect, remember, and innovate what it means to be Kanaka Maoli.

In a Hawaiian cultural environment plagued by constant threats to our collective ability to exist as a people, one of the main things all of these cultural productions have in common is that they do not explicitly engage the question of Hawaiian independence or nation-building. These spaces of performance allow us to examine our future as Kānaka Maoli and to reevaluate what role formalized structures of governance will have in our everyday relations and our ability to be a people. It is no secret or surprise that Kānaka Maoli are torn over the appropriate path to nationhood. The nation-building process took center stage in 2014 when the U.S. Department of the Interior (DOI) held public meetings in Hawai'i where hundreds of Kānaka Maoli lined up to testify against the involvement of the U.S. government in the process of rebuilding the lāhui. Many people told the

DOI to "go home," questioning U.S. jurisdiction in the islands. With a quarter of a million Kānaka Maoli residing in Hawai'i and 45 percent now living on the continent, Kānaka Maoli across the globe have been taking part in moments like these and other public displays of survivance around various issues (the use of GMOs, the struggle at Mauna Kea, militarization, homelessness, cultural appropriation, and other land struggles). There is a deep sense of urgency. And yet many Kānaka Maoli have found themselves disenfranchised, disinterested, and just plain confused about the political process. This signals a profound chasm within our lāhui, indicative of the immense work that must be done to articulate our various desires for the future, allowing us to decide for ourselves what our lāhui ought to look like. Following the DOI meetings, an entity composed of private businesses, community groups, and employed state officials known as Na'i Aupuni attempted to hold a Native Hawaiian–only vote, composed of "registered" Kānaka Maoli, including those in the diaspora, a process that was legally contested, resulting in the cancellation of the election altogether. In February 2016, Na'i Aupuni held an 'aha, or convention, to discuss the path to nationhood, where delegates drafted a constitution and adopted it, with intentions of educating the wider Hawaiian community. As many critics have noted, what was noteworthy about this process was that the so-called nation-building process was led by "professional Hawaiians" who favored a decidedly top-down approach rather than one that was generated within Hawaiian communities. The fraught 'aha process was a reminder of the settler-colonial infrastructure that Hawaiians were being told to work within, affirming the ongoing status of Hawai'i as a U.S. state and the continual presence of the U.S. military, with no apparent intentions of dismantling the settler colonial structures that dispossess the Kanaka Maoli people of our claim to Hawai'i.

Many of the advocates of the vote described the need for Kānaka Maoli to come together in the 'aha despite its flawed evolution. Within the pro-independence communities, there were calls to unenroll in the registry or not to vote. Others were troubled by how divisive participation in the election was, especially when both sides relied on scare tactics. OHA ran ads and distributed mailers with the testimonies of Native Americans who lost their citizenship because they weren't on their tribal rolls, urging Kānaka Maoli that this was our last chance to become a nation. On the other end of the spectrum, there were accusations that Kānaka Maoli who were not in support of full independence were sellouts, unenlightened, or lacked imagination or vision because they were invested in the goodies of

Americanness, that is, colonized. I talked to friends and family members who said that they were being shamed into not feeling Hawaiian enough because pro-independence nationalists were dictating what "real" or "enlightened" Hawaiians are supposed to think. The Hawaiian community is generally divided in two camps: on one side are the pro–federal recognition Kānaka Maoli who are invested in a governing structure generated from the top, and on the other are pro-independence nationalists who are largely portrayed as radicals who aspire to a precolonial Hawaiian lifestyle (even if this is not what they are advocating at all). This split within the modern lāhui is not an anomaly; it has been the norm since the early 1990s, when institutional support for the Hawaiian sovereignty movement gained traction in Hawai'i politics. The Hawaiian Renaissance in the 1970s— specifically the cultural revival and the landing at Kaho'olawe—resulted in the creation of OHA and the implantation of Kanaka Maoli elites in the state and federal governments, which facilitated the growing split in the Hawaiian community between those who choose to work within the system and those who wish to perhaps articulate something else but who for so long have been denied the space to do so or have been completely dismissed altogether. My critiques come from a place of aloha because I know that all the parties involved do have the best interests of the Kanaka Maoli people in mind; they just have radically different perspectives. This process has been and continues to be contentious for the Hawaiian community, and it is isolating for those who do not register (literally and figuratively) as Kānaka Maoli, who are already at risk of losing their claims to indigeneity because they do not appear on the surface to represent the values of Hawaiian culture, be it aesthetically, physically, or politically.

Our governance process must come from many different directions, from places we might not expect and from voices that aren't looked to. Hokulani Aikau explains that it is imperative for us to imagine alternative forms of governance not predicated on statist models. She advocates building an alaloa kīpapa (a long path paved with stones or clouds set closely together) to our Hawaiian ontologies in order to create the conditions of possibility needed for Indigenous resurgence. Building on the work of the First Nations scholars Taiaiake Alfred and Jeff Corntassel, Aikau writes that the alaloa kīpapa can be a path that "focuses on things that restore a sense of individual and communal responsibility for our language, histories, territories, ceremony, and intellectual practices."[1] This path would permit us then to bring our full selves to the task of connecting to our culture, as it was and as it changes. While Aikau's theory at first blush seems to be about returning to a traditional pure "Hawaiian" way of thinking, it is in fact a call to look at our ontologies and revive them in the present in a manner that draws on them and takes action to form a path toward decolonial futures for all of us, not just those the state authorizes.[2]

Rather than bringing us together, the nation-building process has continued to separate us. There are so many Kānaka Maoli who feel that their voices are irrelevant because they were told for too long that they weren't "Hawaiian enough," or because they don't want to give up on America, or because they were rejected by their families for one reason or another. Within the Hawaiian community we continue to restrict what Hawaiianness is supposed to embody. We must make space for these difficult conversations, not just figure certain voices as too radical, as "un-Hawaiian" or out of touch. In many ways we all don't fit "Hawaiianness" because it is a category that became necessary only through the introduction of outsiders who continue to exert power over the way we define ourselves. We cannot return to a precolonial Hawaiian way of being or life, but there are benefits in returning to the source of Hawaiian culture for knowledge or wisdom while also acknowledging how much has changed, how our kupunas change, how culture continues to change. Kānaka have always sustained our culture by creating community, via what scholars like to theorize as Indigenous networks beyond settler governance. These networks cannot be reduced to the administrative gaze or applications for citizenship; they exist in place and travel with people. With social media, they have taken on a new life, but they are profoundly connected to material in-person interactions.

Kānaka Maoli everywhere know that it is our genealogies that make us who we are. We perform our kuleana to them in many different ways and in unexpected genres, and this allows the Kanaka Maoli people to continue. In performance space we negotiate many expectations; these spaces show us that the "spirit of aloha" can impose a violence upon us, while at the same time it serves as a reminder of our cultural resilience in the face of attempts to erase or, at the very least, exploit our culture in the service of settler colonialism. While aloha is what these performance spaces produce, performance space also exposes the limits of aloha because of the way that aloha continues to be appropriated. Thus, these spaces call us to account for the ways in which the spirit of aloha silences, erases, and renders invisible those members of our 'ohana who do not meet the benchmarks of Hawaiian indigeneity. In our commitment to perform our indigeneity for each other, we recenter aloha among ourselves, which in turn allows us to make decolonial claims to life, love, and living as Kānaka Maoli. When we recognize the aloha in one another, we refuse state-based or tourist-infused fantasies of aloha, and we reaffirm aloha as a social relationship between Kanaka Maoli people and our land and non-Natives whom we welcome because they are also committed to this relation, as Trask describes:

> Social connections between our people are through aloha, simply translated as "love" but carrying with it a profoundly Hawaiian sense that is, again, familial and genealogical. Hawaiians feel aloha for Hawaiʻi from whence they come and for their Hawaiian kin upon whom they depend. It is nearly impossible to feel or practice aloha for something that is not familial. This is why we extend familial relations to those few non-Natives whom we feel understand and can reciprocate our aloha. But aloha is freely given and freely returned; it is not and cannot be demanded or commanded. Above all, aloha is a cultural feeling and practice that works among the people and between the people and their land.[3]

Trask's words remind us all that we need aloha and we need each other. We must remember this social relation and cultivate it because the yardsticks of indigeneity and aloha apply to all of us, such as when we are performing in a musical genre that appears antithetical to aloha or even when we are protecting a sacred mountain.

While this book might appear to be about the anxieties around Indigenous identity, it's actually about the materiality of what brings these anxieties into being and how Kānaka Maoli respond. A multitude of marginal performances not coded as "Hawaiian" exist in and outside of Hawaiian communities, because of an artistic desire or purposeful defiance of "Hawaiian" expectations or simply because that is what makes sense to our identities. Trask centers Hawaiʻi as our home, a place we will always belong, and reminds us of our obligation toward the land and to each other. She clarifies that it is a Hawaiian sense that is rooted in genealogy, something that we feel, yet that is still very material. Aloha cannot be demanded or forced, such as in the example of the Aloha State apparatus, where she connects aloha to a practice and a cultural feeling. I have hoped to show the way that these different performance spaces construct and build upon aloha, bringing together different Hawaiian and non-Hawaiian audiences and communities that are predicated on questioning the status quo in Hawaiʻi, a status quo that continues to be invested in constraining and regulating aloha in the service of a tourism industry that confines and codifies the Hawaiian people and our culture.

The nation-building process has been a long time coming, and Naʻi Aupuni is just the latest incarnation of this journey. I am not going to lie: when I got an e-mail from Naʻi Aupuni with my login and voter code, I felt validated and empowered, even when I knew about the problems surrounding the election and this entire process. Maybe I finally felt recognized by my people. I know I am not alone in this, so how do we account for these deeply conflicted feelings within our lāhui? The desire to be recognized and be seen by our lāhui and one another happens through settler colonial governmental forms as well as in subcultural spaces where indigeneity is not known in advance or predetermined by a registry. Accounting for the diverse ways indigeneity is articulated and performed throughout the lāhui will expand our ability to thrive in the future and sustain all of us. Perhaps if the everyday pressures to be Kānaka Maoli were not so stringent, we wouldn't be so invested in colonial structures; or maybe if we made more space for our own contradictions and complexities, we would know and understand ourselves as so many altered elements that are united through genealogy and that our political commitments will continue to be diverse—articulated at times in the diaspora or with Christianity or hip-hop or even federal recognition—but that we have a kuleana to listen to our kupuna and each other and to integrate all kinds of knowledge and expressions in our fight to be Kānaka Maoli. Our visions will vary widely, but we must not forget aloha when we look at these spaces at the edges of the tree, at the edges of the ocean, for they teach us so much about the so-called center. When we look to the margins and center aloha, we are reminded that our indigeneity survives because we continue to do it, because we are committed to having aloha for each other, for the ʻāina, for the lāhui. These are the products and stakes of our performance. By continuing to perform our culture in inventive ways that honor the past and remake the visions of the future, we perform ourselves into existence through aloha.

Notes

Preface

1. I have chosen not to italicize or underline Hawaiian words because Hawaiian is the original language of Hawaiʻi and of Kānaka Maoli. Each Hawaiian word will be followed by a translation the first time it is used.

2. The state of Hawaiʻi distinguishes between the terms "Hawaiian" and "Native Hawaiian," each of which has a contested legality based on blood quantum. I use the term "Kanaka Maoli" to refer any person descended from the Indigenous people inhabiting the Hawaiian Islands before 1778. The term, which has been adopted in recent years, translates into "true people" or "real people" in relation to Hawaiian indigeneity. "Kānaka Maoli" (with the macron over the first *a*) is the plural of "Kanaka Maoli." Please also note that I use the term "Hawaiian" to refer to categories such as "Hawaiian music" or "Hawaiian performance" and "Hawaiian community" because of its common usage. At times I use "Hawaiians" to refer to Kānaka Maoli when contextually appropriate.

3. "Song of Sovereignty" was written and first recorded by Peter Apo and Jeff Rasmussen as part of the *Hawaiian Nation: A Call for Sovereignty* anthology in 1990 on Manu Records. For more on this, see Don Wellr and John Berger, "Hawaii Acts Lead Sovereignty Push," *Billboard Magazine*, April 30, 1994; Hōʻaikane, "Keep Hawaiian Lands in Hawaiian Hands," on A New Beginning Records, 1989; and Bruddah Waltah and Island Afternoon, "Hawaiian Lands," on Island Reggae Records, 1995.

4. Pukui, *ʻOlelo Noʻeau*; Peralto, "Hānau Ka Mauna, the Piko of Our Ea," 233.

5. Goodyear-Kaʻōpua, Hussey, and Wright, *A Nation Rising*.

6. Ibid.

7. Quoted in Carroll, McDougall, and Nordstrom, *Huihui*, 99.

Introduction

1. Osorio, *Dismembering Lāhui*.

2. Ibid.

3. Burlingame, Kasher, and Poole-Burlingame, *Da Kine Sound*; Osorio, "Songs of Our Natural Selves."

4. See, for example, Kameʻeleihiwa, *Native Land and Foreign Desires / Pehea La E Pono Ai?*; Osorio, *Dismembering Lāhui*; Silva, *Aloha Betrayed*.

5. I invoke nationalism in nonspecific terms here to consider how culture is deployed by nationalists rather than naming specific cultural nationalist groups or individuals. Also, I flag cultural nationalism as a loose set of practices that can organize and uplift as well as divide Indigenous communities in the name of "tradition" or "authenticity."

6. Joseph, *Against the Romance of Community*.

7. da Silva, *Toward a Global Idea of Race.*

8. Hokowhitu, "Haka," 291.

9. Raibmon, *Authentic Indians*, 9.

10. Ibid., 3.

11. Deloria, *Playing Indian*, 126.

12. Goeman, "Introduction to Indigenous Performances" 11.

13. Austin, *How to Do Things with Words.*

14. For example, as witnessed in the thousands of testimonies against U.S. federal involvement during the Department of the Interior meetings held in the summer of 2014. See Arvin and Teves, "Recognizing the Aloha in 'No.'"

15. Arista and Kertesz, "Aloha Denied."

16. Milham, "Lanakila Mangauil and the Foundation for Kapu Aloha."

17. Chang, "'We Will Be Comparable to the Indian Peoples,'" 862.

18. Wolfe, "Settler Colonialism and the Elimination of the Native."

19. "Haka" is a type of Maori dance traditionally performed prior to a battle. In the 2000s it was performed on a global stage by the New Zealand All-Blacks Rugby team and has since become especially prominent at sporting events. While the haka is most associated with the Maori people, it is prevalent throughout Polynesia and the Pacific Islander diaspora in Aotearoa, Australia, and the United States.

20. Butler, *Gender Trouble*, 146.

21. Teaiwa, "Native Thoughts," 29; Teaiwa, "Militarism, Tourism and the Native," 55.

22. Diaz and Kauanui, "Native Pacific Cultural Studies on the Edge."

23. Goffman, *The Presentation of Self in Everyday Life.*

24. See also Graham and Glenn, *Performing Indigeneity*, 2–5.

25. See also Wilmer, *Native American Performance and Representation*; Graham and Glenn, *Performing Indigeneity*, 5–7.

26. The Hawaiian term "haole" literally translates to "foreigner," although some have translated it to mean "without breath" (it would be hā'ole instead, which is a separate term). Early foreigners, usually white Europeans, were called haole, although Asian immigrants were also referred to as haole in the early days of the Hawaiian Kingdom. In modern usage it is common to refer to someone as haole if they are white even if they are not a newcomer to the islands. It is not always derogatory, although it certainly can be.

27. Hokowhitu, "The Death of Koro Paka," 116.

28. A. Smith, "Queer Theory and Native Studies," 42.

29. Hokowhitu, "Haka," 293.

30. Ibid.; Graham and Glenn, *Performing Indigeneity.*

31. Thrift, *Non-representational Theory*, 124–25.

32. Chow, "Where Have All the Natives Gone?"

33. S. Lyons, *X-Marks*, 59–61.

34. Raibmon, *Authentic Indians*, 3.

35. Johnson, *Appropriating Blackness*, 8.

36. Silva, *Aloha Betrayed*, 8; Basham, "He Puke Mele Lahui." Kaona was utilized widely during the annexation era. Students and researchers of Hawaiian music have given mele (songs) from this period considerable attention. Noenoe Silva, for in-

stance, explains that during times of oppression (such as following the overthrow in 1893, or before annexation in 1898), kaona was used to express individual feelings and to maintain solidarity against "colonial maneuvers."

37. Arista, "Navigating Uncharted Oceans of Meaning," 666.

38. hoʻomanawanui, "He Lei Hoʻoheno No Nā Kau a Kau"; hoʻomanawanui, "From Ocean to O'shen."

39. McDougall, "Putting Feathers on Our Words," 3–4.

40. Ibid.

41. Scott, *Domination and the Arts of Resistance*, 201.

42. A. Simpson, *Mohawk Interruptus*, 20.

43. Taylor, *The Archive and the Repertoire*, 193.

44. Stillman, "Remembering the History of Hawaiian Hula"; Kaeppler, "Acculturation in Hawaiian Dance."

45. Silva, "'He Kānāwai E Hoʻopau I Na Hula Kuolo Hawaiʻi.'

46. Kanahele, *Hawaiian Music and Musicians*; Diamond, *American Aloha*. Kalākaua held a celebration, referred to as a "jubilee," to celebrate his fiftieth birthday, which involved proud displays of the Hawaiian Kingdom, including a lūʻau, a Lā Kūʻokoʻa (independence day celebration), "historical tableaux," and of course hula performances that brought together the Kanaka Maoli people. For more, see Silva, *Aloha Betrayed*, 118. For more on hula, see Stillman, *Sacred Hula*; Kaeppler, Van Zile, and Tatar, *Hula Pahu*.

47. Stillman, "Textualizing Hawaiian Music," 74.

48. Kanahele, *Hawaiian Music and Musicians*. See Lewis, "Storm Blowing from Paradise," 63.

49. Noland, *A Hawaiian Survival Handbook*, 153.

50. Goodyear-Kaʻōpua, Hussey, and Wright, *A Nation Rising*, 2.

Chapter 1

1. Like many Native populations across the United States, many Kānaka Maoli have median incomes far below state and national averages, high unemployment, lack of educational attainment, drug abuse, and increasing risk of homelessness or unstable living conditions. All of these conditions compromise quality of life. For more information on poverty rates, see U.S. Bureau of the Census, American Community Survey, "Figure Inc-10: Poverty Rates for Families for Whom Poverty Status Is Determined," and "Table Emp-11: Native Hawaiian Employment Status." Also, Kānaka Maoli suffer disproportionately from high rates of cardiovascular disease, hypertension, cancers, diabetes, obstructive lung diseases (asthma, bronchitis, emphysema), chronic kidney disease, metabolic syndrome, and obesity, with the highest rate of diabetes among ethnic subgroups in Hawaiʻi. Kānaka Maoli also have a lower life expectancy and higher rates of cardiovascular and diabetes-related mortality than the population as a whole. Additionally, Kānaka Maoli have higher than average behavioral risk factors for diseases, with higher rates of tobacco use, alcohol consumption, methamphetamine use, and dietary fat intake than the general population, compounded by lower fruit and vegetable intake and decreased physical activity. See

State of Hawai'i, Department of Health, Hawai'i Health Survey, "Figure Hth-01: Chronic and Other Health Conditions."

2. *Ulukau On-line Hawaiian Dictionary*, s.v. "aloha," http://wehewehe.org/.

3. Kanahele, *Kū Kanaka, Stand Tall*, 480.

4. Kanahele, "The Dynamics of Aloha," 205.

5. Mary Kawena Puku'i was a contributor to multiple publications. See, for example, Henry P. Judd, Mary Kawena Puku'i, and John F. G. Stokes, *Introduction to the Hawaiian Language* (Honolulu: Tongg Publishing, 1943); Mary Kawena Puku'i and Samuel H. Elbert, *Hawaiian-English Dictionary*, 3rd ed. (Honolulu: University of Hawai'i Press, 1965); E. S. Craighill Handy and Mary Kawena Puku'i, *The Polynesian Family System in Ka'ū, Hawai'i* (Rutland, VT: C. E. Tuttle Co., 1972); Mary Kawena Puku'i, E. W. Haertig, and Catherine A. Lee, *Nānā I Ke Kumu = Look to the Source*, 2 vols. (Honolulu: Hui Hānai, 1972); Mary Kawena Puku'i and Alfons L. Korn, *The Echo of Our Song: Chants and Poems of the Hawaiians* (Honolulu: University of Hawai'i Press, 1973); Mary Kawena Puku'i, Samuel H. Elbert, and Esther T. Mookini, *Place Names of Hawaii*, rev. and enl. ed. (Honolulu: University of Hawai'i Press, 1974); Mary Kawena Puku'i, *'Olelo No'eau: Hawaiian Proverbs and Poetical Sayings*, Bernice P. Bishop Museum Special Publication (Honolulu: Bishop Museum Press, 1983).

6. Pukui, Haertig, and Lee, *Nānā I Ke Kumu*, Vol. 2: 3.

7. Kanahele, *Kū Kanaka, Stand Tall*, 478–79.

8. Althusser, "Ideology and Ideological State Apparatuses."

9. Ibid., 110.

10. Butler, *The Psychic Life of Power*.

11. Weber, *The Protestant Ethic and the Spirit of Capitalism*, 80.

12. Chow, *The Protestant Ethnic and the Spirit of Capitalism*, 43.

13. Althusser, "Ideology and Ideological State Apparatuses," 158.

14. Ibid.

15. Butler, *The Psychic Life of Power*, 119.

16. Ibid., 99.

17. The "Great Mahele" was enacted in 1848 and is generally regarded as the start of capitalism in Hawai'i. The mahele—defined as division—changed communal land tenure to private ownership, which eventually dispossessed many common people of access to their lands. For details, see Van Dyke, *Who Owns the Crown Lands of Hawai'i*; Cooper and Daws, *Land and Power in Hawaii*.

18. Kanahele, *Hawaiian Music and Musicians*. For more on hula, see Stillman, *Sacred Hula*.

19. Balme, "Dressing the Hula"; Diamond, *American Aloha*.

20. Meyer, *Ho'oulu*, 23–24; Silva, *Aloha Betrayed*.

21. Tengan, *Native Men Remade*, 46; Goodyear-Ka'ōpua, "Domesticating Hawaiians."

22. Kaomea, "Indigenous Studies in the Elementary Curriculum," 31.

23. Ibid., 34; Kaomea, "A Curriculum of Aloha?"

24. Kaomea, "A Curriculum of Aloha?," 335.

25. As Kaomea explains, textbooks full of photographs credited to the Hawai'i's Visitors Bureau promote a curriculum that supports tourism (ibid., 323–324; "Indigenous Studies in the Elementary Curriculum," 38). Textbook examples include *Hawaii the Aloha State* (Honolulu: Bauer, 1982), *Hawaii Our Island State* (Honolulu: Potter, Kasdon, and Hazama, 1979), and several others. See Kaomea, "A Curriculum of Aloha?"

26. Imada, *Aloha America*; Imada, "The Army Learns to Lū'au."

27. Joesting, "Hawaii's Golden Rule Means Aloha."

28. Reverend Abraham Akaka, "Hawaii Statehood Address—Aloha Ke Akua," http://www.akakafoundation.org/sermons.html.

29. Ohnuma, "'Aloha Spirit' and the Cultural Politics of Sentiment as National Belonging," 374–79.

30. Pierce, "'The Whites Have Created Modern Honolulu,'" 128.

31. Halualani, *In the Name of Hawaiians*; Kanahele, "The Dynamics of Aloha."

32. Foucault, *Discipline and Punish*.

33. Okamura, "The Illusion of Paradise," 266–68.

34. Scientists received funding through a Rockefeller Foundation grant (1927–37) to study the effects of racial blending in the islands. Sociologists and anthropologists subsequently referred to Hawai'i as a racial melting pot; see Romanzo Adams, "Hawaii as a Racial Melting Pot," *Mid-Pacific Magazine* 32, no. 3 (Sept. 1926): 213–16 and *Interracial Marriage in Hawaii: A Study of the Mutually Conditioned Processes of Acculturation and Amalgamation* (New York: MacMillan Co., 1937); Andrew Lind, *An Island Community: Ecological Succession in Hawaii* (Chicago: University of Chicago Press, 1938); Lawrence H. Fuchs, *Hawaii Pono: A Social History* (New York: Harcourt, Brace & World, 1961); and work by Glen Grant and Dennis M. Ogawa, "Living Proof: Is Hawaii the Answer?," *Annals of the American Academy of Political and Social Science* 530 (November 1993): 137–54.

35. Fujikane and Okamura, *Asian Settler Colonialism*, 3. As cited in Okamura, "The Illusion of Paradise," the history of Hawai'i over the past century shows evidence of ethnic conflict, such as the overthrow of the Hawaiian monarchy in 1893, the numerous sugar and pineapple workers' and dockworkers' strikes from 1909 through 1958, and the emergence of the anti-Japanese backlash in the mid-1970s (272).

36. Okamura, "The Illusion of Paradise," 274.

37. "The Power of Aloha" is former Lieutenant Governor Duke Aiona of Hawai'i's so-called program of positive thinking; see www.powerofaloha.org.

38. Daws, *Shoal of Time*.

39. Trask, *From a Native Daughter*, 1.

40. Ibid.

41. Halualani, *In the Name of Hawaiians*, 28.

42. Ibid., xiv.

43. Kanahele, "The Dynamics of Aloha."

44. Mak, *Developing a Dream Destination*.

45. The Aloha Spirit Law requests that city employees greet the public using the words "aloha" and "mahalo" (thank you). See L 1959, JR 1, § 1; Supp, § 14-5.1; HRS § 5-7.5.

46. Dingeman, "'Spirit of Aloha' Transplanted into State Law"; "Senate Wants Aloha Spirit in Courtroom"; Reyes, "Legislators Endorse 'Aloha Spirit' as 'Essence of the Law' in Islands"; "'Aloha Spirit' About to Become Official."

47. Hawaiʻi Revised Statutes.

48. "Aloha Spirit as State Policy Gets Hearing."

49. Morita, "'Aloha Spirit' Bill Meets Some Heartfelt Opposition."

50. Osorio, "Kūʻē and Kuʻokoʻa."

51. Van Dyke, "Governor Signs into Law Hawaiʻi's Marriage Equality Bill"; Lincoln, "Hawaii Becomes 15th State to Legalize Same-Sex Marriage."

52. Pierce, "'The Whites Have Created Modern Honolulu,'" 128.

53. Ibid.

54. Diamond, *American Aloha*, 25.

55. Brown, *Regulating Aversion*, 21.

56. For more details about George Helm, see the Hawaiian Patriots Project, http://www.kamakakoi.com/hawaiianpatriots/george.html. (accessed December 2, 2014).

57. Osorio, "Hawaiian Souls."

58. Butler, *The Psychic Life of Power*, 119.

59. For more on settler colonialism in Hawaiʻi, see Okamura, "Why There Are No Asian Americans in Hawaiʻi."

60. Franklin Odo and Susan Yim, "Ethnicity," in *The Price of Paradise*, Vol. 2, edited by R. W. Roth, 225 (Honolulu: Mutual Publishing, 1993), quoted in Okamura, "The Illusion of Paradise," 273.

61. Okamura, "The Illusion of Paradise," 278.

62. For works specifically about settler colonialism in Hawaiʻi, see Fujikane and Okamura, *Asian Settler Colonialism*, and Saranillio, "Seeing Conquest."

63. In government, aspirations for Hawaiian sovereignty produced federal response in the form of the 1993 Apology Resolution. Similarly, numerous Hawaiian sovereignty groups claim to be rightful inheritors of the Hawaiian Kingdom and have created their own structure and process of governing. Several sovereignty groups have lobbied for redress at the United Nations, and there have even been a few court cases brought forward by Kānaka Maoli against the state and the U.S. government. In addition to government and politics, Kanaka Maoli cultural and spiritual practices are protected by the law (e.g., gathering rights and subsistence activities). Hawaiian-language immersion schools are also increasingly common. These activities are evidence of the ways that Kānaka Maoli are asserting their cultural identity in a manner that reaches beyond the Hawaiian community and aspires to influence if not completely transform Hawaiʻi politics.

64. Halualani, *In the Name of Hawaiians*, 24; Okamura, "The Illusion of Paradise." For an example of this rhetoric, see the writings of Ken Conklin, who has published extensive critiques of the Hawaiian sovereignty movement. He especially targets Kanaka Maoli activists and academics, calling into question their "authenticity" and charging them with racial separatism. See Ken Conklin, *Hawaiian Apartheid: Racial Separatism and Ethnic Nationalism in the Aloha State* (Montgomery, AL: E-booktime LLC, 2007). Conklin also heads Aloha for All, a multiethnic group committed to promoting aloha for people regardless of background. The group believes Hawaiian

sovereignty is a Hawaiian supremacist project. The groups' founders are involved with lawsuits against Hawaiian entitlement programs.

65. For detailed analysis of the backlash against sovereignty, see the work of J. Kēhaulani Kauanui, especially her article "Colonialism in Equality."

66. Crabbe's letter can be seen at *Star Advertiser* staff, "OHA Trustees Rescind Letter to Feds on Hawaiian Kingdom's Status," *Honolulu Star-Advertiser*, May 9, 2014, http://www.staradvertiser.com/news/breaking/20140509_oha_seeks_clarity_on _hawaiian_kingdom_status.html?2i. The response from the OHA Board of Trustees chair, College Machado, can be accessed on the *Hawai'i Free Press* site: http://www .hawaiifreepress.com/ArticlesMain/tabid/56/ID/12611/OHA-Chaos-Machado -Crabbe-Dueling-Statements-full-text.aspx.

67. An example of a Kanaka Maoli defying his or her subject position is personified in Trask, *From a Native Daughter*; for an account of a controversy at the University of Hawai'i, see the chapter "The Politics of Academic Freedom as the Politics of White Racism." See also Trask, "Racism against Native Hawaiians at the University of Hawaii."

68. Hall, "'Hawaiian at Heart.'"

69. hooks, *Black Looks*.

70. da Silva, *Toward a Global Idea of Race*.

71. Ibid.

72. Gray, "Subject(Ed) to Recognition."

73. da Silva, *Toward a Global Idea of Race*.

74. For an extended critique of the film *Aloha*, see the collaborative work of Hine-moana of Turtle Island, a collective of Pacific Islander feminists residing in California and Oregon. Their analysis of *Aloha* can be accessed at https://morethantwominutes .wordpress.com/2015/06/16/on-cameron-crowes-aloha-and-indigenous-pacific-films -we-actually-recommend/.

75. Hall, "Which of These Things Is Not Like the Other," 727–28.

76. Meyer, *Ho'oulu*, 4.

77. Also noted by Kanahele, *Kū Kanaka, Stand Tall*, and Ohnuma, "'Aloha Spirit' and the Cultural Politics of Sentiment as National Belonging."

78. Clifford, *Returns*, 302.

79. Butler, *The Psychic Life of Power*, 104.

80. Clifford, *Returns*, 302.

81. Žižek, *The Sublime Object of Ideology*, 42.

82. Hattori, "Model Minority Discourse and Asian American Jouis-Sence."

83. Dolar, "Beyond Interpellation," 92.

84. Chow, *The Protestant Ethnic and the Spirit of Capitalism*, 110; Žižek, *The Sublime Object of Ideology*.

85. Chow, *The Protestant Ethnic and the Spirit of Capitalism*, 112–13.

86. Diaz and Kauanui, "Native Pacific Cultural Studies on the Edge," 317.

87. Chow, *The Protestant Ethnic and the Spirit of Capitalism*, 110.

88. Teaiwa, "Militarism, Tourism and the Native."

89. Diaz and Kauanui, "Native Pacific Cultural Studies on the Edge," 315–42.

90. Chow, *The Protestant Ethnic and the Spirit of Capitalism*, 111.

91. Butler, *The Psychic Life of Power*, 104.

92. Chow, *The Protestant Ethnic and the Spirit of Capitalism*, 111.

93. Butler, *The Psychic Life of Power*, 105.

Chapter 2

1. "Island Mele."

2. As Osumare notes, a hip-hop scene started to coalesce in Honolulu during the early 1980s, evidenced in mainstream acknowledgment on a local television show called *Breakin Hawai'i* in 1984. For more, see Osumare, "Props to the Local Boyz."

3. See Osumare, *The Africanist Aesthetic in Global Hip-Hop*, 16.

4. Kelley, foreword to *The Vinyl Ain't Final*; Mitchell, "Kia Kaha! (Be Strong)"; Ullestad, "Native American Rap and Reggae."

5. Vizenor, "Aesthetics of Survivance," 1.

6. See Tengan, *Native Men Remade*, 66; Diaz, "'Fight Boys til the Last'"; Hokowhitu, "Tackling Maori Masculinity." In terms of military service, see also Tengan and Markham, "Performing Polynesian Masculinities in American Football." Denetdale also notes how the word "warrior" is used to motivate Navajo participation in U.S. wars. She raises questions about how Navajo participation in U.S. wars becomes aligned with a Navajo warrior tradition, making the link between family values and recent legislation such as the Diné Marriage Act of 2005. See Denetdale, "Securing Navajo National Boundaries."

7. I differentiate between "Hawai'i hip-hop" and "Hawaiian hip-hop." "Hawai'i hip-hop" can be any hip-hop coming out of Hawai'i. I use "Hawaiian hip-hop" to refer to artists who explicitly identify themselves as Kanaka Maoli and feature references to Hawaiian life and history in their music.

8. ho'omanawanui, *Voices of Fire*.

9. See "100,000 Hits on YouTube," https://www.youtube.com/watch?v=R5COF zi7oYU. Also "When It's on It's On!," https://www.youtube.com/watch?v=qUwVv WW6Gok.

10. Chun, "Hip-Hop for the Masses"; Chun, "Nanakuli's in the House."

11. See Burgess and Green, *YouTube*; Niesse, "Native Hawaiians Occupy Iolani Palace Grounds."

12. See "Tiki's Taking It to the Streets," http://www.youtube.com/user/tikient#p /u/1/DeHlkA34VB4.

13. I use "local" here rather than "settler" because that is the term that Krystilez uses. "Settler" is still not a common term in Hawai'i.

14. As defined by Stillman (2005) "patterned and contoured use of sustained pitches" (79).

15. There could be multiple interpretations of which style of oli is being referenced, but because of the use of sustained pitches and its incorporation of multiple pitches on the same contour through each phrase (as short as this one is), it fits into the ho'āeae tradition.

16. As defined by Stillman (2005) "funerary wailing" (79).

17. Oliveira, *Ancestral Places*, 65.

18. Place songs are frequent in Hawaiian music, including contemporary songs about a particular place, such as Olomana's "Ku'u Home o Kahalu'u," Ehukai's "Molokai Slide," and Bruddah Waltah's "Kailua-Kona."

19. On the "enduring nature" of Hawaiian music, see Stillman, "Textualizing Hawaiian Music." Unfortunately, the video for "The 'O'" and "Won" has been taken down from YouTube (originally accessed November 13, 2009).

20. Krystilez video for "Shake,"http://www.youtube.com/watch?v=lc-VK-7g7eE &feature=player_embedded. Also posted is a video for "Tha Word," http://www .youtube.com/watch?v=ISodFmUyapY&feature=player_embedded.

21. The video for "Bloodline," http://www.youtube.com/watch?v=LXJKsvGiS5Y. These lyrics are sung in the same rhythm as Tupac's song "Ambitionz Az a Ridah" (1996).

22. "Kamehameha the Great," in brief, is in reference to the Hawaiian chief Kamehameha I, who united all the islands in the late eighteenth century. The Hawaiian "monarchy" that resulted from his consolidation of power reigned throughout the nineteenth century and has a genealogy that is still present today. Kamehameha remains an icon of Hawaiian strength, personified in various cultural productions, including paintings, architecture, statues, and clothing. The shirt referred to draws on these histories. There has also been a surge in Hawaiian-related designs in clothing, especially among some folks in the hip-hop scene who have started their own clothing labels, which is beyond the scope of my analysis here. The prevalence of Native imagery as a source of pride is certainly present in the proliferation of independent clothing labels run by Krystilez and other Hawaiians. These examples show what Jocelyn Linnekin described in the 1990s as an expression of consumerism that is indicative of a "rootedness in a primordial homeland." Linnekin, "Consuming Cultures," 236.

23. The Office of Hawaiian Affairs was created in 1978 to develop, coordinate, and watch over programs and activities relating to Kānaka Maoli.

24. Department of Hawaiian Homelands, "Department of Hawaiian Homelands Annual Report, 2013," 39.

25. Department of Hawaiian Homelands, "Department of Hawaiian Homelands Beneficiary Surveys Update," 36.

26. Ibid.

27. Ibid.; Kauanui, *Hawaiian Blood*, 80.

28. Kauanui, *Hawaiian Blood*, 80.

29. Keanu Sai argues that under international law, the U.S. government is an illegal occupier of Hawai'i because the Hawaiian Kingdom never signed a treaty of cession. His website explains this in detail; see http://www2.hawaii.edu/~anu/. Sai, "American Occupation of the Hawaiian State; Kauanui, *Hawaiian Blood*; "For Get [sic] Hawaiian Entitlement"; Kauanui, "Diasporic Deracination and 'Off-Island' Hawaiians."

30. Arvin, "Still in the Blood."

31. Kauanui, *Hawaiian Blood*, 85.

32. Ibid., 68.

33. Ibid., 85.

34. Krystilez, *The "O."*

35. The comments section for the "Bloodline" video is telling of the different interpretations that the video yields. Some comments aim to represent their own "bloodline," or where someone is from, whereas other comments mock Krystilez and others in the video as gangsta wannabes or shameful examples of Hawaiianness.

36. Krystilez e-mailed this song to me and others in December 2009.

37. Labrador, *Building Filipino Hawai'i.*

38. Krystilez, "Homesteady."

39. "Island Mele"; Genegabus, "In the Mix."

40. Brian Kuwada contends that Hawaiian-language proficiency among Hawaiians is as low as 5 percent. Kuwada, "To Translate or Not to Translate."

41. Quoted in Chun, "Nanakuli's in the House"; http://archives.starbulletin.com /2007/01/26/features/story03.html.

42. Office of Hawaiian Affairs, "The Disparate Treatment of Native Hawaiians in the Criminal Justice System"; Tengan, *Native Men Remade*, 61.

43. Kelley, *Race Rebels.*

44. "Tiki Entertainment Presents 'Bloodline,'" http://www.youtube.com/watch?v =LXJKsvGiS5Y.

45. Rose, *The Hip-Hop Wars.*

46. Forman, *The Hood Comes First*, 126.

47. Johnson, *Appropriating Blackness*, 3.

48. Watkins, *Hip-Hop Matters.*

49. Johnson, *Appropriating Blackness*, 8.

50. C. Smith, "Method in the Madness," 346, quoted in Rivera, *New York Ricans from the Hip-Hop Zone*, 248.

51. An earlier version of this research was presented as a conference paper at the 2008 Pacific Worlds Conference in Salt Lake City, Utah, where it received considerable criticism by the audience, particularly from older Kānaka Maoli who were in attendance. One woman was in tears, expressing concern for the younger generation who, in identifying with hip-hop, forget who they really are. Another audience member, a middle-aged Pacific Islander man, dressed in fatigues, commented that what these young men really need is to be taken outside and taught some "real discipline." Henderson, "Gifted Flows," 300, also explains how Samoan elders criticized Samoan hip-hop artists for trying to act "black."

52. State of Hawai'i, DBEDT, "Top 10 Most Expensive and 10 Least Expensive States to Live."

53. Office of Hawaiian Affairs, *Native Hawaiian Data Book*, 2003.; Kana'iaupuni, Malone, and Ishibashi, "Income and Poverty among Native Hawaiians."

54. Krystilez, "West Side," https://www.youtube.com/watch?v=I46JyN4aErs.

55. Kame'eleihiwa, *Native Land and Foreign Desires / Pehea La E Pono Ai?*, 9.

56. Ibid., 51.

57. Goodyear-Ka'ōpua, "Kuleana Lāhui"; Goodyear-Ka'ōpua, Hussey, and Wright, *A Nation Rising.*

58. The Blount Report was a Foreign Relations Committee report regarding the overthrow of the Hawaiian Kingdom in 1893. President Grover Cleveland appointed

James H. Blount to investigate the activities of the overthrow. Blount concluded that the United States was complicit in the overthrow and called it an "act of war."

59. Video clip of Haunani-Kay Trask from *Journey to Justice: A Conversation with Haunani-Kay Trask*, 2010, https://vimeo.com/39644495.

60. Silva, *Aloha Betrayed*, 130–31. Ohnuma, "'Aloha Spirit' and the Cultural Politics of Sentiment as National Belonging," 380; Goodyear-Kaʻōpua, Hussey, and Wright, *A Nation Rising*.

61. Bacchilega, *Legendary Hawaiʻi and the Politics of Place*, 51.

62. Ibid., 8–9, 36.

63. Lefebvre, *The Production of Space*, 13.

64. Oliveira, *Ancestral Places*, 67.

65. Forman and Neal, *That's the Joint!*

66. Isldsnow, November 12, 2012, comment on "West Side," YouTube, https://www.youtube.com/watch?v=I46JyN4aErs.

67. PUNISHERx808, November 12, 2012, comment on "West Side," YouTube, https://www.youtube.com/watch?v=I46JyN4aErs.

68. Junior Boy, November 12, 2012, comment on "West Side," YouTube, https://www.youtube.com/watch?v=I46JyN4aErs.

69. According to OHA, *Native Hawaiian Data Book*, 2013. The number of Hawaiians living outside of Hawaiʻi has increased 46 percent between 2000 and 2010. Population forecasts show that the percentage of the Kanaka Maoli population living outside of Hawaiʻi will continue to increase due to the state's high cost of living and limited economic opportunities. Fifty-five percent of the Kanaka Maoli population lives in Hawaiʻi, and there are large populations of Kānaka Maoli in California, Washington, Nevada, and Texas. See also Kauanui, "Diasporic Deracination and 'Off-Island' Hawaiians."

Chapter 3

1. As a point of clarification, I refer to Cocoa Chandelier with female pronouns because in drag culture drag queens generally refer to one another that way. I am analyzing her as a performer and therefore refer to her in the gender pronoun she performs as.

2. A fund-raiser for travel to a drag competition.

3. "Erotica" (1992), "Justify My Love" (1990), "Cherish" (1989), "Hung Up" (2005).

4. Chinatowns were historically noted as havens for illicit behavior, most notably drug use, undocumented immigration, and prostitution, and as places where disease was prevalent. Shah, *Contagious Divides*, 43. In an article on the rise of the artist community in Chinatown, Ragnar Carlson writes, "Now, a new generation of urban pioneers is remaking the street. Just steps from thriving Nuʻuanu Avenue, artists, musicians and entrepreneurs—savvy with experience gained elsewhere and driven by passion for the street—are looking to help the strip step out of its rough-and-tumble past and into a new life as an artistic and cultural mecca." Chinatown is also known for its māhū sex workers. For more on Honolulu's Chinatown revitalization, see R. Carlson, "Hotel Street: From Skid Row to Pacific Soho," *Honolulu Weekly*, June 15, 2005.

5. In 2003, the "First Friday Honolulu Art Walk" started in downtown Honolulu and Chinatown to promote local art galleries, shops, and restaurants. What began as a small art walk geared toward the local community has exploded into a full-blown monthly festival inundated by tourists. The monthly event is celebrated by some and bemoaned by others.

6. "Butchie" is a term often used in Hawai'i to refer to lesbians; it does not necessarily refer only to lesbians who appear "butch" or masculine. "Muffie" is a word used to describe gay men.

7. Kaina Jacobs was Universal ShowQueen 2001.

8. Cocoa Chandelier also appeared as the Hawaiian mythological character Lohi'au, Pele's lover, in Iona Pear's rendition of Hawaiian mythology. Enomoto, "Modern Myth."

9. Giinko Marischino is a collective of dancers founded in the mid-1990s, specializing in the collaborative process as a method of participatory art making. With a base in butoh (a dance form that originated in Japan) and in modern dance, Giinko includes other realms of art such as drag, comedy, installation, music, and video in its eclectic performance events. See http://www.facebook.com/pages/GIINKO -MARISCHINO/81348636162#!/pages/GIINKO-MARISCHINO/81348636162?v =info. Giinko specializes in butoh, a form of dance about darkness and haunting, evading definition. See Sondra Horton Fraleigh, *Dancing into Darkness*. Pittsburgh, PA: University of Pittsburgh Press, 1999; *Butoh: Metamorphic Dance and Global Alchemy*, Chicago, IL: University of Illinois Press, 2010.

10. She has also appeared in Albert Wendt's *Songmaker's Chair*, Chinese Opera Jinju, and was part of the first all-Hawaiian-language stage production in 2015, *Lā'ieikawai*.

11. "Māhū" is a term used in Hawai'i to describe persons who embody both masculine and feminine abilty, insight, feeling and spirit. Used in the present day to refer to gay men, drag queens, and transwomen.

12. Muñoz, *Disidentifications*, 11.

13. For more, see Chow, *The Protestant Ethnic and the Spirit of Capitalism*, 107.

14. To "queer" something means to look at how something disrupts the norm; it is an analytic that comes from queer theory.

15. See Fleetwood, *Troubling Vision*, 7.

16. Foucault, *Discipline and Punish*, 187.

17. Basham, "I Mau Ke Ea O Ka Aina I Ka Pono"; Kame'eleihiwa, *Native Land and Foreign Desires / Pehea La E Pono Ai?*

18. That is not to say that there aren't comparable terms to mark someone "queer." "Māhū" and "butchie" are often terms used to degrade nonnormative gender performance in Hawai'i.

19. McMullin, "Fa'afafine Notes."

20. Besnier and Alexeyeff, introduction to *Gender on the Edge*, 2.

21. Wallace, *Sexual Encounters*; O'Brien, *The Pacific Muse*.

22. Morgensen, *Spaces between Us*.

23. "Fa'afafine" is term used in Samoan culture to describe a man who lives in the manner of a woman, "fa'a" meaning "in the manner of" and "fafine" meaning "woman." "Fakaleiti" is a Tongan term to describe a man who behaves in an effeminate manner.

24. I use LGBTQ2 here because it is used by the editors of *Queer Indigenous Studies*. The "2" refers to people who identify as two-spirited individuals. However, "two-spirit" is not typically used in Hawai'i, so I have chosen not to use LGBTQ2 when talking about the LGBTQ community Hawai'i.

25. Driskill et al., *Queer Indigenous Studies*, 212.

26. Bailey, *Butch Queens Up in Pumps*, 130; See, *The Decolonized Eye*, 138.

27. Newton, *Mother Camp*, 3.

28. Muñoz, *Disidentifications*, 99.

29. Butler, "Critically Queer," 160.

30. See, *The Decolonized Eye*, 128.

31. Ibid., 138.

32. See A. Smith, "Queer Theory and Native Studies: The Heteronormativity of Settler Colonialism," 45. Also see Chuh, *Imagine Otherwise*. Chuh argues that Asian American studies (and by extension other ethnic studies) should be defined by its critique, not by its subjects and objects.

33. Ethnographic entrapment is a process by which Natives present a version of themselves that would make them "universal," as subjects with a culture that is worthy of universal humanity. In other words, this means that Natives must prove that they are worthy by showing that they have a redeemable essence or essential being that is of worth to everyone. As Smith argues, this makes Natives into natural objects to be discovered, to create and renew the life of non-Natives at the expense of the Native. A. Smith, "Queer Theory and Native Studies," 42–43; da Silva, *Toward a Global Idea of Race*.

34. Cocoa Chandelier, Cocoa Chandelier's Facebook Page, https://www.facebook .com/330778506937221/photos/a.632835693398166.1073741826.330778506937221 /632835703398165/?type=3&theater.

35. Bailey, *Butch Queens Up in Pumps*, 55.

36. Ibid., 56.

37. Raibmon, *Authentic Indians*, 9.

38. Bailey, *Butch Queens Up in Pumps*, 66–67.

39. Simpson, *Mohawk Interruptus*, 15.

40. Bailey, *Butch Queens Up in Pumps*, 66–67.

41. Chandelier, Cocoa Chandelier's Facebook Page.

42. Kame'eleihiwa, *Native Land and Foreign Desires / Pehea La E Pono Ai?*

43. Muñoz, *Disidentifications*, 74.

44. Ibid.

45. "TBT Diva of Polynesia Cocoa Chandelier 2006," https://www.youtube.com /watch?v=s7ni4lgE6ic.

46. Bailey, *Butch Queens Up in Pumps*, 132; See, *The Decolonized Eye*.

47. Muñoz explains that disidentifying subjects both hold onto the loss of the subject and invest in it a new kind of life. Muñoz, *Disidentifications*, 12.

48. Kamehameha I was the first Hawaiian chief to unite all the islands, in the late eighteenth century. The Hawaiian "monarchy" that resulted from his consolidation of power reigned throughout the nineteenth century and has a genealogy that is still present today. Kamehameha remains an icon of Hawaiian strength and is

personified in various cultural productions, including paintings, architecture, statues, and clothing.

49. For examinations of how Hawaiians are invoked in urban planning, see Marek, "Waikiki Virtual Reality."

50. The film was released in 2002 and was the third Bollywood version to be produced but the first in full color. It is still the most expensive Bollywood film ever produced. It has been released in English, French, German, Mandarin, Thai, and Punjabi. At the time, it was the highest-grossing Bollywood film ever.

51. Kavita Krishnamurthy, "Dola Re Dola," on the *Devdas* soundtrack, Fontana Indian, Universal Music India Pvt. Ltd., 2002.

52. Also featured prominently is Panjabi MC, "Beware of the Boys," Sequence Records, 2003. The single features a remix with Jay-Z.

53. da Silva, *Toward a Global Idea of Race*.

54. Ibid., xxxv.

55. Coulthard, *Red Skin, White Masks*; Coulthard, "Subjects of Empire."

56. Office of Hawaiian Affairs, *Native Hawaiian Data Book*; Kanaʻiaupuni, Malone, and Ishibashi, "Income and Poverty among Native Hawaiians."

57. Povinelli, *The Cunning of Recognition*.

58. Phelan, *Unmarked*. Phelan reads Foucault's *History of Sexuality* (1979), noting that his usage of the "confession" is akin to how power operates in many forms of performance. She argues that "women and performers" are the ones who are scripted to sell or confess, but I would add here that this is applicable to anyone "underrepresented" who must confess or sell themselves to be included.

59. On November 26, 2008, a Pakistan-based military organization coordinated bombing attacks throughout South Mumbai, India. The attacks lasted two days, killing over 150 people and wounding over 300.

60. Phelan, *Unmarked*, 163. See also Alsultany, "Selling American Diversity and Muslim American Identity through Non-Profit Advertising Post-911," 619.

61. For more on music and appropriation, see Born and Hesmondahalgh, *Western Music and Its Others*.

62. Jamal and Naber, *Race and Arab Americans before and after 9/11*. Puar's chapter "The Turban Is Not a Hat" in *Terrorist Assemblages* is also an example of this conflation.

63. Ahmed, "Western Ethnocentrism and Perceptions of the Harem."

64. Sunaina Maira explains that the opening up of India's economic market has caused India to be a nation of cheap labor, goods, and emergent markets and trends.; Maira, "Henna and Hip-Hop."

65. See, *The Decolonized Eye*, 129.

66. Ibid., 128–29.

67. Personal communication with Cocoa Chandelier, December 21, 2009.

68. A. Simpson, "On Ethnographic Refusal," 74.

69. Phelan, *Unmarked*, 148–49.

70. Taylor, *The Archive and the Repertoire*, 143.

71. Phelan, *Unmarked*, 149.

72. Ibid., 148.

73. Ibid., 146–47.

74. Muñoz, *Disidentifications*, 189.

Chapter 4

1. Linnea, *Princess Ka'iulani*; Rivenburgh, *Princess Kaiulani*; Stanley and Stanley, *The Last Princess*.

2. Wood, *Displacing Natives*, 15.

3. M. Carlson, *The Haunted Stage*, 5.

4. Burns, *Puro Arte*, 91.

5. Krystilez, "Karma."

6. Byrd, *The Transit of Empire*, 38.

7. Roach, *Cities of the Dead*, xi.

8. Shaughnessey, "She Lived, and Worked, behind the Scenes," http://www.lowellsun.com/ci_8602523.

9. Derrida, *Spectres of Marx*; Gordon, *Ghostly Matters*.

10. Gordon, *Ghostly Matters*, xvi.

11. Tuck and Ree, "Glossary of Haunting," 642.

12. Kosasa, "Critical Sights/Sites," 56.

13. Vizenor, "Aesthetics of Survivance."

14. Marek, "Waikīkī Virtual Reality."

15. Herman, "Kala'aina—Carving the Land," 357–58.

16. Kosasa, "Critical Sights/Sites," 119; Marek, "Waikīkī Virtual Reality."

17. Kosasa, "Critical Sights/Sites."

18. Bergland, *The National Uncanny*.

19. Gonser and Hoover, "Glen Grant Was Teacher, Storyteller."

20. Grant et al., *Chick'n Skin*; Vandertuin et al., *Scary Stories*.

21. Grant, *Obake*, 1.

22. Fujikane and Okamura, *Asian Settler Colonialism*, 1–40.

23. Kam, "The Legacy of 'Āinahau," 55–56.

24. Kapanui, "Kawēkiu."

25. "Letters of Congratulations."

26. "Princess Kaiulani Proclaimed Heir of the Crown."

27. "Her Only Plaint."

28. "Letters of Congratulations."

29. Miss Kekoaohiwaikalani, "He Inoa No Kalaninuiahilapalapa." Translations are mine.

30. Goodyear-Ka'ōpua, "Domesticating Hawaiians," 19.

31. Miller, *From Liberation to Conquest*.

32. Hall, "Navigating Our Own 'Sea of Islands.'"

33. Taouma, "Gauguin Is Dead . . . There Is No Paradise," 13.

34. Silva, *Aloha Betrayed*.

35. Taylor, *The Archive and the Repertoire*, 29.

36. Raheja, *Reservation Reelism*, xiii.

37. Ibid., x.

38. Ibid., xi.

39. There is a Facebook page dedicated to "Princess Kaiulani Movie Facts" as an educational website (https://www.facebook.com/pages/Princess-Kaiulani-Movie-Facts/124227770929213?fref=ts). The majority of the page has historical images of Kaʻiulani and posts by users advocating for Hawaiian sovereignty, referring to the illegal overthrow. It was made by the creators of BarbarianPrincessMovie.com as a way to spread awareness of the film's inaccuracies (http://BarbarianPrincessMovie.com/). There is also a Facebook page for the movie *Princess Kaiulani* (https://www.facebook.com/PrincessKaiulaniMovie?fref=ts). Local newscasts covered reactions to the premiere; KITV.com, *Princess Kaiulani Movie Debuts*, video, YouTube.com, 2010.

40. Raheja, *Reservation Reelism*, xi.

41. Hearne, *Native Recognition*, 269.

42. Ibid., 275; Ortiz, "History of Right Now," 6.

43. Hearne, *Native Recognition*, 276.

44. Raheja, *Reservation Reelism*, xiii.

45. Free Hawaiʻi Broadcasting Network, *Princess Kaʻiulani Movie Facts Get the Ax* (2010).

46. Moketananda, *Protest the Taping of Kaʻiulani*. In a couple of video postings on YouTube, Palani Vaughan discusses how during preproduction of the film, one of the line producers perished by falling off a balcony at the Princess Kaʻiulani Hotel. I heard a similar story about this during the first ghost tour I took of ʻIolani Palace in 2008. See Moketananda, *Protesting the Filming of Barbarian Princess Kaʻiulani*.

47. Gordon, *Ghostly Matters*, 65–66. Gordon draws on Walter Benjamin, "Theses on the Philosophy of History." In Walter Bejamin, *Illuminations*, translated by Harry Zohn, edited by Hannah Arendt, 253–64. New York: Penguin Randomhouse, 1969.

48. Svaton, "A Woman's Place in the World."

49. Stevenson, *Songs of Travel and Other Verses*.

50. L. Simpson, *Dancing on Our Turtle's Back*, 96.

51. Gordon, *Ghostly Matters*, 65–66.

52. Ibid., 65.

53. Ibid., 134–35.

54. Vizenor, "Aesthetics of Survivance," 11.

55. L. Simpson, *Dancing on Our Turtle's Back*, 145.

Chapter 5

1. Office of Hawaiian Affairs, "Native Hawaiian Databook," 2013.

2. Haunani-Kay Trask, quoted in Kelly and Kuleana Works Production, "Noho Hewa." See also James Cave, "Culture Cave: Life at the Other End of Honolulu's Brain Drain," http://www.civilbeat.com/2015/03/culture-cave-life-at-the-other-end-of-honolulus-brain-drain/; Eric Pape, "Living Hawaiʻi: Some Reasons Not to Start a Career in Honolulu," http://www.civilbeat.com/2015/05/living-hawaii-some-reasons-not-to-start-a-career-in-honolulu/.

3. Kauanui, "Diasporic Deracination and 'Off-Island' Hawaiians," 146.

4. For example, Kānaka Maoli who live in the continental United States are often viewed as disconnected from Hawaiian culture and unaware of political issues faced by Kānaka Maoli in Hawai'i. During the 2015–2016 Na'i Aupuni election process, many candidates running to be delegates in the Hawaiian convention were explicitly against Kānaka Maoli on the continent being allowed to vote or to access any benefits that may become available.

5. Kelly and Kuleana Works Production, *Noho Hewa*.

6. Ka'ili, "Tauhi Va," 86.

7. See *Ulukau On-line Hawaiian Dictionary*, s.v. "Wā": "Space, interval, as between objects or time; in music, one of the four spaces of the staff; channel," http://www.wehewehe.org.

8. Ibid., 92.

9. David Gegeo, quoted in Aikau, "Indigeneity in the Diaspora," 480. For more, see Gegeo, "Cultural Rupture and Indigeneity," 494–95.

10. Aikau, "Indigeneity in the Diaspora," 480.

11. Ibid.; Ramirez, *Native Hubs*.

12. Ramirez, *Native Hubs*.

13. Diaz and Kauanui, "Native Pacific Cultural Studies on the Edge," 317.

14. Hau'ofa, *We Are the Ocean*, 104.

15. Ibid.

16. DeLoughrey, *Routes and Roots*, 2.

17. Ibid.

18. Gopinath, *Impossible Desires*, 28; Eng, *The Feeling of Kinship*.

19. Aikau, "Indigeneity in the Diaspora," 479–80.

20. "Kū Kia'i Mauna—We Are Mauna Kea," https://www.google.com/maps/d/viewer?mid=zpOxLeECNO-8.k4xAbeh21Qgk; Ian Scheuring, "Local Celebrities Take to Social Media and Mauna Kea Protests," http://www.hawaiinewsnow.com/story/28730585/local-celebrities-take-part-in-mauna-kea-protests; "Photos: 'We Are Mauna Kea' Movement Goes Global," http://www.hawaiinewsnow.com/slideshow?widgetid=151714.

21. Kauanui, "Diasporic Deracination and 'Off-Island' Hawaiians," 146.

22. Ulises, "Tacit Subjects," 339.

23. Waitt and Markwell, *Gay Tourism*.

24. D'Emilio, "Capitalism and Gay Identity," 102–103.

25. Morgensen, "Settler Homonationalism," 106.

26. Driskill, "Doubleweaving Two-Spirit Critiques," 75.

27. Ibid., 71.

28. Manolo Guzman, "Sexile," quoted in La Fountain-Stokes, *Queer Ricans*, 175.

29. O'Brien, *The Pacific Muse*; Wallace, *Sexual Encounters*; Kame'eleihiwa, *Native Land and Foreign Desires / Pehea La E Pono Ai?*; Morris, "Aikane."

30. Merry, *Colonizing Hawai'i*.

31. Ulises, "Tacit Subjects," 339.

32. Pukui, Haertig, and Lee, *Nana I Ke Kumu*.

33. "Moana Nui" is a term frequently used to refer to the Pacific Ocean in Polynesia. "Moana" means ocean and "nui" means great or large.

34. Jolly, "On the Edge?," 419.

35. Ibid., 425.

36. Teaiwa, "Native Thoughts," 19.

37. Ladislav Zgusta, "Diaspora: The Past in the Present" *Studies in the Lingusitic Sciences* 31:1, Spring 2001: 291–97. See also Jarrod Hayes, "Queering Roots, Queering Diaspora," in *Rites of Return: Diaspora Poetics and the Politics of Memory*, edited by Marianne Hirsch and Nancy K. Miller, 73 (New York: Columbia University Press, 2011).

38. DeLoughrey, *Routes and Roots*, 45.

39. F. Williams, "The Canoe Is the People."

40. Lyons and Tengan, "Introduction: Pacific Currents."

41. DeLoughrey, *Routes and Roots*, 142.

42. Diaz and Kauanui, "Native Pacific Cultural Studies on the Edge," 315.

43. Trask, "Fighting the Battle of Double Colonization."

44. Kauanui, "Blood Reproduction of (the) Race in the Name of Hoʻoulu Lāhui," 110–12; Arvin, Tuck, and Morrill, "Decolonizing Feminism"; Arvin, "Still in the Blood," 690.

45. Young, "From a Native *Trans* Daughter," 90.

46. Hall, "Navigating Our Own 'Sea of Islands,'" 16.

47. L. Simpson, "The Place Where We All Live and Work Together," 18–20.

48. Eng, *The Feeling of Kinship*.

49. Harvey and Thompson, *Indigenous Diasporas and Dislocations*, 10.

50. Fuifuilupe Niumeitolu, "Pacific Islanders March for Self-Determination," https://morethantwominutes.wordpress.com/2015/03/02/pacific-islanders-march-for-self-determination/.

51. DeLoughrey, *Routes and Roots*, 45.

52. Kanaʻiaupuni and Malone, "This Land Is My Land."

Conclusion

1. Aikau, "Following the Alaloa Kīpapa of Our Ancestors," 656.

2. Ibid., 657.

3. Trask, *From a Native Daughter*, 141.

Bibliography

Ahmed, Leila. "Western Ethnocentrism and Perceptions of the Harem." *Feminist Studies* 8, no. 3 (1982): 521–34.

Aikau, Hokulani. "Following the Alaloa Kīpapa of Our Ancestors: A Trans-Indigenous Futurity without the State (United States or Otherwise)." *American Quarterly* 67, no. 3 (2015): 653–61.

———. "Indigeneity in the Diaspora: The Case of Native Hawaiians at Iosepa, Utah." *American Quarterly* 62, no. 3 (2010): 477–500.

"'Aloha Spirit' About to Become Official." *Honolulu Advertiser*, April 15, 1986.

"Aloha Spirit as State Policy Gets Hearing." *Honolulu Star-Bulletin*, February 16, 1986.

Alsultany, Evelyn. "Selling American Diversity and Muslim American Identity through Non-profit Advertising Post-911." *American Quarterly* 59, no. 3 (2007): 593–622.

Althusser, Louis. "Ideology and Ideological State Apparatuses." In *Lenin and Philosophy and Other Essays*. New York: Monthly Review Press, 1971.

Arista, Noelani. "Navigating Uncharted Oceans of Meaning: *Kaona* as Historical and Interpretive Method." *Modern Language Association of America* 125, no. 3 (2010): 663–69.

Arista, Noelani, and Judy Kertesz. "Aloha Denied." *Hawaiʻi Independent*, February 25, 2014. http://hawaiiindependent.net/story/aloha-denied.

Arvin, Maile. "Still in the Blood: Gendered Histories of Race, Law, and Science in *Day v. Apoliona*." *American Quarterly* 67, no. 3 (2015): 681–703.

Arvin, Maile, and Stephanie Nohelani Teves. "Recognizing the Aloha in 'No.'" *Hawaiʻi Independent*, July 7, 2014. http://hawaiiindependent.net/story/recognizing-the-aloha-in-no.

Arvin, Maile, Eve Tuck, and Angie Morrill. "Decolonizing Feminism: Challenging Connections between Settler Colonialism and Heteropatriarchy." *Feminist Formations* 25, no. 1 (2013): 8–34.

Austin, J. L. *How to Do Things with Words*. 2nd ed. Oxford: Clarendon Press, 1975.

Bacchilega, Cristina. *Legendary Hawaiʻi and the Politics of Place*. Philadelphia: University of Pennsylvania Press, 2007.

Bailey, Marlon M. *Butch Queens Up in Pumps: Gender, Performance, and Ballroom Culture in Detroit*. Ann Arbor: University of Michigan Press, 2013.

Balme, Christopher B. "Dressing the Hula: Iconography, Performance and Cultural Identity Formation in Late Nineteenth Century Hawaii." *Paideuma* 45 (1999): 233–55.

Basham, Leilani. "He Puke Mele Lāhui: Nā Mele Kūpaʻa, Nā Mele Kūʻē a Me Nā Mele Aloha O Nā Kānaka Maoli." MA thesis, University of Hawaiʻi, 2002.

———. "I Mau Ke Ea O Ka Aina: He Puke Mele No Ka Lahui Hawaii." PhD Diss., University of Hawai'i, 2007.

Bergland, Renée L. *The National Uncanny: Indian Ghosts and American Subjects.* Hanover, NH: University Press of New England, 2000.

Besnier, Niko, and Kalissa Alexeyeff. Introduction to *Gender on the Edge*, edited by Niko Besnier and Kalissa Alexeyeff, 1–32. Honolulu: University of Hawai'i Press, 2015.

Bhansali, Sanjay Leela. *Devdas.* DVD. India: Mega Bollywood Pvt. Ltd, 2002.

Born, Georgina, and David Hesmondahalgh, eds. *Western Music and Its Others: Difference, Representation, and Appropriation in Music.* Berkeley: University of California Press, 2000.

Brown, Wendy. *Regulating Aversion: Tolerance in the Age of Identity and Empire.* Princeton, NJ: Princeton University Press, 2008.

Burgess, Jean, and Joshua Green. *YouTube: Online Video and Participatory Culture.* Malden, MA: Polity Press, 2009.

Burlingame, Burl, Robert Kamohalu Kasher, and Mary Poole-Burlingame. *Da Kine Sound: Conversations with the People Who Create Hawaiian Music.* Kailua, Hawai'i: Press Pacifica, 1978.

Burns, Lucy Mae San Pablo. *Puro Arte: Filipinos on the Stages of Empire.* New York: New York University Press, 2012.

Butler, Judith. "Critically Queer." In *Performance Studies*, edited by Erin Striff, 152–65. Houndmills, UK: Palgrave Macmillan, 2003.

———. *Bodies That Matter.* New York: Routledge, 1993.

———. *Gender Trouble.* New York: Routledge, 1990.

———. *The Psychic Life of Power: Theories in Subjection.* Stanford, CA: Stanford University Press, 1997.

Byrd, Jodi A. *The Transit of Empire: Indigenous Critiques of Colonialism.* Minneapolis: University of Minnesota Press, 2011.

Carlson, Marvin. *The Haunted Stage: The Theatre as Memory Machine.* Ann Arbor: University of Michigan Press, 2001.

Carlson, Ragnar. "Hotel Street: From Skid Row to Pacific Soho." *Honolulu Weekly*, June 15 2005.

Carroll, Jeffrey, Brandy Nālani McDougall, and Georgeanne Nordstrom. *Huihui: Navigating Art and Literature in the Pacific.* Honolulu: University of Hawai'i Press, 2015.

Chang, David A. "'We Will Be Comparable to the Indian Peoples': Recognizing Likeness between Native Hawaiians and American Indians, 1834–1923." *American Quarterly* 67, no. 3 (2015): 859–86.

Chow, Rey. *The Protestant Ethnic and the Spirit of Capitalism.* New York: Columbia University Press, 2002.

———. "Where Have All the Natives Gone?" In *Writing Diaspora: Tactics of Intervention in Contemporary Cultural Studies.* Bloomington: Indiana University Press, 1993.

Chuh, Kandice. *Imagine Otherwise: On Asian Americanist Critique.* Durham, NC: Duke University Press, 2003.

Chun, Gary C. W. "Hip-Hop for the Masses." *Honolulu Star-Bulletin*, May 9, 2006.

———. "Nanakuli's in the House." *Honolulu Star Bulletin*, January 26, 2007.

Chun, Malcolm Nāea. *No Nā Mamo: Traditional Hawaiian Beliefs and Practices.* Honolulu: University of Hawai'i Press, 2011.

Clifford, James. *Returns.* Cambridge, MA: Harvard University Press, 2013.

Cooper, George, and Gavan Daws. *Land and Power in Hawaii: The Democratic Years.* Honolulu: University of Hawai'i Press, 1990.

Coulthard, Glen. *Red Skin, White Masks: Rejecting the Colonial Politics of Recognition.* Minneapolis: University of Minnesota Press, 2014.

———. "Subjects of Empire: Indigenous Peoples and the 'Politics of Recognition.'" *Contemporary Political Theory* 6 (2007): 437–60.

Daws, Gavan. *Shoal of Time: A History of the Hawaiian Islands.* Honolulu: University of Hawai'i Press, 1968.

Deloria, Phillip. *Playing Indian.* New Haven, CT: Yale University Press, 1999.

DeLoughrey, Elizabeth M. *Routes and Roots: Navigating Caribbean and Pacific Island Literatures.* Honolulu: University of Hawai'i Press, 2007.

D'Emilio, John. "Capitalism and Gay Identity." In *Powers of Desire: The Politics of Sexuality*, edited by Ann Snitow, Christine Stansell, and Sharan Thompson, 100–13. New York: Monthly Review Press, 1983.

Denetdale, Jennifer Nez. "Securing Navajo National Boundaries: War, Patriotism, Tradition, and the Diné Marriage Act of 2005." *Wicazo Sa Review* 24, no. 2 (Fall 2009): 131–48.

Department of Hawaiian Homelands. "Department of Hawaiian Homelands Annual Report, 2013." Honolulu: State of Hawai'i, 2014.

———. "Department of Hawaiian Homelands Beneficiary Surveys Update." Honolulu: State of Hawai'i, 2014.

Derrida, Jacques. *Spectres of Marx.* London: Routledge, 2006.

Diamond, Heather A. *American Aloha: Cultural Tourism and the Negotiation of Tradition.* Honolulu: University of Hawai'i Press, 2008.

Diaz, Vicente M. "'Fight Boys til the Last': Football and the Remasculinization of Identity in Guam." In *Pacific Diasporas*, edited by Paul Spickard, Joanne Rondilla, and Deborah Hippolyte Wright, 165–94. Honolulu: University of Hawai'i Press, 2002.

Diaz, Vicente M., and J. Kēhaulani Kauanui. "Native Pacific Cultural Studies on the Edge." *Contemporary Pacific* 13, no. 2 (Fall 2001): 315–42.

Dolar, Mladen. "Beyond Interpellation." *Qui Parle* 6, no. 2 (1993): 73–96.

Driskill, Qwo-Li. "Doubleweaving Two-Spirit Critiques: Building Alliances between Native and Queer Studies." *GLQ: A Journal of Lesbian and Gay Studies* 16 (2010): 69–92.

Driskill, Qwo-Li, Chris Finley, Brian Joseph Gilley, and Scott Lauria Morgensen. *Queer Indigenous Studies: Critical Interventions in Theory, Politics, and Literature.* Tucson: University of Arizona Press, 2011.

Eng, David L. *The Feeling of Kinship: Queer Liberalism and the Racialization of Intimacy.* Durham, NC: Duke University Press, 2010.

Enomoto, Catherine Kekoa. "Modern Myth: Hawaiian Legends Wax Eclectic." *Honolulu Star-Bulletin*, May 27, 1997.

Fleetwood, Nicole R. *Troubling Vision: Performance, Visuality, and Blackness*. Chicago: University of Chicago Press, 2011.

Forman, Murray. *The 'Hood Comes First: Race, Space and Place in Rap and Hip-Hop*. Middletown, CT: Wesleyan University Press, 2002.

Forman, Murray, and Mark Anthony Neal. *That's the Joint! The Hip-Hop Studies Reader*. New York: Routledge, 2004.

Foucault, Michel. *Discipline and Punish: The Birth of the Prison*. New York: Vintage Books, 1977.

Free Hawai'i Broadcasting Network. 2010. "Princess Ka'iulani Movie Facts Get The Ax." Last modified May 19, 2010. https://www.youtube.com/watch?v=fsjCMLD3bZU.

Fujikane, Candace, and Jonathan Y. Okamura, eds. *Asian Settler Colonialism: From Local Governance to the Habits of Everyday Life in Hawai'i*. Honolulu: University of Hawai'i Press, 2008.

Gegeo, David Welchman. "Cultural Rupture and Indigeneity: The Challenge of (Re)visioning 'Place' in the Pacific." *Contemporary Pacific* 13 (2001): 491–507.

Genegabus, Jason. "In the Mix: Krystilez Keeps Making Waves." *Honolulu Pulse*, June 7, 2014.

Goeman, Mishuana. "Introduction to Indigenous Performances: Upsetting the Terrains of Settler Colonialism." *American Indian Culture and Research Journal* 35, no. 4 (2011): 3–18.

Goffman, Erving. *The Presentation of Self in Everyday Life*. Garden City, NY: Doubleday, 1959.

Gonser, James, and Will Hoover. "Glen Grant Was Teacher, Storyteller." *Honolulu Advertiser*, June 20, 2003.

Goodyear-Ka'ōpua, Noelani. "Domesticating Hawaiians: Kamehameha Schools and the 'Tender Violence' of Marriage." In *Indian Subjects: Hemispheric Perspectives on the History of Indigenous Education*, edited by Brian Klopotek and Brenda Childs, 16–47. Santa Fe, NM: School for Advanced Research Press, 2014.

——. "Kuleana Lāhui: Collective Responsibility for Hawaiian Nationhood in Activists Praxis." *Affinities* 5, no. 1 (2011): 130–63.

Goodyear-Ka'ōpua, Noelani, Ikaika Hussey, and Erin Kahunawaika'ala Wright. *A Nation Rising: Hawaiian Movements for Life, Land, and Sovereignty*. Durham, NC: Duke University Press, 2014.

Gopinath, Gayatri. *Impossible Desires: Queer Diasporas and South Asian Public Cultures*. Durham, NC: Duke University Press, 2005.

Gordon, Avery. *Ghostly Matters: Haunting and the Sociological Imagination*. Minneapolis: University of Minnesota Press, 1997.

Graham, Laura R., and Penny H. Glenn. *Performing Indigeneity: Global Histories and Contemporary Experiences*. Lincoln: University of Nebraska Press, 2014.

Grant, Glen. *Obake: Ghost Stories in Hawai'i*. Honolulu: Mutual Publishing, 1994.

Grant, Glen, Scott Eilif Sorensen, KGMB, and Lee Enterprises. *Chick'n Skin [II]: Tales of Supernatural Hawaii*. VHS. Honolulu: Lee Enterprises, 1996.

Gray, Herman. "Subject(ed) to Recognition." *American Quarterly* 65, no. 4 (December 2013): 771–98.

Hall, Lisa Kahale'ole. " 'Hawaiian at Heart' and Other Fictions." *Contemporary Pacific* 17, no. 2 (2005): 404–13.

———. "Navigating Our Own 'Sea of Islands': Remapping a Theoretical Space for Hawaiian Women and Indigenous Feminism." *Wicazo Sa Review* 24, no. 2 (2009): 15–38.

———. "Which of These Things Is Not Like the Other: Hawaiians and Other Pacific Islanders Are Not Asian Americans, and Not All Pacific Islanders Are Hawaiian." *American Quarterly* 67, no. 3 (2015): 727–47.

Halualani, Rona T. *In the Name of Hawaiians: Native Identities and Cultural Politics*. Minneapolis: University of Minnesota Press, 2002.

Harvey, Graham, and Charles Johnson, eds. *Indigenous Diasporas and Dislocations*. Burlington, VT: Ashgate, 2005.

Hattori, Tomo. "Model Minority Discourse and Asian American Jouis-Sence." *differences* 11, no. 2 (1999): 228–47.

Hau'ofa, Epeli. *We Are the Ocean: Selected Works*. Honolulu: University of Hawai'i Press, 2008.

Hawai'i State Department of Business, Economic Development & Tourism (DBEDT). "Top 10 Most Expensive and 10 Least Expensive States to Live: 2014." Table 14.22. Honolulu: Department of Business, Economic Development & Tourism, 2014.

Hayes, Jarrod. "Queering Roots, Queering Diaspora," in *Rites of Return: Diaspora Poetics and the Politics of Memory*, edited by Marianne Hirsch and Nancy K. Miller, 72–87. New York: Columbia University Press, 2011.

Hearne, Joanna. *Native Recognition: Indigenous Cinema and the Western*. Albany: State University of New York Press, 2012.

Henderson, April. "Gifted Flows: Engaging Narratives of Hip Hop and Samoan Diaspora." PhD Diss., History of Consciousness, University of California Santa Cruz, 2006.

Herman, Doug. "Kala'aina—Carving the Land: Geography, Desire and Possession in the Hawaiian Islands." MA thesis, University of Hawai'i, 1995.

"Her Only Plaint." *Morning Call* 73, no. 92 (1893): 1. http://chroniclingamerica.loc .gov/lccn/sn94052989/1893-03-02/ed-1/seq-1/.

Hokowhitu, Brendan. "The Death of Koro Paka: 'Traditional" Māori Patriarchy.' " *Contemporary Pacific* 20, no. 1 (Spring 2008): 115–41.

———. "Haka: Colonized Physicality, Body-Logic, and Embodied Sovereignty." In *Performing Indigeneity*, edited by Laura R. Graham and Penny H. Glenn, 273–304. Lincoln: University of Nebraska Press, 2014.

———. "Tackling Maori Masculinity: A Colonial Genealogy of Savagery and Sport." *Contemporary Pacific* 16, no. 2 (Fall 2004): 259–84.

hooks, bell. *Black Looks: Race and Representation*. Boston, MA: South End Press, 1992.

ho'omanawanui, ku'ualoha. "From Ocean to O'shen: Reggae, Rap, and Hip Hop in Hawai'i." In *Crossing Waters, Crossing Worlds*, 273–308. Durham, NC: Duke University Press, 2006.

———. "He Lei Ho'oheno No Nā Kau a Kau: Language, Performance and Form in Hawaiian Poetry." *Contemporary Pacific* 17, no. 1 (Spring 2005): 29–81.

———. *Voices of Fire: Reweaving the Literary Lei of Pele and Hi'iaka*. Minneapolis: University of Minnesota Press, 2014.

Imada, Adria. *Aloha America*. Durham, NC: Duke University Press, 2012.

———. "The Army Learns to Lū'au: Imperial Hospitality and Military Photography in Hawai'i." *Contemporary Pacific* 20, no. 2 (Fall 2008): 328–61.

"Island Mele: Krystilez Lets Off Some Steam." *Honolulu Star-Advertiser*, June 17, 2011.

Jamal, Amaney A., and Nadine Christine Naber. *Race and Arab Americans before and after 9/11: From Invisible Citizens to Visible Subjects*. Syracuse, NY: Syracuse University Press, 2008.

Joesting, Edward. "Hawaii's Golden Rule Means Aloha." *Honolulu Star-Bulletin*, February 20, 1979.

Johnson, E. Patrick. *Appropriating Blackness: Performance and the Politics of Authenticity*. Durham, NC: Duke University Press, 2003.

Jolly, Margaret. "On the Edge? Deserts, Oceans, Islands." *Contemporary Pacific* 13 (2001): 417–66.

Joseph, Miranda. *Against the Romance of Community*. Minnesota: University of Minnesota Press, 2002.

Kaeppler, Adrienne L. "Acculturation in Hawaiian Dance." *Yearbook of the International Folk Music Council* 4, no. 25 (1972): 38–46.

Kaeppler, Adrienne, Judy Van Zile, and Elizabeth Tatar. *Hula Pahu: Hawaiian Drum Dances*. Honolulu: Bishop Museum Press, 1993.

Kahakauwila, Kristiana. *This is Paradise*. New York: Penguin Random House, 2013.

Ka'ili, Tevita O. "Tauhi va: Nurturing Tongan Sociospatial Ties in Maui and Beyond." *Contemporary Pacific* 17, no. 1 (2005): 83–114.

Kam, Ralph Thomas. "The Legacy of 'Āinahau: The Genealogy of Ka'iulani's Banyan." *Hawai'i Journal of History* 45 (2011): 49–68.

Kame'eleihiwa, Lilikalā. *Native Land and Foreign Desires / Pehea La E Pono Ai?* Honolulu: Bishop Museum Press, 1992.

Kanahele, George. "The Dynamics of Aloha." In *Pacific Diasporas*, edited by Paul Spickard, Joanne Rondilla, and Deborah Hippolyte Wright, 195–218. Honolulu: University of Hawai'i Press, 2002.

———. *Hawaiian Music and Musicians: An Illustrated History*. Honolulu: University of Hawai'i Press, 1979.

———. *Kū Kanaka, Stand Tall: A Search for Hawaiian Values*. Honolulu: University of Hawai'i Press, Waiaha Foundation, 1986.

Kanaʻiaupuni, S. M., N. J. Malone, and K. Ishibashi. "Income and Poverty among Native Hawaiians: Summary of Ka Huakaʻi Findings." Honolulu: Kamehameha Schools, 2005.

Kanaʻiaupuni, S. M., and Nolan Malone. "This Land is My Land." In *Race, Ethnicity, and Place in a Changing America*, edited by John W. Frazier, 287–300. Buffalo, NY: SUNY Press, 2012.

Kaomea, Julie. "A Curriculum of Aloha? Colonialism and Tourism in Hawaiʻi's Elementary Textbooks." *Curriculum Inquiry* 30, no. 3 (2000): 319–44.

———. "Indigenous Studies in the Elementary Curriculum: A Cautionary Hawaiian Example." *Anthropology and Education Quarterly* 36, no. 1 (2005): 24–42.

Kapanui, Lopaka. "Kawēkiu." http://ghostsnextdoor.blogspot.com/2014/10 /kawekiu.html.

Kauanui, J. Kēhaulani. "Blood Reproduction of (the) Race in the Name of Hoʻoulu Lāhui—A Hawaiian Feminist Critique." *Pacific Studies* 30, nos. 1 and 2 (2007): 110–16.

———. "Colonialism in Equality: Hawaiian Sovereignty and the Question of U.S. Civil Rights." *South Atlantic Quarterly* 17, no. 4 (2008): 635–50.

———. "Diasporic Deracination and 'Off-Island' Hawaiians." *Contemporary Pacific* 19, no. 1 (Spring 2007): 138–60.

———. "For Get [*sic*] Hawaiian Entitlement: Configurations of Land, 'Blood,' and Americanization in the Hawaiian Homes Commission Act of 1921." *Social Text*, no. 29 (1999): 123–44.

———. *Hawaiian Blood: Colonialism and the Politics of Sovereignty and Indigeneity*. Durham, NC: Duke University Press, 2008.

Kekoaohiwaikalani, Miss. "He Inoa No Kalaninuiahilapalapa." *Leo o ka Lahui*, March 21, 1893. Published electronically March 5, 2015. http://nupepa-hawaii .com/2015/03/05/ellen-prendergasts-mele-inoa-for-princess-kaiulani-1893/.

Kelley, Robin D. G. Foreword to *The Vinyl Ain't Final: Hip-Hop and the Globalization of Black Popular Culture*, edited by Sidney Lemelle and Dispannita Basu, xi–xii. Ann Arbor, MI: Pluto Press, 2006.

———. *Race Rebels: Culture, Politics, and the Black Working Class*. New York: Free Press, 1996.

Kelly, Anne Keala, and Kuleana Works Production. *Noho Hewa: The Wrongful Occupation of Hawaiʻi*. Film. Honolulu: Kuleana Works Production, 2009.

KITV.com. *Princess Kaiulani Movie Debuts*. Video. YouTube.com, 2010.

Kosasa, Karen. "Critical Sights/Sites: Art Pedagogy and Settler Colonialism in Hawaiʻi." PhD Diss., University of Rochester, 2002.

Krystilez. "Homesteady." In *Empires of Funk: Hip-Hop and Representation*, edited by Mark R. Villeagas, Kandi Kuttin, Roderick N. Labrador, and Jeff Chang, 293–96. San Diego: Cognella Academic Publishing, 2013.

———. "Karma." 2014. Video. https://www.youtube.com/watch?v=rDbq4aq45jo.

———. *The "O."* Honolulu: Tiki Entertainment, 2006. CD.

Kuwada, Brian. "To Translate or Not to Translate: Revising the Translating of Hawaiian Language Texts." *Biography* 32, no. 1 (2009): 54–65.

Labrador, Roderick N. *Building Filipino Hawai'i*. Urbana: University of Illinois Press, 2015.

La Fountain-Stokes, Lawrence M. *Queer Ricans: Cultures and Sexualities in the Diaspora*. Minneapolis: University of Minnesota Press, 2009.

Lefebvre, Henri. *The Production of Space*. London: Basil Blackwell, 1991.

Lemelle, Sidney, and Dipannita Basu, eds. *The Vinyl Ain't Final: Hip-Hop and the Globalization of Black Popular Culture*. Ann Arbor, MI: Pluto Press, 2006.

"Letters of Congratulations." *Pacific Commercial Advertiser* 20, no. 18 (1875): 2. Published electronically October 2014. https://nupepa.files.wordpress.com/2014/10/pca_10_20_1875_2.png.

Lewis, George H. "Storm Blowing from Paradise: Social Protest and Oppositional Ideology in Popular Hawaiian Music." *Popular Music* 10, no. 1 (1991): 53–67.

Lincoln, Mileka. "Hawaii Becomes 15th State to Legalize Same-Sex Marriage." *Hawaii News Now*, November 13, 2013.

Linnea, Sharon. *Princess Ka'iulani: Hope of a Nation, Heart of a People*. Grand Rapids, MI: Eerdmans Books for Young Readers, 1999.

Linnekin, Jocelyn. "Consuming Cultures: Tourism and the Commoditization of Cultural Identity in the Island Pacific." In *Tourism, Ethnicity, and the State in Asian and Pacific Societies*, edited by Robert E. Wood and Michel Picard, 215–50. Honolulu: University of Hawai'i Press, 1997.

Lyons, Paul, and Ty Kāwika Tengan. "Introduction: Pacific Currents." *American Quarterly* 67, no. 3 (2015): 545–574.

Lyons, Scott Richard. *X-Marks: Native Signatures of Assent*. Minneapolis: University of Minnesota Press, 2010.

Maira, Sunaina. "Henna and Hip-Hop: The Politics of Cultural Production and the Work of Cultural Studies." *Journal of Asian American Studies* 3, no. 3 (2000): 329–69.

Mak, James. *Developing a Dream Destination: Tourism and Tourism Policy Planning in Hawai'i*. Honolulu: University of Hawai'i Press, 2008.

Marek, Serge. "Waikīkī Virtual Reality: Space, Place and Representation in the Waikīkī Master Plan." MA thesis, University of Hawai'i, 1997.

McDougall, Brandy Nālani. "Putting Feathers on Our Words: Kaona as Decolonial Aesthetic Practice in Hawaiian Literature." *Decolonization: Indigeneity, Education and Society* 3, no. 1 (2014): 1–22.

McMullin, Dan Taulapapa. "Fa'afafine Notes: On Tagaloa, Jesus, and Nafanua." In *Queer Indigenous Studies*, edited by Qwo-Li Driskill, Chris Finley, Brian Joseph Gilley, and Scott Lauria Morgensen, 81–96. Tucson: University of Arizona Press, 2011.

Merry, Sally Engle. *Colonizing Hawai'i: The Cultural Power of Law*. Princeton, NJ: Princeton University Press, 2000.

Meyer, Manulani. *Ho'oulu: Our Time of Becoming*. Honolulu: 'Ai Pohaku Press, 2003.

Milham, Ka'iulani. "Lanakila Mangauil and the Foundation for Kapu Aloha." *Hawai'i Independent*. August 26, 2015. http://hawaiiindependent.net/story/lanakila-mangauil-and-the-foundation-for-kapu-aloha.

Miller, Bonnie M. *From Liberation to Conquest: The Visual and Popular Cultures of the Spanish-American War of 1898.* Amherst: University of Massachusetts Press, 2011.

Mitchell, Tony. "Kia Kaha! (Be Strong): Maori and Pacific Islander Hip-Hop in Aotearoa—New Zealand." In *Global Noise: Rap and Hip-Hop Outside the USA*, edited by Tony Mitchell, 280–305. Middletown, CT: Wesleyan University Press, 2001.

Moketananda. *Protesting the Filming of Barbarian Princess Ka'iulani.* YouTube Video, March 27, 2008. https://www.youtube.com/watch?v=ssMqZoAMGUM.

———. *Protest the Taping of Ka'iulani.* YouTube Video, March 25, 2008. https://www.youtube.com/watch?v=bBv5Wxc7HiI.

———. *Protest the Taping of Ka'iulani at the Palace.* YouTube Video, March 26, 2008. https://www.youtube.com/watch?v=letKqPGeqbo.

Morgensen, Scott Lauria. "Settler Homonationalism: Theorizing Settler Colonialism within Queer Modernities." *GLQ: A Journal of Lesbian and Gay Studies* 16 (2010): 105–31.

———. *Spaces between Us: Queer Settler Colonialism and Indigenous Decolonization.* Minneapolis: University of Minnesota Press, 2011.

Morita, Stirling. "'Aloha Spirit' Bill Meets Some Heartfelt Opposition." *Honolulu Star-Bulletin*, March 4, 1986.

Morris, Robert J. "*Aikane*: Accounts of Hawaiian Same-Sex Relationships in the Journals of Captain Cook's Third Voyage (1776–1780)." *Journal of Homosexuality* 19, no. 4 (1990): 30–54.

Muñoz, José Esteban. *Disidentifications: Queers of Color and the Performance of Politics.* Minneapolis: University of Minnesota Press, 1999.

Newton, Esther. *Mother Camp: Female Impersonators in America.* Chicago: University of Chicago Press, 1979.

Niesse, Mark. "Native Hawaiians Occupy Iolani Palace Grounds." *Maui News*, May 1, 2008.

Noland, Brother. *A Hawaiian Survival Handbook.* Honolulu: Watermark Publishing, 2014.

O'Brien, Patty. *The Pacific Muse: Exotic Femininity and the Colonial Pacific.* Seattle: University of Washington Press, 2006.

Office of Hawaiian Affairs. "The Disparate Treatment of Native Hawaiians in the Criminal Justice System." Honolulu: Office of Hawaiian Affairs, 2010.

———. *Native Hawaiian Data Book.* Honolulu: Office of Hawaiian Affairs, 2003.

———. *Native Hawaiian Data Book.* Honolulu: Office of Hawaiian Affairs, 2013.

Ohnuma, Keiko. "'Aloha Spirit' and the Cultural Politics of Sentiment as National Belonging." *Contemporary Pacific* 20, no. 2 (Fall 2008): 365–94.

Okamura, Jonathan. "The Illusion of Paradise: Privileging Multiculturalism in Hawai'i." In *Making Majorities: Constituting the Nation in Japan, Korea, China, Malaysia, Fiji, Turkey, and the United States*, edited by Dru C. Gladney, 264–84. Stanford, CA: Stanford University Press, 1998.

———. "Why There Are No Asian Americans in Hawai'i: The Continuing Significance of Local Identity." *Social Process in Hawai'i* 35 (1995): 161–78.

Oliveira, Katrina-Ann Rose-Marie Kapāʻanaokalāokeola Nākoa. *Ancestral Places: Understanding Kanaka Geographies*. Corvallis: Oregon State University Press, 2014.

Ortiz, Simon. "History of Right Now." In *Beyond the Reach of Time and Change: Native American Reflections on the Frank A. Rinehart Photograph Collection*, edited by Simon J. Ortiz, 3–8. Tucson: University of Arizona Press, 2004.

Osorio, Jonathan Kamakawiwoʻole. *Dismembering Lāhui: A History of the Hawaiian Nation to 1887*. Honolulu: University of Hawaiʻi Press, 2002.

———. "Hawaiian Souls: The Movement to Stop the U.S. Military Bombing of Kahoʻolawe." In *A Nation Rising: Hawaiian Movements for Life, Land, and Sovereignty*, edited by Noelani Goodyear-Kaʻōpua, Ikaika Hussey, and Erin Kahunawaikaʻala Wright, 137–60. Durham, NC: Duke University Press, 2014.

———. "Kūʻē and Kuʻokoʻa: History, Law, and Other Faiths." In *Law and Empire in the Pacific, Fiji, and Hawaiʻi*, edited by S. E. Merry and D. Brennis, 213–38. Santa Fe, NM: SAR Press, 2004.

———. "Songs of Our Natural Selves: The Enduring Voice of Nature in Hawaiian Music." Paper presented at the 8th Annual Pacific History Association Conference, Mangilao, Guam, 1992.

Osumare, Halifu. *The Africanist Aesthetic in Global Hip-Hop: Power Moves*. New York: Palgrave Macmillan, 2007.

———. "Props to the Local Boyz: Hip-Hop Culture in Hawaiʻi." In *The African Aesthetic in Global Hip-Hop*, 105–46. New York: Palgrave, 2007.

Peralto, Leon Noʻeau. "Hānau Ka Mauna, the Piko of Our Ea." In *A Nation Rising: Hawaiian Movements for Life, Land, and Sovereignty*, edited by Noelani Goodyear-Kaʻōpua, Ikaika Hussey, and Erin Kahunawaikaʻala Wright, 233–43. Durham, NC: Duke University Press, 2013.

Phelan, Peggy. *Unmarked*. New York: Routledge, 1993.

Pierce, Lori. " 'The Whites Have Created Modern Honolulu': Ethnicity, Racial Stratification, and the Discourse of Aloha." In *Racial Thinking in the United States*, edited by Paul Spickard and G. Reginald Daniel, 124–54. Notre Dame, IN: University of Notre Dame Press, 2004.

Povinelli, Elizabeth A. *The Cunning of Recognition: Indigenous Alterities and the Making of Australian Multiculturalism*. Durham, NC: Duke University Press, 2002.

"Princess Kaiulani Proclaimed Heir of the Crown." *Hawaiian Gazette*, March 17, 1891, 4. Published electronically February 6, 2014. http://nupepa-hawaii.com /2014/02/06/kaiulani-the-heir-to-the-throne-1891/ - more-11897.

Puar, Jasbir. *Terrorist Assemblages: Homonationalisms in Queer Times*. Durham, NC: Duke University Press, 2007.

Pukuʻi, Mary Kawena. *ʻOlelo Noʻeau: Hawaiian Proverbs and Poetical Sayings*. Bernice P. Bishop Museum Special Publication. Honolulu: Bishop Museum Press, 1983.

Pukuʻi, Mary Kawena, E. W. Haertig, and Catherine Lee. *Nānā I Ke Kumu = Look to the Source*. Vols. 1 & 2. Honolulu: Hui Hanai, 1972.

Raheja, Michelle H. *Reservation Reelism: Redfacing, Visual Sovereignty, and Representations of Native Americans in Film*. Lincoln: University of Nebraska Press, 2010.

Raibmon, Paige Sylvia. *Authentic Indians: Episodes of Encounter from the Late-Nineteenth-Century Northwest Coast.* Durham: Duke University Press, 2005.

Ramirez, Renya. *Native Hubs: Culture, Community, and Belonging in Silicon Valley and Beyond.* Durham, NC: Duke University Press, 2007.

Reyes, Donna. "Legislators Endorse 'Aloha Spirit' as 'Essence of the Law' in Islands." *Honolulu Advertiser*, April 18, 1986.

Rivenburgh, Viola K. *Princess Kaiulani, a Fictional Biography.* Honolulu: Tongg Publishing, 1960.

Rivera, Raquel. *New York Ricans from the Hip-Hop Zone.* New York: Palgrave Macmillan, 2003.

Roach, Joseph. *Cities of the Dead.* New York: Columbia University Press, 1996.

Rose, Tricia. *The Hip-Hop Wars.* New York: Perseus, 2008.

Sai, Keanu David. "American Occupation of the Hawaiian State: A Century Unchecked." *Hawai'i Journal of Law and Politics* 46 (2004): 46–81.

Saranillio, Dean Itsuji. "Kewaikaliko's *Benocide*: Reversing the Imperial Gaze of *Rice v. Cayetano* and Its Legal Progeny." *American Quarterly* 62, no. 3 (September 2010): 457–76.

———. "Seeing Conquest: Colliding Histories and the Cultural Politics of Hawai'i Statehood." PhD Diss., University of Michigan, 2009.

Scott, James. *Domination and the Arts of Resistance.* New Haven, CT: Yale University Press, 1990.

See, Sarita. *The Decolonized Eye: Filipino American Art and Performance.* Minneapolis: University of Minnesota Press, 2009.

Sellers-Young, Barbara, and Anthony Shay, eds. *Belly Dance: Orientalism, Transnationalism, and Harem Fantasy.* Costa Mesa, CA: Mazda Publishers, 2005.

"Senate Wants Aloha Spirit in Courtroom." *Honolulu Advertiser*, April 2, 1986.

Shah, Nayan. *Contagious Divides: Epidemics and Race in San Francisco's Chinatown.* Berkeley: University of California Press, 2001.

Shaughnessey, Dennis. "She Lived, and Worked, behind the Scenes." *Lowell Sun*, March 17, 2008. http://www.lowellsun.com/ci_8602523.

Silva, Denise Ferreira da. *Toward a Global Idea of Race.* Minnesota: University of Minnesota Press, 2007.

Silva, Noenoe. *Aloha Betrayed: Native Hawaiian Resistance to American Colonialism.* Durham, NC: Duke University Press, 2004.

———. " 'He Kānāwai E Hoʻopau I Na Hula Kuolo Hawaiʻi': The Political Economy of Banning the Hula (1857–1870)." *Hawaiian Journal of History* 34 (2000): 29–48.

Simpson, Audra. *Mohawk Interruptus: Political Life across the Borders of Settler States.* Durham, NC: Duke University Press, 2014.

———. "On Ethnographic Refusal: Indigeneity, 'Voice' and Colonial Citizenship." *Junctures: The Journal for Thematic Dialogue* 9 (2007): 67–80.

Simpson, Leanne Betasamosake. *Dancing on Our Turtle's Back: Stories of Nishnaabeg Re-creation, Resurgence and a New Emergence.* Winnipeg: Arbeiter Ring Publishing, 2011.

———. "The Place Where We All Live and Work Together: A Gendered Analysis of Sovereignty." In *Native Studies Keywords*, edited by Stephanie Nohelani

Teves, Andrea Smith, and Michelle Raheja, 18–24. Tucson: University of Arizona Press, 2015.

Smith, Andrea. "Queer Theory and Native Studies: The Heteronormativity of Settler Colonialism." *GLQ: A Journal of Lesbian and Gay Studies* 16, no. 1–2 (2010): 42–68.

Smith, Christopher Holmes. "Method in the Madness: Exploring the Boundaries of Identity in Hip-Hop Performativity." *Social Identities* 3 (1997): 345–74.

Spahr, Juliana. *Fuck You, Aloha, I Love You*. Middletown, CT: Wesleyan University Press, 2001.

Stanley, Fay, and Diane Stanley. *The Last Princess: The Story of Princess Kaʻiulani of Hawaiʻi*. New York: Four Winds Press, 1991.

State of Hawaiʻi, Department of Health. Hawaiʻi Health Survey. "Figure Hth-01: Chronic and Other Health Conditions (Prevalence per 1,000—Age Adjusted in the State of Hawaiʻi: 2010." Honolulu: State of Hawaiʻi Department of Health, 2010.

Stevenson, Robert Louis. *Songs of Travel and Other Verses*, edited by Sidney Colvin. London: Chatto and Windus, 1896.

Stillman, Amy K. "Remembering the History of Hawaiian Hula." In *Cultural Memory: Reconfiguring History and Identity in the Postcolonial Pacific*, edited by Jeannette Marie Mageo, 187–204. Honolulu: University of Hawaiʻi Press, 2001.

———. *Sacred Hula: The Historical Hulaʻalaʻapapa*. Honolulu: Bishop Museum Press, 1998.

———. "Textualizing Hawaiian Music." *American Music* (Spring 2005): 69–91.

Svaton, Eleanor. "A Woman's Place in the World—Kaʻiulani at Kumu Kahua Theatre." March 31, 2015. http://www.hittingthestage.com/a-womans-place-in -the-world-kaiulani-at-kumu-kahua-theatre/.

Taouma, Lisa. "Gauguin Is Dead . . . There Is No Paradise." *Journal of Intercultural Studies* 25, no. 1 (2004): 35–46.

Taylor, Diana. *The Archive and the Repertoire: Performing Cultural Memory in the Americas*. Durham, NC: Duke University Press, 2003.

Teaiwa, Teresia. "Militarism, Tourism and the Native: Articulations in Oceania." PhD Diss., University of California, Santa Cruz, 2001.

———. "Native Thoughts: A Pacific Studies Take on Cultural Studies and Diaspora." In *Indigenous Diasporas and Dislocations*, edited by Graham Harvey and Charles Johnson, 15–36. Burlington, VT: Ashgate, 2005.

Tengan, Ty Kāwika. *Native Men Remade: Gender and Nation in Contemporary Hawaiʻi*. Durham, NC: Duke University Press, 2008.

Tengan, Ty Kāwika, and Jesse Makani Markham. "Performing Polynesian Masculinities in American Football: From Rainbows to Warriors." *International Journal of the History of Sport* 6, no. 16 (2009): 2412–31.

Thrift, Nigel J. *Non-representational Theory: Space, Politics, Affect*. London: Routledge, 2008.

Trask, Haunani-Kay. "Fighting the Battle of Double Colonization: The View of a Hawaiian Feminist." *Annual Journal of Ethnic Studies* 2 (1984): 196–213.

———. *From a Native Daughter: Colonialism and Sovereignty in Hawaiʻi*. 2nd ed. Honolulu: University of Hawaiʻi Press, 1999.

———. "Racism against Native Hawaiians at the University of Hawaii: A Personal and Political View." *Amerasia Journal* 18, no. 3 (1992): 33–50.

Tuck, Eve, and C. Ree. "Glossary of Haunting." In *Handbook of Autoethnography*, edited by Stacey Holman Jones, Tony E. Adams, and Carolyn Ellis, 639–58. Walnut Creek, CA: Left Coast Press, 2013.

Ulises, Decena Carlos. "Tacit Subjects." *GLQ: A Journal of Lesbian and Gay Studies* 14, no. 2–3 (2008): 339–59.

Ullestad, Neal. "Native American Rap and Reggae: Dancing to the Beat of a Different Drummer." In *Ethnomusicology: A Contemporary Reader*, edited by Jennifer Post, 331–50. New York: Routledge, 2006.

U.S. Bureau of the Census. American Community Survey. "Figure Inc-10: Poverty Rates for Families for Whom Poverty Status Is Determined." 2012. https://factfinder.census.gov/faces/tableservices/jsf/pages/productview.xhtml?src=bkmk.

———. "Table Emp-11: Native Hawaiian Employment Status: State of Hawai'i 2010–2014." U.S. Bureau of the Census, 2014. http://www.ohadatabook.com/T-EMP-11-15.pdf .

Vandertuin, Catherine, Laha Ku, Nyla Fuji, Glen Grant, Gaye Glaser, and Oceanic Cablevision. *Scary Stories*. Vol. 20. Honolulu: Oceanic Cablevision, 1987.

Van Dyke, Jon M. *Who Owns the Crown Lands of Hawai'i?* Honolulu: University of Hawai'i Press, 2008.

Van Dyke, Michelle Broader. "Governor Signs into Law Hawaii's Marriage Equality Bill." *Buzzfeed*, November 13, 2013. https://www.buzzfeed.com/mbvd/governor-signs-into-law-hawaiis-marriage-equality-bill?utm_term=.dmWWKnvN9v-.rizJZKnzgn.

Vizenor, Gerald. "Aesthetics of Survivance." In *Survivance: Narratives of Native Presence*, edited by Gerald Vizenor, 1–24. Lincoln: University of Nebraska Press, 2008.

Waitt, Gordon, and Kevin Markwell. *Gay Tourism: Culture and Context*. New York: Haworth Hospitality Press, 2006.

Wallace, Lee. *Sexual Encounters: Pacific Texts, Modern Sexualities*. Ithaca, NY: Cornell University Press, 2003.

Watkins, S. Craig. *Hip-Hop Matters: Politics, Pop Culture, and the Struggle for the Soul of a Movement*. Boston: Beacon Press, 2005.

Weber, Max. *The Protestant Ethic and the Spirit of Capitalism*. New York: Scribner, 1958.

Williams, Frith. *The Canoe Is the People: Indigenous Navigation in the Pacific*. Paris: UNESCO, 2005.

Williams, Patricia J. *Seeing through a Color-Blind Future: The Paradox of Race*. New York: Noonday Press, 1997.

Wilmer, S. E. *Native American Performance and Representation*. Tucson: University of Arizona Press, 2009.

Wolfe, Patrick. "Settler Colonialism and the Elimination of the Native." *Journal of Genocide Research* 8, no. 4 (2006): 387–409.

Wood, Houston. *Displacing Natives: The Rhetorical Production of Hawai'i*. Lanham, MD: Rowman and Littlefield, 1999.

Young, Kalaniopua. "From a Native Trans Daughter: Carceral Refusal, Settler Colonialism, Re-routing the Roots of an Indigenous Abolitionist Imaginary." In *Captive Genders: Trans Embodiment and the Prison Industrial Complex*. 2nd ed., edited by Eric Stanley and Nat Smith, 83–96. Oakland, CA: AK Press, 2015.

Zambucka, Kristin. *A Cry of Peacocks*. Videocasette. Directed by Duccio K. Marignolie and John Wray. Green Glass Productions, 1993.

Žižek, Slavoj. *The Sublime Object of Ideology*. London: Verso, 1989.

Index

Italic page numbers indicate figures.

Abercrombie, Neil, 35
Aboriginal Lands of Hawaiian Ancestry
    (ALOHA), 36
Ai, Olana, 42
Aikau, Hokulani, 149, 172
'Āinahau, 125
Akaka, Abraham, 31
Akaka, Daniel, 4
Alfred, Taiaiake, 172
Aloha, xv–xvi; and agency, 30;
    appropriation of, 2, 5; and authentic-
    ity, 34; betrayal of, 38–39; call of, 28,
    43–44, 84, 100, 109–11; and capital-
    ism, 27, 122; and Christianity, 28, 24,
    31; and colonialism, 9, 27; commer-
    cialization of, 1, 42–43; commodifica-
    tion of, 2, 8, 31, 44; and community,
    25; constructedness of, 98; contradic-
    tions of, 23; and decolonization, 6–7,
    173; as disciplining force, 8, 24, 33, 36,
    39; discourse of, 36; epistemology of,
    25; as essentialist, 24, 31; as floating
    signifier, 39; as "gift to the world," 2,
    8, 24, 32–33, 39–40; in the Hawaiian
    diaspora, 46, 149; and Hawaiianness,
    5, 20, 30–31, 33, 38–39, 46–48, 98, 105,
    110; history of, 23–25; as ideology, 29,
    33, 35; and indigeneity, 7–9, 21, 24, 48;
    limits of, 173; meaning of, 1, 24–25,
    45; and multiculturalism, 27, 34;
    naturalization of, 103; performance
    of, 2–3, 7–11, 24, 30, 34, 42, 44–46,
    48–49, 51, 86, 88, 105, 148–49, 173–74,
    175; and policing of behavior, 24; as
    refusal, 78; rejection of, 26–27, 46,
    48–49, 53, 84, 98, 110–11, 173–75; and

settler colonialism, 25, 122; spirit of,
    26; as state ideology, 35–36, 43;
    sustainable, 21; as term, 1; and tourism,
    21, 27, 32–34; translations of, 24–25.
    See also Aloha 'āina; Aloha Spirit Law
Aloha (film), 41, 183n74
Aloha 'āina, 8, 36–37, 42, 45, 58, 71;
    epistemology of, 72; and Hawaiian
    hip-hop, 71; and Hawaiian indigene-
    ity, 45; and Hawaiian Renaissance,
    72; and kuleana, 72; and lāhui, 77;
    and "West Side" (song), 71–72, 73.
    See also Aloha
Aloha 'Āina o Nā Wahine (Hawaiian
    Women's Patriotic League), 131
Aloha for All, 182n64
Aloha in drag, 46, 84, 85, 88, 108; as act
    of refusal, 84; and knowledge
    production, 93; as performance, 98;
    and shared cultural understanding,
    99. *See also* Chandelier, Cocoa
Aloha Spirit Law, 8, 24, 32–34, 37, 47,
    181n45
Althusser, Louis, 24, 26, 27
Angry Locals (rap group), 52
Apo, Peter, 177n3
Arista, Noelani, 8, 17
Articulation, 45
Arvin, Maile, 8, 163
Asian Americans, in Hawai'i, 123
Asians: erasure of, 124; as "local"
    community, 31, 49; as settlers, 7, 14,
    37, 122–23, 124; subjugation of, 36
Austin, J. L., 7
Authenticity: and aloha, 34; arbitrari-
    ness of, 17; and blood quantum, 64;

209

Authenticity (cont.)
and colonialism, 13, 26; and cultural nationalism, xiv, 177n4; and culture, 2–3; and essentialism, 14–15; in Hawaiian music, 71; and Hawaiian nationalism, xiii, 20; and Hawaiian Renaissance, in hip-hop, 52, 68, 69–70; and hula, xiii; and inclusion, 4–5; and indigeneity, xiii–xiv, 5–7, 15, 69–70; and interpellation, 43; of Kapu Aloha, 9–10; of "the Native," 148; and performance, 52, 91; and racism, 69; and realness, 90. *See also* Hawaiianness; Indigenous realness

Bacchilega, Cristina, 73
Bailey, Marion, 90, 92
Benjamin, Walter, 136–37
Blackness, 70; "acting black," xii, 70, 186n51; antiblackness, 53; appropriation of, 61
Blood quantum, 20; and authenticity, 64; and colonialism, 85; and defiant indigeneity, 11; and homesteads, 63–65; and Indigenous identity, 65; and Kānaka Maoli, 63–66; and "Native Hawaiian," 177n2; and race, 64–65; and racial exclusion, 163
Blount, James, 72, 187n58
Blount Report, 186n58
Bodies That Matter (Butler), 12
Brathwaite, Kamau, 149
Butler, Judith, 12, 26, 46; on drag, 89
Butoh, 83, 188n9
Byrd, Jodi, 118

Campbell, Abigail Kuaihelani, 131
Campbell, Alice Kamokila, 141
Capitalism: and aloha, 27, 122; and colonialism, 30; and exploitation, 8; in Hawai'i, 28, 180n17; and hula, 28; and inclusion, 4; and performance, 109; and progress, 144; and representation, 109
Carroll, Dennis, 113, 115, 134

Chandelier, Cocoa, 6, 20, 187n1; aliases of, 83; as ali'i, 91, *91*, 93, 95–96, 111–12, 116; aloha, refusal of, 110–11; and appropriation, 107; "Cocoa Chandelier's Confessional," 81–84; defiant indigeneity of, 96; as disidentifying subject, 99; Hawaiianness, refusal of, 96–98; Hawaiian performance, queering of, 88, 107; indigeneity, refusal of, 96; oeuvre of, 83, 188n8, 188n10; Orientalism in, 100, 103, 105–7; play in, 107; *RuPaul's Drag Race*, campaign for, 111–12; Universal ShowQueen performance (2008), 99–103, *101*, 104–6, 108–10. *See also* Aloha in drag
Chang, David, 10
Chow, Rey, 1; on coercive mimeticism, 85; on ethnic performance, 2; on interpellation, 44; on Weber, 27
Christianity: and aloha, 28, 31, 24; and Hawaiian education, 29; interpellation of, 24, 28; and Kānaka Maoli, 19, 28, 94–95, 157, 163–64; missionaries in the Pacific, 19, 25, 28, 163; and sexuality, 87; sexual morality of, 64, 157, 160, 163–64
Chuh, Kandice, 189n32
Chun, Malcolm Nāea, 24–25
Cleghorn, Archibald Scott, 125
Cleveland, Grover, 186n58; in *Princess Ka'iulani*, 131
Clifford, James, 43
Colonialism, 117, 124; and aloha, 9, 27; and authenticity, 13, 26; and blood quantum, 85; and capitalism, 30; and cultural performance, 103–4; and defiant indigeneity, 53; and diaspora, 151; and gender, 92; and Hawaiian culture, 30; and Hawaiianness, 106–7; and heteronormativity, 85, 155; and heteropatriarchy, 159; and Indigenous presence, 91; and "the Native," 16, 92; and the other, 105; and performance, 4–5; and performativity, 170;

resistance to, 132; and sovereignty, xii; and tourism, 33. *See also* Settler Colonialism

Colonization: and Christian domesticity, 160; and cultural appropriation, 121; and cultural difference, 2; as gendered process, 13; and geography, 12. *See also* Colonialism; Settler Colonialism

Coming out, 156–57; in "The Old Paniolo Way," 153–54, 157, 158, 167

Committee of Safety, 49

Confession: in Cocoa Chandelier's work, 82–84; coming out as, 157; in ethnic studies, 84; in Native studies, 84; and performance, 84, 190n58

Conklin, Ken, 182n64

Corntassel, Jeff, 172

Coulthard, Glen, 103

Crabbe, Kamana'opono, 38

Cry of Peacocks, A (documentary), 115

Cultural advisors, 4–5, 136

Cultural nationalism, 43, 145; and authenticity, xiv, 177n4. *See also* Nationalism; Nationalism, Hawaiian

Culture: and authenticity, 2–3; and difference, 2; and indigeneity, 2; performance of, 2, 29–30; and race, 103

Culture, Hawaiian: accommodation of, 4; and colonialism, 30; and hula, 118–19; and race, 103; and settler colonialism, 4. *See also* Aloha; Hawaiianness

David Kalākaua (king), 19, 126, 179n46; hula, reviving of, 28; in *Princess Ka'iulani*, 133

Davies, Clive, in *Princess Ka'iulani*, 129–30, 132

Davies, Theophilus Harris, 129

Decolonization, 14, 57; and aloha, 6–7, 173; and cultural difference, 104; and gender, 164–65; and indigeneity, 11, 18; of Kānaka Maoli, 133, 164–65, 173; and nostalgia, 118

Deedy, Christopher, 121

Defiant indigeneity, 3; and antiblackness, 53; and blood quantum, 11; of Cocoa Chandelier, 96; and colonialism, 53; contradictions of, 62; heteropatriarchy in, 53; knowledge in, 18; of Krystilez, 49, 61–62, 70; and lāhui, 53; and "the Native," 11; performance of, 11, 49, 84; and settler colonialism, 11

Deloughrey, Elizabeth, 149, 160, 162; on state-based nationalisms, 168

Denetdale, Jennifer Nez, 184n6

Derrida, Jacques, 122

Devdas (film), 101, 106, 190n50

Diamond, Heather, 36

Diaspora: and colonialism, 151; etymology of, 160; heteropatriarchal discourse of, 160; and home, 166; LGBTQ communities in, 152–54, 168; as masculine discourse, 162; and masculinity, 166; as performance, 167; queer of color, critiques of, 155; and settler colonialism, 151

Diaspora, Indigenous, stigma of, 168

Diaspora, Kānaka Maoli, 77, 145–48, 175, 187n69, 193n4; aloha, performance of, 46, 149; and assimilation, 146; connectedness of, 147; and federal recognition, 150–51; gay diaspora, 152–53; queer, 163; reasons for leaving, 145; visibility of, 150

Diaspora, Pacific Islanders: connectedness of, 147; queering of, 149; as traditional, 158

Diasporic indigenes, 149

Diaz, Vicente, 148, 162

Disarticulation, 45

Disidentification, 84, 99; and subjectivity, 189n47

Dole, Sanford P., 116; in *Princess Ka'iulani*, 131, 136

Drag, 84–85, 88–89, 187n1; recognizability of, 99; and tradition, 87

Drag performances: and gender presentation, 88; and sexuality, 87; as transgressive, 99; as Western, 87. *See also* Aloha in drag; Chandelier, Cocoa

Driskill, Qwo-Li, 88, 155

Elderts, Kollin, 121

Epistemology: of aloha, 25; of aloha ʻāina, 72; Indigenous, 149, 159, 165; of Kānaka Maoli, 61. *See also* Knowledge production

Essentialism: and aloha, 24, 31; and authenticity, 14–15; and indigeneity, 15; and "the Native," 12, 15

Ethnic studies, 189n32; the confession in, 84

Faʻafafine, 87, 188n23

Fahrni, Jennifer, 115

Fakaleiti, 87, 188n23

Feminism: of *Kaʻiulani* (play), 141; Kānaka Maoli, 165; Native, 163

Feminist philosophy, 12

Filipinos, 66

Film: Hawaiian tropes in, 41, 133–34; and knowledge production, 134; limits of, 131; Native people in, 133, 136

Fleetwood, Nicole, 85

Forman, Murray, 69

Foucault, Michel, 32, 190n58

From a Native Daughter: Colonialism and Sovereignty in Hawaiʻi (Trask), xii, 183n67

Gegeo, David, 147

Gender Trouble (Butler), 12

Ghost stories, 122–23; settler ideology of, 123

Ghost tours, 7, 119–20, 124–27, 143–44, 192n46; and erasure of Hawaiian indigeneity, 120; in Hawaiʻi, 7, 52, 115, 119–20, 122

Globalization: as masculine discourse, 162; of media, 31, 50; Native, 146

Goeman, Mishuana, 7

Goodyear-Kaʻōpua, Noelani, xv, 29, 129

Gordon, Avery, 120, 136–37, 143

Grant, Glen, 122–23; Obake Files series, 122, 124

Great Mahele, 28, 180n17

Guzman, Manolo, 155

Haka, 11, 178n19

Hall, Lisa Kahaleʻole, 165

Halualani, Rona, 33

Haoles: defined, 178n26; hegemony of, 36–37; and locals, 31, 121; settler guilt of, 123; and sovereignty movement, xii; tourists, xi, 7

Hauʻofa, Epeli, 147, 148

Hawaiʻi: aliʻi of, 116–19, 121, 126, 134, 141–44, 163; as Aloha State, 8, 24, 31, 33–34, 47, 93, 174; annexation of, 49, 64, 113, 129, 179n36; banning of same-sex marriage in, 156; capitalism in, 28, 180n17; Christianization of, 94; and colonialism, 114; colonization of, xiv, 29; education in, 29, 181n25; ethnic conflict in, 181n35; exceptional multiculturalism of, 32, 181n34; feminization of, 113, 128, 130; independence of, 170–71; institutional racism in, 36; leaving from, 152–53; LGBTQ community in, 93–94, 109, 152; martial law in, xi; as melting pot, 32, 36; nation-building of, 68, 78, 170, 173, 175; performance space in, 82; queer indigeneity in, 88; racism in, 59; recognition of, 68; social protest in, 39; sovereignty movement, xii–xiii, 34, 38, 123, 137, 172, 182n64; statehood of, xi, 28, 31–32; territory period, xi, 28–29, 31, 63; tourist economy of, 30, 156; U.S. militarization of, 1; U.S. occupation of, xiv, 4, 126, 132, 145, 185n29. *See also* Hawaiian Kingdom

Hawaiian Homes Commission Act (HHCA), 63–64

Hawaiian Kingdom, xi, 95, 185n22, 189n48; Apology Resolution, 3,

182n63; land tenure, shifts in, 64; legal status of, 38; memorialization of, 117; modernizing of, 134; mourning for, 46; nostalgia for, 97, 117–18; overthrow of, 28–29, 49, 63–64, 72, 114, 116–17, 127–28, 137–38, 185n29, 186n58; and performance, 118; as thing of the past, 126, 130

Hawaiian language: decline of, 28–29; immersion schools, 182n63; in *Princess Ka'iulani*, 134; proficiency in, 67, 186n40; recovery of, xiv; suppression of, 19; translation of, 24–25

Hawaiian music, 20; and authenticity, 74; mainstream, 45–50, 74; and nostalgia, 19; place in, 77, 185n18; radio stations, 68; and sovereignty, xiii. *See also* Hip-hop, Hawaiian

Hawaiianness: and aloha, 5, 20, 30–31, 33, 38–39, 46–48, 85, 98, 105, 110; and Cocoa Chandelier, 96–98; and colonialism, 106–7; and heteronormativity, 163–64; and outsiders, 173; and performance, xiv 7, 20, 27, 85, 105–7; queering of, 84; refusal of, 96–98; visibility of, 102. *See also* Aloha; Authenticity

Hawaiian Political Action Council, 35

Hawaiian Renaissance, 3, 34, 172; and aloha 'āina, 72; and authenticity, 20; and performance, 20

Hawaiians: diasporic, 99, 187n69; gender expression of, 90; and "Native Hawaiians," 177n2; racialization of, 104; reparations for, 113–14; self-determination of, 90; self-governance of, 95; stereotypes of, 49. *See also* Kānaka Maoli

Hawaiian studies: and knowledge production, 84; queering of, 86

Hawaiian Survival Handbook, A 21

Helm, George, 37

Heteronormativity: and colonialism, 85, 155; and Hawaiianness, 163–64; within LGBTQ community, 164–65; and nationalism, 163

Heteropatriarchy: and colonialism, 159; critique of, 141; in defiant indigeneity, 53; and diaspora, 160; in Krystilez, 50, 61–62; and nationalism, 149, 161–62; and nonheteronormative relations, 87; and women's agency, 161

Hinemoana of Turtle Island, 41, 183n74

Hip-hop, xv; authenticity in, 69–70; Filipinos in, 66–67; in Hawai'i, 49–50, 184n2; mainstream, 60, 74; misogyny in, 49; Native, 51; Native scholarship on, 51; place in, 74; underground, 74; women in, 68–69. *See also* Hip-hop, Hawaiian; Krystilez

Hip-hop, Hawaiian, 49, 175; and aloha 'āina, 71; and authenticity, 70, 186n51; digital space, use of, 75, 77–78; masculinity in, 50–51, 76; and race, 103; radio airplay, lack of, 68; social media, use of, 68. *See also* Hawaiian music; Hip-hop; Krystilez

History, Hawaiian: and Hawaiian indigeneity, 71; rewriting of, 3. *See also* Hawai'i; Hawaiian Kingdom

Hokowhitu, Brendan, 5, 14

Homesteads, 49, 53–54, 61–66, 78; administration of, 62; in "Bloodline," 62, 65–66; and blood quantum, 63–65

Homonormativity, within LGBTQ community, 164–65

Honolulu: Chinatown, 81–82, 187n4, 188n5; urban renewal in, 82. *See also* Waikīkī

ho'omanawanui, ku'ualoha, 51

Hui Hawai'i Aloha 'Āina, 72

Hula: as apolitical, 89; and authenticity, xiii; banning of, 19, 28; and capitalism, 28; commodification of, 2; and Hawaiian culture, 118–19; and Hawaiian knowledge, 118–19; in *Ka'iulani* (play), 142; revival of, 28; and tourism, 19, 28

Identity: and blood quantum, 64–65; commodification of, 107; Hawaiian, 39, 58, 106–7; Indigenous, 16, 92, 174; Kānaka Maoli, 30, 50–51, 53, 70, 76–80, 104, 108, 182n63; and performance, xiv–xv, 9; and place, 61, 64, 73; as politics of evading, 89; queer, 89, 164; and sexuality, 89, 154, 164, 167, 169. *See also* Indigeneity; Indigeneity, Hawaiian; Subjectivity

Ideological State Apparatuses (ISAs): and aloha, 36; and subjectivity, 26. *See also* Interpellation

Ideology, 43–44; aloha as, 29, 33, 35; and interpellation, 26–27, 43–44; settler ideology, 123; and subjectivity, 45, 84

Imada, Adria, 30

Indigeneity: and activism, 50; and authenticity, 5–7, 15, 69–70; and colonization, 13; and decolonization, 11, 18; and essentialism, 15; and fluidity, 12; and genealogy, xv; and lāhui, xv; and land, xv, 145, 151, 159–60; and movement, 160; myths of, 14; and "the Native," 12, 15–16; in Native studies, 13; and nature, 61; performance of, xiv, 5, 15, 98, 160; as performative process, 12–13, 51; and place, 146, 152, 170; queer, 88; queering of, 149; and race, 2; and settler colonialism, 10, 118; and sovereignty, 103. *See also* Defiant indigeneity

Indigeneity, Hawaiian: and aloha, 7–9, 21, 24, 48, 99; and aloha ʻāina, 45; and authenticity, xiii–xiv, 3; erasure of, 120–22; future of, 117; and Hawaiian history, 71; as performance, 15–16, 20, 46, 49, 104; and performativity, 17. *See also* Defiant indigeneity

Indigenous people: and the past, 118; relation to nation-state, 38; sovereignty, claims to, 103; visibility of, 104. *See also* Diaspora, Indigenous; Kānaka Maoli; Performance, Indigenous

Indigenous realness, 85, 90–93; and knowledge production, 93. *See also* Authenticity; Chandelier, Cocoa

Interpellation, 6, 26–27; through aloha, 43; Althusser on, 24, 26–27; and authenticity, 43; of Christianity, 24, 28; and ideology, 26–27, 43–44; and subjectivity, 26–27, 43, 84

IZ Real, 59–60, 62, 65

Jacobs, Kaina, 82, 188n7

Jawaiian music, xiii. *See also* Hawaiian music

Jay-Z, 100, 102, 105

Johnson, E. Patrick, 70

Jolly, Margaret, 159

Kaʻahumanu (queen), 90, 94–95

Kaʻahumanu Society, 95

Kaʻeo, Kaleikoa, 146

Kahakauwila, Kristiana, 7, 19, 146; diaspora in, 152; *This Is Paradise*, 146. *See also* "Old Paniolo Way, The"

Kahoʻolawe, 36

Kaʻili, Tevita, 147

Kaʻiulani (Princess Victoria Kawēkiu Kaʻiulani Kalaninuiahilapalapa Cleghorn), 18; death of, 113–14, 128–29; death of broken heart trope, 128–29; as foil for Liliʻuokalani, 130–32; as "half-breed," 131; haunting of, 127; as "hope of Hawaiʻi," 142; in *Kaʻiulani* (play), 138; Kawananakoa, relationship with, 113, 132–33; legacy of, 114–15, 116; lineage of, 126; name songs for, 128; normative beauty of, 127–28, 143. See also *Kaʻiulani* (play); *Princess Kaʻiulani* (film)

Kaʻiulani (play), 7, 113, 114, 115, 137–44; death of Kaʻiulani in, 141–43; feminism of, 141; heteropatriarchy, critique of, 141; hula in, 142; Kaʻiulani as Everywoman in, 138, 140; multiple actresses, use of, 138, *139*; oli

in, 142; production history of, 137.
    See also Ka'iulani

Same-sex marriage, 156
Satawal, 160
See, Sarita, 89, 97, 107
Self-determination: and difference, 104; of Kānaka Maoli, 4, 32, 50, 64, 90
Settler colonialism, 8, 50, 115, 144; and aloha, 25, 122; and cultural experts, 5; and culture, 4; and defiant indigeneity, 11; and diaspora, 151; and difference, 104; in Hawai'i, 133–34; and historical amnesia, 122; and home, 146; and homonationalism, 155; and inclusion, 4; and indigeneity, 10, 118; and Indigenous hauntings, 119–20; and nostalgia, 117; and recognition, 4; and space, 121–22
Settlers: Asians as, 7, 14, 37, 122–23, 124; guilt of, 123–24; ideology of, 123
Sexuality: of Kānaka Maoli, 157; in the Pacific, 86–87
Sheraton Princess Ka'iulani Hotel, 115, 121; ghost tour of, 125–27; haunting of, 119; images of ali'i in, 126
Silva, Denise Ferreira da, 103
Silva, Noenoe, 28, 42, 72, 178n36
Simpson, Audra, 18, 93, 107
Simpson, Leanne Betasasmoke, 165
"Song of Sovereignty," xiii, 177n3
Sovereignty: and home, 165; and indigeneity, 103; and nationhood, 18; Native claims to, 103
Sovereignty, Hawaiian, 4, 137, 182n63; challenges to, 132; Kānaka Maoli claims of, 14, 32, 108, 122, 150–51; of lāhui, 72; movement for, xii–xiii, 34, 38, 123, 137, 172, 182n64; protests for, xii; settler state, challenge to, 37–38; and U.S. colonialism, xii
Spahr, Juliana, 23
Speech acts, 7
Stevenson, Robert Louis, 138
Subjectivity, 1; and disidentification, 189n47; gendered, 92; and ideology, 45, 84; Indigenous, 15; and interpella-

tion, 26–27, 43; modern, 15; and "the Native," 12; of Natives, 189n33; and ontology, 44; Pacific, 159–60; and performance, 15; racial, 92

Taylor, Diana, 108, 133
Teaiwa, Teresia, 12, 44–45, 159
Te Moana Nui, 125
Tengan, Ty Kāwika, 29, 50
The "O" (Krystilez album), 53–55, 57–62, 71; "Bloodline," 61–62, 64–66, 68, 71–74, 78, 170, 186n35; oli in, 57–58, 184n15; "Shake," 60; and supporting locals, 55; "The 'O' " (song), 57, 59–60; "Who I Am," 66; "Won," 59–60. *See also* Krystilez
This Is Paradise (Kahakauwila), 7
Tidalectics, 149, 166
Tiki Entertainment, 57, 59, 60, 65
Tourism: and aloha, 21, 27, 32–34; and Hawaiian economy, 30, 156; and hula, 19, 28; and Kānaka Maoli, 67, 99; and the settler state, 121; and U.S. colonialism, 33; in Waikīkī, 120–21
Tradition: and drag, 87; Indigenous, 58, 79, 177n5; and Kapu Aloha, 9; and modernity, 5, 8, 159; and movement, 160; Native, 155; performance of, xiii–xiv, 10, 13; and place, 66
Trask, Haunani-Kay, xii, xv–xvi, 42, 183n67; on aloha, 174; on aloha 'āina, 72; and Hawaiian nationalism, 163; "Lovely Hula Hands," 33; on tourism, 33
Trask, Mililani, xii
Tuck, Eve, 120

Ulises, Decena Carlos, 154
U.S. Department of the Interior (DOI), 38
U.S. military: Hawai'i, militarization of, 1; Hawai'i, occupation of, xiv, 4, 126, 132, 145, 185n29; Pacific, occupation of, 41
USS *Arizona* Memorial, xi

Vaughan, Palani, 136, 192n46

Visibility: of Hawaiianness, 102; of Indigenous people, 104; of Kānaka Maoli, 85, 102, 106; of Kānaka Maoli diaspora, 150; and misrepresentation, 85; and misrecognition, 85

Vizenor, Gerald, 50, 120

Waikīkī, 6; erasure of Hawaiian indigeneity in, 120–22; ghost tours in, 7, 115; "Hawaiianness" of, 120, 126; homeless in, 121; Kānaka Maoli in, 55; revitalization of, 99; royal past of, 126; tourist industry in, 120–21

War on Terror, 105

Weber, Max, 26–27

"West Side" (Krystilez song), 53, 54, 71, 73; as aloha 'āina, 71–72, 73; kuleana in, 71; music video for, 73, 75, 79–80; place in, 71, 74; viewer comments on, 75, 186n35. *See also* Krystilez

Whiteness: of LGBTQ life, xv, 155 and masculinity, 114, 141

White supremacy, 40; indigeneity, celebration of, 118; struggle against, 5, 40

Williams, Patricia, 70

Women, Hawaiian, domestication of, 160–61

Women, Native: annexation, resistance to, 131; as collaborators with colonizers, 131

Women, Pacific: domestication of, 160–61; "dusky maiden" trope, 130–31; as navigators, 160–61

Yorihito, Higashifushimi, 133

Young, Kalaniopua, 164

Žižek, Slavoj, 43–44

www.ingramcontent.com/pod-product-compliance
Lightning Source LLC
Chambersburg PA
CBHW030313270326
41926CB00010B/1341